THE GREAT PAGEANT

How I Learned About the Lives and Journeys of Birds

Eldon Remy

Enjoy Mother Natures gift of birds!
Eldon Remy

PublishingWorks, Inc.
Exeter, NH
2008

Back cover: Three sets of bird silhouettes, placed across the map of Eastern North America, depict spring migration routes of hawks, songbirds, and waterfowl, as described in the text.

All photographs and diagrams are by the author. The relief maps were provided by the U.S. Geologic Survey. Osprey in flight on the front cover is courtesy "sbbyland" of StockXpert.com

PublishingWorks, Inc.,
60 Winter Street
Exeter, NH 03833
603-778-9883
For Sales and Orders:
1-800-738-6603 or 603-772-7200

Designed by: K. Mack

LCCN: 2008921300
ISBN: 1-933002-67-0
ISBN-13: 978-1-933002-67-5

Printed in China

THE GREAT PAGEANT

For Jessa, Ryan and Nathan
and
In Memory of Jane

Contents

May

June

Preface

The Great Pageant is one of Mother Nature's great wonders: countless birds, worldwide, perpetually fulfilling prehistoric, predestined missions, including migration.

When I was a young Boy Scout at summer camp, the nature counselor directed that anyone interested in an early-morning bird walk tie a sock around the end of his cot, so that he would know to awaken those boys for the walk. This I did, and was enthralled at what I experienced that morning. I have been a birder ever since. Over the years, I became more and more aware that as a novice birder, my limited knowledge was preventing me from receiving as much satisfaction as I might from this very popular pastime. I had not yet thought of it as the Great Pageant, but I had perceived that it was something big. I asked myself, "How does one acquire sufficient knowledge to comprehend, and appreciate, this colossal phenomenon?" I was unable to find a source that could substantially help in my quest. Consequently, after I retired, I vowed to answer the question and document my progress. To learn about the Great Pageant I spent a full year, and portions of following years, sampling the eastern North American portion of this spectacle from the uniquely favorable south shore of Lake Ontario. I documented my frequent field trips, usually under the tutelage of local knowledgeable birders. I recorded my questions, their answers, and my increasing perceptions, as my knowledge expanded.

My notes resulted in this book. I hope it will accelerate, and deepen, your appreciation of the Great Pageant.

Eldon Remy
Rochester, New York
February 7, 2007

Acknowledgments

I could not have written this book without the help of a number of very capable people. A special thanks is due to Elaine Cummings, whose years of experience as an English and writing teacher were substantially challenged by my early versions of the manuscript. Thanks also to Steve Remy and Diane Vervalin, who offered hundreds of corrections and suggestions.

The book is about the skilled, competent, local birders who spent hundreds, perhaps thousands, of hours in the field with me, sharing their knowledge and experience. My learning, which was a demanding, extensive experience spanning an entire year and portions of following years, is the subject of this book. Those special people, whom I quote extensively throughout the book to document my learning process, include Betsy Brooks and Bob McKinney from Braddock Bay Bird Observatory; John Bounds, Brett Ewald, Jerry Liguori, Frank Nicoletti, Trish Stanko, Jason Franz, and Dave Tetlow from Braddock Bay Raptor Research; Carolyn Cass; Mike Davids; Kevin Griffith; Bob Marcotte; Neil and Laura Moon; Bill Symonds; and many others whom I met along the way.

Jerry Liguori has since written a book, *Hawks from Every Angle*, which is considered to be arguably the best book on identification of hawks in flight. Bob Marcotte has published the beautifully illustrated book *Birds of the Genesee*. Brett Ewald has published several scholarly monographs on waterfowl migration along Lake Ontario. Frank Nicoletti has been mentioned as a valued source in most books on hawks. Betsy Brooks and Bob McKinney have authored several scholarly monographs on bird banding. Neil and Laura Moon have published several papers on their hawk-watching project at Braddock Bay.

What I have described in this book is the way in which I slowly learned from these qualified experts. It was bit by bit, step by step, as I learned the significance of the Great Pageant.

Introduction

My Favorite Example of the Great Pageant

A tiny, rich blue warbler glistened brilliantly in the sun. Another warbler, vivid black and orange, swept by. One accommodatingly posed: rufous, olive, white, and yellow. Melodic notes came from a bright yellow songster. Birds were everywhere, moving in all directions among the trees, shrubbery, or on the ground. In seconds I had seen, or heard, at least twenty birds of a dozen different species. They kept coming, one group after another, high, low, close, at a distance. Call notes and singing came from all directions, spectacular in diversity: high, sweet songs; short, sharp call notes; warbles of one rendition or another; flute-like haunting notes; repetitious notes of one pitch or another. Within twenty minutes in this small area of the woods I had found more than fifty birds of at least twenty species; about half were warblers in the most beautiful and diverse collection of colors and designs imaginable. I was exuberant, relaxing now from the concentrated effort to see, hear, sort, differentiate, and identify.

What is this marvelous event that I await with anticipation each year? Mother Nature synchronizes several key factors: a date in May, during the annual spring migration; a warm night with southerly winds over a large area to the south, which triggers millions of small birds to migrate northward toward their ancestral nesting grounds; a rainstorm, which the flyers do not encounter until they reach my neighborhood in the early morning hours, abruptly bringing them to the ground, called a "fallout"; an inviting habitat, such as a woods along the lakeshore, for them to rest and feed, before they attempt to fly across the barrier of Lake Ontario.

But a "fallout" is only a very small part of the phenomenon that I have found so fascinating, spurring my lifelong, absorbing pursuit. I will introduce you to the gripping hobby of following the Great Pageant, and how to experience it as it occurs in the northeastern United States. But first, be aware that this is a global phenomenon.

Global View of the Pageant

Around the world, millions of birds travel from one region to another. They are not haphazard movements; the birds' ancestors have followed the same prodigious master plan for thousands of years, perhaps millions. Some birds traverse thousands of miles on their intercontinental travels; a few never move but a few miles during their life span. Each species knows just what to do: where to live, the routes to travel, how to find food and survive.

Many ornithologists believe that the retreat of glaciers from the last ice age enabled many species to gradually shift their nesting grounds northward, migrating to where there is less competition for food, and where more daylight permits the young to be fed almost around the clock to hasten their maturity. Most species have adopted some form of migration to improve their chances for survival.

Many birds avoid migrating across seas and large lakes, preferring safer and more food-abundant land routes. While skirting large bodies of water, their migration paths are narrowed, bringing traveling flocks closer together. At such locations their concentrated numbers provide astounding views of the birds' numbers. Several locations are especially well known:

1. The continents of Asia and North America nearly meet in the Bering Sea, where the fingers of Alaska and Siberia come within a few miles. Every spring many Asian birds fly north along the east coast of Asia, funneling through the gap between Siberia and Alaska to arrive at their nesting grounds in the Arctic. At the same time, many North American species, also on their way to the Arctic, fly northward along the west coast of North America, and through the same gap as the Asian birds. Sea birds, after having wintered in the South Pacific, fly the same route to their nesting grounds in the Arctic. St. Lawrence Island, on this multi-tracked migration route, is visited by countless birds from Asia, America, and Oceania during late May and early June. The island's tiny Eskimo village, Gambell, is the site for witnessing this breathtaking event. I stayed there in the home of one of the village elders, a retired whaler, to see this phenomenon for myself.

2. Many birds that have nested in either western Asia or eastern Europe migrate to Africa in the fall by skirting the

eastern end of the Mediterranean Sea. The European birds arrive via Turkey to avoid the Black Sea. The birds from western Asia fly over Iran, to avoid the Caspian Sea, Persian Gulf, Red Sea, and Indian Ocean. Both groups are funneled through Syria and Israel, turn south to Egypt, and then disperse throughout Africa for the winter. Elat, at the southern tip of Israel, the northern end of the Red Sea, is one of the best sites to see birds from both continents migrating in highly concentrated numbers. Some species, however, need not take this roundabout route; they are well adapted for flying directly across large bodies of water.

3. In fall, birds leaving their nesting sites in eastern Asia fly south along the east coast of Asia, as far as Southeast Asia, then follow the Peninsula of Malaysia south and east to Indonesian islands. There they disperse for the winter, or continue on to Australia or New Zealand. In late July 1999, on the island of Bali, my guide excitedly pointed high above a large rice field. "Flying ahead of the rainstorm is a flight of white-throated needletails and fork-tailed swifts. This is as early as I have seen them here; they nest in China and are now on their way to winter in Australia."

4. Another concentrated migration area is the Great Lakes of North America. In spring, birds from South and Central America fly northward following either the East Coast, or more broadly up the east-central part of the continent. Portions of the two routes converge at the Great Lakes, which are large obstacles in their way. The birds select narrow paths through the maze of the lakes. Emerging north of the lakes, the birds disperse to their breeding grounds throughout Canada.

Why I Call It "The Great Pageant"

I call this annual worldwide set of events "The Great Pageant" because it occurs according to a script played out every year, under the direction of Mother Nature. She has assigned specific roles to each of the Pageant's actors. Some have intriguing personalities for us to discover, and each species has ancient rituals to conduct, extensive punctual geographic travels to undertake, and multiple costume changes to make. Some are graced with breathtaking beauty—an artist could not create more handsome color schemes for our amazement. The Pageant plays continuously throughout the year, because each species has its own timetable; some species are nesting while others are migrating. The Pageant is colorful, dynamic, and expansive. Although the Pageant is ritualistic, its immensity and diversity is always presenting aspects and variations that entertain and surprise us.

Although the Pageant is global and continuous, we can only be in one place at a time to sample the event. To a limited extent the different actors or species assist our need to sample the Pageant from one site. Each species arrives at the site at its appointed time, then departs, leaving the stage, my sampling site, for the next group that follows, often reappearing later in the Pageant's year in other costumes.

Most birds live only a few years, but the ancient script does not suffer from the turnover in the cast. Each bird, when born, is programmed by Mother Nature to play its role as did its ancestors. Like birds, we humans also are allocated a limited time on earth, so while here we should observe and enjoy one of the more profound and interesting natural aspects of our planet—the Great Pageant. Mother Nature has largely obscured it from the casual viewer. Consequently, it takes considerable time and dedication to learn, interpret, observe, understand, and appreciate the Pageant. But when we are sufficiently accomplished and have experienced it, it is like having discovered a portion of Mother Nature's plan, an intimate connection to her secrets.

Acquiring the necessary knowledge and skills to experience the Pageant is an enjoyable journey in itself, but it is also demanding. It can take years. So, as to not miss any local parts of the Pageant, what species should we be looking for? How? Where? When? When we see a bird, we can identify it from a field guide, and read about its habitats, but that is not enough. We need to know how it fits into the Pageant: Where has it been? Where is it going? What route is it taking? Why? What triggers its movements? What costume changes (plumages) must we recognize? What does it do when not migrating? Mother Nature has formulated these centuries-old pieces of information and placed them into her script for the Pageant. My goal: to learn about, and experience, as much of the script as possible, for the more I know about the Pageant, the more I can experience and appreciate it.

My Sampling of the Pageant

Just a few miles from where I live near Rochester, New York, is a twenty-mile stretch of the south shore of Lake Ontario. It is one of those very special concentrated migration locations. Waterfowl use that part of the lake during migration as an east-west highway, an extension of the coastal route. Thousands of hawks, having worked their way north, skirt the south shores of lakes Erie and Ontario, to be funneled into a narrow flight pattern where the shoreline makes an abrupt turn at Braddock Bay's famous Hawk Lookout. Millions of small birds, reluctant to fly over the lake without sufficient rest and fuel, stop overnight in the many small woodlots near the lakeshore, before continuing their journey into Canada and their nesting grounds. These factors make the site a microcosm of the eastern North American part of the Pageant, ideal for me to sample the great show.

Most eastern United States bird species are widely distributed, so what is seen of the Pageant from this special site can be experienced throughout much of the East, but perhaps in a less concentrated form.

Especially since my retirement some years ago, I have birded the site on almost a daily basis, often with knowledgeable, skilled local birders who helped me discover many aspects necessary to deeply experience the Pageant.

My mentors, in turn, have benefited from those before them: experienced birders of the Atlantic Coast have learned much about waterfowl habits; hawk watchers from the Appalachian ridges have finely honed techniques for identifying distant hawks; other experienced birders across the East have methods for finding and identifying the many species of warblers and other small birds. We have benefited from the accumulated knowledge of this long lineage of perceivers; they have shed much light on the Pageant.

I have recorded my learning process, and view that effort as having documented portions of the Pageant's script. It would be presumptuous of me, however, to think I could observe the many aspects of the Pageant from a single sampling location; I have merely documented a few excerpts from Mother Nature's great script.

Suggestions for the Reader

The reader should have a field guide for reference to the appropriate color plate of the species being described, and for viewing the range maps I frequently mention while depicting a species' role in the Pageant

Most bookstores have a selection of excellent field guides from which you can choose. Be aware that some guides cover only the eastern half of the country, others just the western half. Some cover the entire country. If you don't yet have binoculars, field guides discuss how to select a pair. Also, bookstores usually carry tapes and CDs of bird calls. You might select one to hear the calls and songs that I describe verbally. Last, the reader does not need to come to my neighborhood to bird and see the Pageant. After reading my accounts, you will know how to look for birding habitats on your own. Better yet, ask an experienced birder in your area where he or she goes birding. As a further help, the subject index has habitat descriptions by species, as well as other subjects to assist in your study.

The reader will see in the book that some species names are in bold print. This is done where information about the species is discussed. If the species is merely mentioned as part of another subject, or contained in the discussion that already has bold print, bold print is not used. The same differentiation between major discussion and passing mention is carried out also in the Index by Species at the end of the book. This is done to facilitate the reader in finding the most useful information on a species as quickly as possible.

PLATE 1. *In midsummer, look carefully at each downy woodpecker for a few scruffy red feathers mixed with the black on the top of its head. That would be the seldom recognized juvenile plumage, which lasts only several weeks*

PLATE 2. *The hairy woodpecker and downy have nearly identical plumage. Note the main difference between the two species is the Hairy's relatively larger bill.*

PLATE 3. *The female cowbird laid her eggs in a chipping sparrow's nest. Here, the larger fledgeling cowbird seeks food from the chippy that raised it, which sadly, was at the expense of her own offspring.*

PLATE 4. *One can hear the woodcocks' mating calls in spring, but one seldom sees them in their secretive haunts in the damp woods.*

PLATE 5. *Late summer on the beach provides a study in similar plumages: two Caspian terns, an adult and immature ring-billed gulls, and the larger herring gull.*

PLATE 6. *The pied-billed grebe is not a duck. It has lobed, not webbed feet, and note its chicken-like bill. It is more accomplished in the water than most ducks, especially at diving. Its ability to lower its body so most of it is submerged is a fascinating trick to watch. We see this interesting little fellow in summer on ponds and lakes.*

PLATE 7. *The white-breasted nuthatch nearly always is going headfirst down a tree trunk. Even woodpeckers don't go down a tree upside down. This is a typical pose, his head held back so he can see us watching him. The jet-black on his head marks him as a male.*

PLATE 8. *Male and female buffleheads are a charming addition to the winter scene along the ice build up of the lake shore. In spring they will move north to nest.*

PLATE 9. *A "kettle" of broad-winged hawks gains altitude using a thermal of rising warm air to assist in migration. The hawks wintered in South America, and are now skirting Lake Ontario en route to Canada to nest.*

PLATE 10. *At night in early spring, saw-whet owls migrate along the lake shore, following a route similar to what the hawks follow during the day. Here, a saw-whet has found its preferred daytime resting site: in a spruce, near the trunk.*

PLATE 11. *The white-crowned sparrow's elegance comes from his erect posture, and clear gray neck and chest.*

PLATE 12. *The white-throated sparrow differs from the white-crowned by its white throat, yellow eye spot, and its often hunched posture.*

PLATE 13. *The huge pileated woodpecker is a thrilling sight, especially when he brandishes his powerful bill. With it, he can quickly chisel a large hole in a dead tree in search of insects.*

PLATE 14. *A tree swallow (left), only a few weeks old, is in its first set of feathers. Soon it will be blue like its parent (right). Look closely to see a few tiny spots of blue starting to show.*

PLATE 15. *Nothing in birding compares to experiencing the spring warbler migration in the north-eastern part of our country. The large numbers, and great diversity of artistically colorful plumage are impossible to describe in words. The chestnut-sided, Wilson's, and magnolia (above) in the hand of their bander, offer hints into mother nature's all out effort to provide a climax to the Great Pageant's spring migration.*

June

1. The Pageant's Opening Act (June 21)

Baby birds have just hatched, and it is the beginning of life for many of the birds I will be seeing throughout the year. This is the opening act of Mother Nature's Pageant!

Only the summer residents are present now, compared to the more dramatic parts of the birding year to come, the fall and spring migrations. The more stable array of species is an easier, opportune time for me to start honing my skills for sampling the Pageant.

I have been invited to join several experienced local birders to search out marsh birds spending the summer here, along the shore of Lake Ontario. Rails, marsh wrens, swamp sparrows, bitterns, red-winged blackbirds, and wood ducks are the most likely species we will see. For the most part, these are the same species that a birder would see in, say, Ohio, Tennessee, or the Carolinas. In other words, we will be sampling the eastern United States portion of the worldwide Pageant.

2. Secrets of a Cattail Marsh

It was 5:30 a.m. when I met Mike Davids, Carolyn Cass, Brett Ewald, and John Bounds. The sun rises grotesquely early this time of year.

Mike is one of our premier local birders. He is especially interested in any unusual species that can be found locally, and always eager to verify its presence personally. He is also very likely to be the person who first finds the unusual bird. He has a knack, based on keen knowledge, for knowing when and where to look for a species that may come to the area once every decade or so—an unusual aspect of the Pageant. On several occasions I have received a call from Carolyn, the instructor for our local museum's course on birding, notifying me that Mike had just found a special bird, telling me where to go to find it. When I would arrive at the site, a number of other birders would already be there, willing to show me the special bird.

Brett is a senior researcher with Braddock Bay Raptor Research (BBRR), and has conducted the hawk count at the nearby Braddock Bay Hawk Lookout for several years. He has also held similar responsibilities at the Cape May Bird Observatory in New Jersey. He founded the Hamlin Beach Lake Watch, now conducted every fall at Hamlin Beach State Park, fifteen miles west of Braddock Bay, to conduct a census of migrating birds, especially waterfowl.

John, also with BBRR, has been its owl migration census taker, and is a skilled birder, especially knowledgeable of hawk identification and migration.

We drove down the Lake Ontario Parkway following the shoreline of Lake Ontario to where Brush Creek flows through an area of cattails and under a bridge a few hundred yards south of the parkway. I told Brett I didn't know much about rails, so he filled me in en route: "Rails are fairly common nesters in the area but are seldom seen because they rarely fly, spending their time on the ground in impenetrable cattail marshes. Rails arrive in the northern marshes in the spring, nest, raise their young, and return to the South in fall, almost always without having been seen by a human being. Birders must be content with finding them by ear; their calls are usually given at dawn or dusk. In fact, hearing them is how we know they are as common as they are—it is certainly not from seeing

While Lying on our bellies, our faces held close to the muddy base of the cattails, the handsome, seldom seen, Virginia rail moved close into view.

them! The best way to increase chances of hearing rails is to repeatedly play a tape of their calls. It may cause them to answer, or better yet, coax them in close enough so they can be seen."

When we arrived at the bridge and cattails, Mike explained why he had brought us here. "This site is well known for **Virginia rails**; I hope we can find one.

Rails nest and feed here in the cattails close to the road, so we have the convenience of looking for them without leaving the road. Most of the other sites in the area where rails are common are in huge expanses of cattails, making it next to impossible to find the birds without a canoe. Rails are most active at dawn, when they are more apt to call or react to other rails calling." Mike had another reason for coming here. "This is north of the normal range of the **king rail**, but one has been reported here recently. I certainly would like to see it."

I reviewed the pages in my field guide that described the two rails. Their pictures looked much the same, the king rail larger than the Virginia.

Carolyn turned on her tape player. She explained, "The Virginia rail often reacts to the calls of the king rail because its call is similar; both calls are a series of evenly timed clucks. I'll play the king's call." She held the player low to the ground, close to the edge of the cattails, and played it several times. No results. She moved down the road a few feet, away from the bridge, and tried again.

After a few minutes we started to hear strange noises; we were not even sure they were coming from a bird. As Carolyn continued to play the tape, the noises came closer. Eventually we heard them often enough and well enough that we decided they were a bird's call notes, but they did not sound at all like the tape. As the calls continued to come closer, our curiosity, anticipation, and alertness heightened.

John whispered, "Just caught a glimpse of a bird walking in the mud, but it's hard to see it among the many cattails." I quickly moved close to John, positioning myself so I could see what he was seeing. We were on our hands and knees now, looking into the cattails at ground level, where the foliage was less dense and where the bird would be seen. Carolyn continued to play the tape. The noises were getting closer, suggesting they were given in response to the tape. I saw it! John said he could see it too. We both watched as it came closer and became more easily seen. With its long toes spreading out over the muddy surface it continued to move very slowly, stepping deliberately over last year's dead cattails. It appeared to be looking for something to eat, and every few seconds gave a call note. Then, when it was less than ten feet away, it came into full view, surrounded by an enchanting and restrictive scene of thick cattails. It had a chestnut-brown body, blue-gray face, and a long bill. A magnificent Virginia rail! Carolyn whispered, "Isn't it gorgeous?" Brett whispered back, "Fantastic!" We were all lying on the ground, eyes at ground level so we could peek into its secret lair.

The rail's beauty was far more stunning than could be depicted in the field guide. Immensely rich colors were artistically combined into exquisite patterns; a noble gray face, outlined by a white throat, blended into the chestnut-brown breast. I don't know how long we watched; I was totally absorbed in this gorgeous and rare sight. Eventually the rail slowly moved away, but not until we all had sufficient time to thoroughly enjoy and study the special treat.

My first Virginia rail! I was thrilled. Lying on the ground, peeking into the secluded midst of the cattails and mud to make a sighting few people have been privileged to experience, was like having been initiated into a secret society. What an auspicious beginning for my project—a look into one of the more secretive parts of Mother Nature's Pageant!

3. Bustle in the Marsh

Carolyn stopped playing the tape; she had just wanted to pique the interest of the rail, but didn't want to run the risk of stressing it. We moved away from our rail-observing positions, stretching to relax from the intense last few minutes. I was now ready for the next find, confident my companions would turn up another actor in the Pageant.

Mike and Brett, ever alert, moved to the other side of the road, where they had heard a **marsh wren** singing. The rattle-like trill came from nearby cattails bordering Brush Creek. The call had a unique quality: it was not musical, but sounded like it could have been made by a mechanical device or toy, rather than a singing bird. Listening carefully, I could hear faint notes sounding like *tea-cup*, two softly given notes preceding the mechanical trill.

Mike then called my attention to a singing **swamp sparrow**, also nearby. I compared the wren's and sparrow's calls as they took turns singing. I described my comparison to Mike: "The swamp sparrow's song is also a rattle-type trill but it has a musical quality rather than the wren's mechanical sound." He agreed, informing me that "the chipping sparrow and junco also have rattle-type calls like the swamp sparrow, but they prefer upland habitats, so there is no problem confusing them here in the swamp."

I told Mike, that I had rarely seen marsh wrens, and then only fleeting glimpses as they drop back among the cover of cattails. Swamp sparrows, however, seem to be much easier to see. He explained why. "Like rails, marsh wrens live in cattails and only rarely pop up so you can see them. We know where they are because they sing profusely throughout the day and sometimes into the night. Swamp sparrows, on the other hand, are more easily seen because they can be found in almost any kind of damp habitat, not just cattails."

Mike started to *spish*, to improve my chances of a good look at the wren. "Spishing" is a technique used by birders to pique the interest of birds, and hopefully get them to come out of their hiding places. He made a *pp* sound followed by a long *shhhhh* noise. I have watched a number of birders spish, and each has his or her own way of doing it, like a fisherman selecting a preferred lure. Brett, Carolyn, and John came over to see if Mike's "spishing" technique would get results.

After a few well-selected spishes, a marsh wren, as if acting on cue, darted out of the cattails and flew across the stream. It landed momentarily on a tall protruding stalk in full view, allowing us a short but clear look at its white throat, eye line, and the black and white stripes on its back. It then dropped down into the cattails out of sight.

We were congratulating Mike on his spishing skills when Mother Nature showed us another seldom-seen resident of the marshes. Bursting straight up out of the cattails, from where it had been hiding near the wren, the bird looked like a miniature heron, only the size of a grackle but with longer legs. It flew across the stream, then quickly dropped out of sight again. The least bittern is the smallest member of the heron family, tan with obvious black patches on the outer third of its wings. Never before had I seen a **least bittern** so close, just thirty feet away. We each commented on how the closeness enabled us to see the wing pattern so clearly. Another great sighting among the cattails!

Our sightings in the last few minutes were unusual because of the birds' impenetrable habitat and reclusive habits. Mother Nature had been benevolent this morning.

A hundred yards upstream were several families of **wood ducks** cruising a wider portion of the creek. Each family had six to eight young, just big enough to swim along with their parents. The adult males, normally the most beautiful of all ducks, were now molting and looked much like their relatively drab, gray mates. It was a charming, serene view. Surrounded by cattails, amid quiet waters, the young chicks were on one of their first outings with their parents. This domestic scene illustrated where we were in the Pageant: the time when the young birds were being raised and prepared for the upcoming fall migration. They had a great deal of growing and learning to do before they were ready. No wonder their parents were so attentive, keeping them well fed and teaching them necessary skills, ensuring that progress stayed on schedule.

July

4. The Decline of Early-Morning Sounds (July 20)

From early spring until recently I was serenaded from the woods and hedgerow behind my house. Robins presented their predawn chorus; then, as light came, cardinals, chipping sparrows, a red-bellied woodpecker, and a house wren joined the concert. This morning all I hear is an occasional distant crow cawing or a blue jay giving his jay-jay call as he hurries by. The silence is an obvious sign that the lives of the birds have progressed. They no longer sing to attract a mate or protect their nesting territory. The early spring hatchlings are now able to care for themselves; those hatched more recently are being fed and supervised by busy parents. The birds' activities have shifted, marking a new section of the Pageant's script. I wanted to observe more of how the passage of recent weeks had affected the birds.

5. Midsummer Activities at an Eastern Pond

Adjacent to Island Cottage Woods is a steep bank. Below it, a ribbon of water, part of Round Pond, extends to the left and right. Beyond is a panoramic view of a huge cattail marsh. The early morning hour, cool and still, added to the beauty and serenity I enjoyed.

A bird sang, breaking the silence; later, a different call alternated with the first. Having been caught up by tranquility, I didn't know how long they had been singing. I recognized both calls, having heard them a month ago at Brush Creek: the mechanical trill was a **marsh wren**, the more musical trill a **swamp sparrow**.

The extensive marsh, with a large pond's finger in the foreground, is the habitat for bitterns, moorhens, swallows, and other species.

I saw neither, but by being able to recognize their calls I learned something else about them: by this date most birds had ceased singing, but these two species persist into late summer.

As singing echoed across the marsh, several **barn swallows** flew by, patrolling the narrow arm of the pond. They flew far to the left, and in a few seconds flew far to the right, remaining low to the water, sometimes barely off the surface, attacking swarming insects. The swallows repeatedly swept back and forth. From my position on the steep bank, I could look almost straight down onto their bright blue backs, and watch their direct flight path, occasionally adjusted by a sideward dart to grab an insect. Their quick change in direction was accomplished by spreading their long, forked tails to one side or another. I interpreted their soft, twittering flight notes to mean they were having great fun gobbling up a bountiful breakfast with their acrobatic maneuvers.

On the far side of the pond two **common moorhens** caught my attention with their bright red bills and foreheads, contrasting with the dark gray of their bodies and the surrounding mud. Each bird carefully lifted one foot at a time out of the mud and deliberately placed it down again so as not to sink too deeply, an efficient manner of walking through the squishy marsh. The moorhens worked their way along the water's edge, sometimes hidden by cattails, other times in the open, pecking away at the tender shoots of aquatic plants. They looked similar to barnyard chickens: small heads; short, heavy, slightly curved bills; and long-toed feet.

Another moorhen was behind a clump of cattails, and ten more were in a line along the narrow, muddy edge of the cattails. Four had the dark-colored bills of juveniles, only a few weeks old, but already as large as their parents. How fast the summer had progressed for them and their parents! The marsh was beautiful and peaceful. How productive a site it was for the moorhens to raise their chicks.

Suddenly shaking me from my reverie, a huge brown form, wingspan over three feet, burst from the cattails. It lumbered about thirty yards and then dropped into the cattails again, out of sight before I realized what I was seeing. I remembered black patches on warm-brown wings. An **American bittern**! I was startled but not surprised: bitterns are usually seen, unexpectedly, taking a short flight over cattails.

Like the other marsh birds I had discussed with Mike Davids and Brett Ewald several weeks ago, American bitterns are seldom seen because of their secretive behavior and the inaccessibility of their habitat to humans. We are more apt to learn of their presence by hearing their strange gulping noises, usually in early morning or evening. A serious birder can assess the population of land birds by walking a defined area of a woods, field, or hedgerow daily, listening and watching attentively, and over time determine with some accuracy the numbers of each species nesting there. In a marsh, however, such a study would be very difficult, even with a canoe. I wondered how many bitterns were in the large marsh in front of me. One pair? Five? Ten? I had no idea.

A pair of **belted kingfishers** also shared the overlook site. One was perched on a dead branch. Periodically it would fly from the branch, hover over a minnow, and then plunge headfirst into the water from a height of ten to twenty feet. Catching lunch in its bill, it returned to its perch, where it skillfully juggled the minnow to swallow it head first. Should its name be king of jugglers rather than king of fishers? I noticed the kingfisher's profile: a large, stout head and bill, a short stout neck, relatively short wings, and not much of a tail—an appropriate design for surviving a lifetime of high-speed plunges through the water's surface tension.

The other kingfisher behaved differently. It repeatedly flew up and down the long slender finger of water at high speed, excitedly giving its rattle-like call to reveal its independent, straightforward personality. It liked what it was doing and wanted me to know it. It seemed to deliberately draw my attention by loudly calling as it flashed by at high speed, looking for food it could catch in a big, splashy dive. I had to chuckle—was it really expecting to find a minnow while participating in such antics? I never saw this kingfisher catch a minnow.

6. A Handsome Late-Summer Songster: Indigo Bunting

While walking back to my car I heard a clear, musical song coming from high in the trees bordering the parking lot. Looking in the direction of the singing I saw an **indigo bunting** perched on a dead branch. His song had an easily discernible pattern: most notes were repeated as pairs. I intently watched and listened, imprinting his unique style of vocalization on my memory while enjoying his magnificence: his brilliant blue was made even more exquisite by the sun's shining from behind me. His feathers glistened with the richest blue imaginable. He was aptly named.

Nearly all the indigo buntings I have seen have been males. The females are usually silent and are a drab brown, making them easily overlooked or dismissed as sparrows. Was there a female nearby that I had overlooked? I looked around briefly in a vain attempt to spot a female.

I remembered a conversation I had with Mike several weeks ago about my not having seen a bunting yet this year. He suggested listening for the song. "For each indigo bunting you see there are about fifty songs that you hear. Fortunately it is one of the last songbirds to stop singing in the late summer, so you still have time to hear one." He went on to describe the song. "It consists of high-pitched repeated two-syllable phrases, sung quite clearly and often given from a high open perch." Mike went on to say that birds sing primarily to attract a mate and announce their territory. I thought it interesting that the bunting continues to sing after the reasons for doing so, that we know about, have passed.

Mike was certainly right! If the bunting had not been singing, I probably would not have noticed him. And it was long after most other birds had stopped singing.

While leaving the pond and bunting, it occurred to me that the species I had seen this morning were probably the same species I'd see in similar habitats no matter where in the East I might be. What I had just seen and heard this morning was typical of many places in the East: Maine, the Carolinas, Pennsylvania, or Ohio.

7. Dispersal Flights: Ploys Within the Pageant

It was a clear, sunny day, so after leaving the bunting I drove west a few miles to Braddock Bay. From the Hawk Lookout observation platform one has a magnificent, expansive view of the bay and its surrounding marsh, as well as Lake Ontario.

Brett Ewald was there, and he explained the hawk watch he was conducting for BBRR. "We are monitoring the hawks now to learn more about their late-summer movements. This is in addition to the census we take during spring migration. During late summer there are random movements of many hawks along the lakeshore. This is not yet a fall migration, but a dispersal after the nesting season is over. We see mostly immature **red-tailed hawks**."

He explained further, recalling statistics he had often given to groups of visitors: "Immature hawks are now fully grown and have been evicted from the nesting site by their parents—a not-so-subtle way of telling them that they are old enough to be on their own. Some of the young red-tails are moving north; one theory suggests they are looking for breeding areas for next year. Another theory is they are just wandering with the prevailing southwest winds of late summer. On August 17, 1991, we counted 2,218 immature red-tailed hawks at Hawk Lookout. We banded 125 of them. On the same day we counted 1,112 broad-winged hawks. The 1991 data called attention to how large summer hawk movements can be, and that more information is needed to understand them."

Brett talked about the prospects for young hawks. "Mortality is about 50 percent for the first year, due mostly to their inexperience in catching prey and coping with hazards."

A hawk flew by, spreading its tail to bank a turn. The light was coming from behind it, so I fully expected to see red in its tail, but there was no red. Brett explained that immatures don't develop red in their tails until their second year.

Over the next two hours we saw about thirty red-tails and several broad-winged as they gradually filtered through, flying across the bay on an easterly route. As near as we could tell, the red-tails were all immatures.

By two o'clock the hawk sightings had become few and far between. I was considering leaving when Brett excitedly pointed out three **great egrets** flying by. They were magnificent—impressive size, a wing span of four feet with slow, deep wing beats, and sensational pure white plumage. Their long legs were stretching out behind them. We tracked them with our binoculars as they gracefully spanned the open waters of the bay, flew over the marsh, and out of sight. Brett clarified: "The three we just saw, like the hawks, are on a dispersal flight. Many species of birds are known to roam at this time of year; it's their summer vacation." "How do you know they are on a dispersal flight?" I asked. "If they had been nesting in the vicinity we would have known about it: their pure white plumage and preference for feeding in open areas would have made their earlier presence obvious. Also, it is highly unlikely they would nest here, being we are well north of their normal nesting range."

8. Enlightenment While Relaxing on My Patio (July 23)

I had never seen a juvenile **downy woodpecker** before, at least that I had recognized as such. It was clinging awkwardly to a tree, some twenty feet from where I was enjoying morning coffee on the patio. I assumed it was just a baby; it held its wings in an unusual position, and moved unsteadily around the trunk. Its mother, having collected breakfast at the suet feeder, flew to the tree above her baby. She chased her offspring around the trunk several times; it seemed strange that it would avoid its mother's attempts to feed it. Finally, the mother caught up, and the baby downed the suet she offered. It was then that I noticed the red feathers on the top of the baby's head. I had a vague recollection that that was the mark of juvenile plumage, which I verified in the field guide. [See Plate 1]

Why, I wondered, during my many years of birding had I never recognized the juvenile plumage of a downy? One possible explanation, or perhaps excuse, was that the red on the forehead was not obvious—it was dark red, and mixed with a few of the surrounding black feathers. The red was not what I would call a standout marking. Today's situation offered the time and relaxed opportunity to study the young woodpecker with more thoroughness than did my typical observations in the field. Also, juvenile plumage lasts only through July and August, when I have not birded much.

From my patio, I watched many birds raise their young to maturity. Also from there, I learned about the juvenile plumage of woodpeckers.

It has been my habit to relax on my patio in the early mornings. I enjoy the quiet serenity of the flowers on the patio, the surrounding stone wall I had labored so to build, and beyond—the hedgerow, field, and woods. The lazy days of summer—what could be more relaxing? I had given little thought to birding, even though familiar birds occasionally flew by or hopped into view. Birds were not migrating, nor were they singing much. This seeming lack of activity had lured me into thinking there was little for me to observe of the Pageant. But, in fact, the birds were extremely busy with the most important part of their lives: raising young. The young were feverishly learning the skills they would need to survive. They would be on their own soon.

My seat on the patio was perfect for viewing and learning about an important act of the Pageant. Sitting here alone it seemed as though Mother Nature was revealing it just to me, at my own convenience. The ostensibly private showing of this act of the Pageant was one that was very important, not only in the lives of the birds, but for the perpetuation of the Pageant itself!

There were at least two downy families with juveniles that had been coming to the feeder frequently, and, to my delight, a family of the less-common **hairy woodpeckers**. From my frequent, careful, morning observations of both species, two questions persistently puzzled me. None of the juvenile downys or hairys had red spots on the back of their heads to indicate they were males. Could they all be females by coincidence, or do they not acquire the male spot until after they lose their juvenile plumage? Also, I was seeing at least one **downy** that was behaving very much like a young, awkward juvenile, being fed by its mother, but it did not have the reddish spot of a juvenile on its forehead. I sent an e-mail message to my longtime friend Bob McKinney, a very astute observer of birds, and a licensed bander for many years. I asked him for explanations.

Bob's reply solved my puzzles. "This time of year, both young-of-the-year **downy** and **hairy woodpeckers** are in their first plumage. They *may* have red on top of the head, but not all do. They lose this during the first pre-basic molt, when males develop red at the back of the head. At this latitude, and after October 1, downys and hairys lacking red at the back of the head may safely be called female. It is not safe to identify young birds as to sex, with or without red, before October 1."

Over the next two weeks, I watched the young become adept at feeding themselves at the feeder. They even starting coming by themselves, more frequently than their parents. To my surprise they acquired a liking for the shelled sunflower seeds in a cylindrical feeder hanging adjacent to the suet. Although the downys, both adult and juveniles, still ate mostly suet, the hairys spent as much time eating seeds. Noting that they had no difficulty in changing to eating shelled sunflower seeds, and that the warm weather had been melting the suet, I ceased providing the latter.

9. A Very Busy Nursery

On early July mornings, between noting activities around the feeders, along the hedgerow, and back in the woods, I would also scan the sky. At a distance I would see different species: a night heron beating a very direct route toward the large ponds and cattails along the lakeshore several miles away, a ring-billed gull winging high as it wandered away from the lakeshore in search of a Dumpster with fast-food scraps, a soaring red-tailed hawk in search of breakfast, a family of chimney swifts combing the breezes for a swarm of insects.

Back on the ground, some species were frequenting the feeders with almost frenzied rapidity, taking seeds back to their nesting spouses, or to newly hatched, hungry babies. It may have been the lazy days of summer for me, but not for them. Those species not attracted to the feeder would disclose their presence by call notes, or I would catch glimpses of them as they busily searched for their preferred sources of food. Throughout my daily morning hour on the patio I was kept very busy, scanning high, observing low, and distinguishing songs or call notes.

A **chickadee** took a seed, then flew over my head toward a small stand of trees, where its nest undoubtedly was located. It would repeat the trip practically nonstop over long periods of time. Male and female chickadees look the same, but one was obviously feeding the other, which was sitting on the eggs. Eventually, after the eggs hatched, I would see both adults at the same time making numerous trips to feed their nestlings. Taking seeds, rather than their usual fare of insects, was undoubtedly an expedient during this busy time for them. I was glad to help them out, and was surprised they didn't make more use of the suet, when I was providing it, which was closer to their natural diet.

After a couple of weeks I could pick out the young chickadees. They were clumsy in their movements, and were hanging around the feeder, anxiously waiting to be fed. Eventually, they too, were helping themselves. I now had no way of determining which were the young, and which were adults. The juveniles' plumage was identical to that of the adults.

There were two family groups of **chipping sparrows** living nearby. I prized these occupants of the nursery—their artfully designed heads, with chestnut caps and black and white eye lines; sleek, slender bodies; elegant and pure slate-gray chests; and serenades of long-lasting, rattling songs that frequently filled the otherwise quiet morning air. Very often, one or two chippies, sometimes more, would explore the base of the stone wall beside the feeders. They would hop to the top of the wall, then to the ground below, curiously exploring nooks and holes in the wall. One would fly away to be replaced by another, singing its prolonged vocalization. As they became old enough to make the short flight, several juveniles were added to the group at the base of the wall, waiting for an adult to offer them seeds. None of the chippies seemed to care that I was closely observing their busy, curious nature.

About midway through my second cup of coffee, I would hear a **cardinal's** call note. The metallic nature of the *clink* was what I recognized. After he announced his approach, I would see an adult male at the feeder. He would then retreat back into the hedgerow with seeds, where two juveniles—the same dull color of the female, but with dark bills, not yet the reddish of the adults—anxiously awaited their breakfast. As the days passed, the juveniles became more adventuresome, hopping onto the stone wall closer to the feeder, showing their impatience. Day after day, the male would feed them. I assumed the female was hatching the second brood; I seldom saw her.

The male **red-bellied woodpecker** typically hatches the eggs, so the female was the regular at the feeder; she was apparently taking food to him. Then, after a couple of weeks, I started seeing the male. Both adults were then making numerous trips to the feeder as they fed their nestlings. Since the juvenile downys and hairys were now frequent visitors, I was anxious to spot a juvenile red-bellied to verify their successful nesting too. After three concerned weeks of waiting, the first juvenile red-bellied appeared on the tree beside the feeder, waiting to be fed. By this time it was full-sized, but with a totally gray head, lacking the distinctive Chinese red that made the adults so eye-catching. I looked carefully to see if there were other juveniles. The comings and goings made it difficult, but finally I was able to see two juveniles at the same time. Over time, I watched both parents care for their young until they had matured sufficiently to feed themselves. They too, like the downys and hairys, were most willing to eat sunflower seeds, alternating with suet when it was available.

Periodically, a song sparrow sang from farther down the hedgerow. Only occasionally would I see it near the feeder, even though it was a seed eater. A meow from a catbird penetrated the underbrush daily, often followed by its appearance at the bird bath. Mourning doves would scan the ground at the base of the feeder, then fly to a rooftop to loudly coo.

Several family groups of robins were always present, but not at the feeder. They were searching for worms on the lawn, and at times, harvesting freshly ripened berries from some of the bushes in the hedgerow.

The summer days on my patio were a wonderful, relaxing experience for me. However, It had been enormously busy for the birds, playing one of the most important roles they had in Mother Nature's Pageant!

August

10. Late-Summer Activity at the Beach
(August 1)

It was still early in the morning when I arrived at Hamlin Beach State Park. The beach is nearly a mile long and several hundred feet wide, one of the few large beaches along the south shore of Lake Ontario. It was a habitat well suited to attract large numbers of water-loving species such as gulls, terns, and shorebirds.

I considered it a good omen that Mike Davids and Bill Symonds were there; they were hoping to see birds' dispersal movements or early migration. I looked forward to benefiting from their expertise, and learning as much as possible in order to experience the Pageant to the fullest. We started walking the beach in a westerly direction so the sun would be to our backs when we looked at the birds.

11. Habits and Appearance of Gulls

We walked awhile without seeing any birds, except an occasional ring-billed gull far out over the lake. I savored the gentle breeze, mild temperature, clear blue sky, and the gentle wave action while waiting for our first sighting.

Looking far down the shoreline, I could see several jetties segmenting the beach at regular intervals. The Army Corps of Engineers had built them to protect against beach erosion.

We soon came to the first jetty. It consisted of huge blocks of rock piled six feet above the waterline and out into the lake for about a hundred yards. Inland from the shoreline, sand had accumulated around the rocks. After stepping over protruding rocks and watching our balance in the loose sand, we emerged on the other side of the jetty to our first sighting—about three hundred **ring-billed gulls**.

From a distance they looked to be in a compact huddle, but as we moved closer, I could see that they were equally spaced about a foot apart, each gull having its own space. They were all facing into the wind to minimize the resistance of the stiff breeze against their feathers. They all looked alike—white with a light grayish-blue back, and a black ring around the bill. This was their adult plumage. "I thought we would see a lot of immatures this time of year," I remarked. Mike answered, "The immatures have probably remained close to where they hatched—small islands at the east end of Lake Ontario about one hundred miles from here. The adults, however, are now dispersing over a larger area."

Knowing I wanted to learn as much as possible about what I was seeing, Bill obliged. "Several other species of gulls have rings on their bills, but only when they are immature. A ring-billed, however, has a ring as an adult, hence its name. Ring-billeds are by far the most numerous of our gulls throughout the year. We see them inland at shopping center parking lots, athletic fields, and farmers' fields. Here along the lake, however, other species of gulls can be seen."

While Bill and Mike carefully scanned the group, looking for more species that might be among them, another fifty ring-billeds flew in from the parking lot. They seamlessly incorporated themselves into the group, taking up the proper distance from each other and facing into the wind.

Bill pointed to three large gulls standing near the water's edge: "**Adult herring gulls**." I had no difficulty recognizing them. Though their plumage was almost identical to that of the ring-billeds, the herrings were much larger. "Look at the other differences," Bill said. "The herring does not have a ring around its bill, but on its lower mandible, or bill, it has a red dot. And, the herring's feet are pink; the ring-billed's, yellow." These two obviously closely related species had just subtle differences, but were very different in size.

Bill found a dark-colored immature herring gull not far from the adults. He knew it had hatched this spring because it had no sign of emerging adult plumage. "The immatures of both gull species are spotted brownish gray, taking on more white on the body and gray on the back each year. It takes several years for a gull to acquire its full adult plumage; the ring-billeds take three years, the herring four." Mike pointed out the ring around the immature herring's bill. "It will lose the ring in three years," he said. I remembered reading in my field guide about two-year, three-year, and four-year gulls, the number of years a species takes to reach full adult plumage. Our discussion prompted me to leaf through the guide to refresh my memory on what it showed as immature plumage. I noticed that, in general, the larger the species of gull, the longer it takes to acquire its adult plumage. The exception is the **little gull**, the smallest gull, which is a three-year gull, not a two-year.

Moving farther down the beach, we came upon another large congregation of ring-billeds. I deliberately searched the group for an immature, a herring gull, or something that we had not yet seen. At the periphery of the group something very different appeared in my binoculars—two **great black-backed gulls** standing near the shoreline. They were nearly twice as large as the ring-billeds, even larger than the herrings. What caught my eye, however, was that they had black backs, as opposed to the very light gray backs of the ring-billeds and herrings.

How dignified the black-backs looked! I decided that their demeanor was due to a combination of their much larger size; their posture, which was much more erect than that of the ring-billeds; and their black and white plumage, reminiscent of formal attire. Perhaps part of their dignified appearance was an aura due to their age and experience; they are believed to be one of the longest-lived birds. Most individuals of a bird species tend not to survive their first year or two, and small songbirds rarely live ten years. Some of the larger birds that live on large lakes or the ocean such as gulls and ducks tend to live longer.

One black-backed, apparently deciding it didn't want us looking at it any more, flew farther down the beach. It was as impressive in flight as it had been standing on the beach. Its huge, black wings were edged in pure white, and its wing beat was slow and powerful. What a contrast it made with the several smaller, lighter colored, and quicker-winged ring-billeds flying nearby. "I find a few black-backs along the lakeshore year 'round, but more abundantly in fall and winter," Bill offered. "Incidentally," he said, "the black-backed is a four-year gull."

Mike had found two **Caspian terns** among the group of ring-billed gulls. Even though he told me exactly where to look, I had to scan back and forth several times before seeing the two bright orange splotches of color—the Caspians' large, distinctively colored bills. I wondered how I could have missed them; their bills were so obvious and eye-catching. Looking at them again, I noticed black on the crown portion of their heads, a feature common to all adult terns. As I looked at the terns and the gulls that surrounded them, I realized how well the terns blended in with the larger group. The terns were the same size and overall color as the ring-billed gulls, they were facing in the same direction, into the wind, and were equally spaced like the gulls. That is why I had trouble seeing them at first.

After a few minutes the terns took off, cruising back and forth along the beach about a hundred yards from shore. They were looking for lunch. As they searched the water below for fish, their downward-pointed bills were easily seen from a distance.

A minute or so later Bill called my attention to the terns' flight call, a loud, rough-sounding *kawk*. Looking in the direction of the repeatedly given calls, we saw the terns coming our way, their bills still pointed downward. When they passed in front of us I studied their silhouettes— their wings were slightly narrower and their bodies more slender than the ring-billeds flying nearby.

Then something I wasn't expecting occurred. One of the terns stopped in midair, hovered for several seconds, then partly closed its wings and fell from the sky, a headfirst high-speed dive from about forty feet. A spectacular splash! The tern quickly emerged from the water and returned to its patrolling altitude. I tried to see if it had caught a minnow or fish, but its body was blocking my view of its bill. Mike explained, "You just saw a typical tern dive. You'll never see a gull dive headfirst." Thinking about it, I have seen gulls make water landings so abruptly that they looked like dives, but they were not headfirst. "In a few weeks," Bill added, "the **common tern** will arrive. It has markings similar to the Caspian but is only half its size." A few steps farther on, Bill spotted four **Bonaparte's gulls** standing behind the group of ring-billeds. The Bonaparte's are small gulls, much smaller even than the ring-billeds. What was most noticeable about them was that their heads were all black, not just black-crowned like the Caspians, and completely different from the all-white heads of the other gulls. "Bonies," as Bill called them, "start showing up this time of year after having nested in northern Canada. Using Lake Ontario as a highway for migration, they're on their way to the Atlantic coast to spend the winter. We'll see many more of them in September and October. The birds we are looking at now probably nested along the south shore of Hudson Bay."

As we continued our walk along the beach, I thought about how the five species we had just seen fit into the Pageant. Summarizing in my mind what I had just experienced, I had to admit to a little bewilderment.

The ring-billeds, herrings, and black-backs nest in large, concentrated colonies at other locations in the Great Lakes region, such as the islands at the east end of Lake Ontario. Once they finish nesting, they disperse from the crowded colonies. Then—and this is where it becomes complex—some come here to stay until the next nesting season, and some non-breeding young adults may remain here throughout the next summer. They do not migrate as we normally think of it. Others of their species do migrate; they move to sites along the Atlantic coast for the winter. So birds within a single species may have different parts to play in the Pageant.

The Bonies and Caspians we just saw, on the other hand, are truly migrating. They are on their way to Florida and the West Indies for the winter.

It is a complex picture, that's for sure! It certainly would be interesting to quiz each gull we had just seen and ask it what its upcoming travel plans were. I knew Mother Nature would never give up her secrets. The best we can hope for is to sample her Pageant, enjoy what we can see, and appreciate the mystery of the remaining secrets. [See Plate 5]

12. Surprise! An Enormous Visitor from Hudson's Bay: A Whimbrel

We continued walking the beach, leaving the large groups of gulls behind. The only birds now were occasional ring-billeds soaring at a distance offshore. The temperature now was quite warm. I was becoming lethargic, but the feeling was to be short lived.

Out of the corner of my eye I spotted a large bird flying toward us from the lake. It was the size of a gull, but a dark color, so I assumed it was an immature gull. When the bird saw us standing where it had intended to land on the beach, it quickly swerved, showing its profile. I could hardly believe what I saw: a very long, slender neck, and an extremely long down-curved bill at least four inches long. "A **whimbrel**!" Mike called out loudly. Its appearance was dramatic, the largest shorebird I had ever seen, and my first whimbrel!

It flew over the nearby rock jetty and dropped down behind it. We scampered over the jetty, ignoring the precarious footing, to get another view. We were well rewarded. The large, powerfully built bird was strolling the beach with huge, decisive, authoritative strides. He owned the beach! "Its down-curved bill tells us it is a member of the curlew family, not a godwit, the other family of large shorebirds," Mike explained. Bill added, "It's my guess that it had spotted the accumulation of algae on the beach and was intending to inspect it for insects and other aquatic life, when we surprised it." He explained further. "It had nested on the Arctic tundra, perhaps Hudson's Bay, and is now going to the southern coast of the United States or South America for the winter. I see several whimbrels here almost every year. I was wondering if we would see one today. They are early migrants, so this is not too early to expect them."

We completed our walk along the beach. I thanked Bill and Mike for their help in making it a fruitful and enlightening field trip.

13. Sampling Shorebirds' Migration to the East Coast (August 9)

Many shorebird species nest in the high Arctic. They remain at their nesting site only long enough to raise their young; then, in July, they begin their journey south to the East Coast. They start migration while numerous other birds are still in dispersal. Large numbers of shorebirds follow the shore of Hudson Bay south into Georgian Bay, then to Lake Ontario. From there it is a day's flight to the Atlantic Coast. The route maximizes the shoreline habitats of mudflats and beaches needed for feeding.

The Genesee River flows north, emptying into Lake Ontario at the City of Rochester. A quarter-mile-long public beach stretches west from the mouth of the river. Few other beaches or mudflats of significant size are nearby; therefore, Ontario Beach attracts many of the shorebirds en route to their wintering grounds.

Considering the date, I decided a trip to Ontario Beach was in order. I knew it would be a hit-or-miss situation, depending upon whether recent weather and winds farther north had been favorable for migration.

A group of about twenty shorebirds were gathered at the shoreline. So as not to alarm them, I slowly walked toward them, then stopped, deciding not to go closer and risk them flying away.

It was a flock of peeps, a collective term applied to the several species of very small shorebirds. Obvious among the flock was a much larger and plumper shorebird, gray above and lighter below. Its legs and bill were not long in comparison to most other shorebirds' proportions. It looked familiar, but I couldn't remember its name; I should not have left my field guide in the car.

Luck was with me. Kevin Griffith had just come by on his morning bicycle ride; he would be better than a field guide. "You're looking at a **red knot**," he said. "It's in its gray winter plumage now; in spring it is reddish brown, hence its name." Over the next few minutes I was to learn much about shorebirds that would help me understand the Pageant. Kevin, an elementary school teacher, loves to teach people about birds, so I encouraged him by asking, "Why is there only one knot?" "The knot is alone now because it had nested on the northern shores of Hudson's Bay, where it had maintained a large nesting territory, isolated from other knots," Kevin replied. "However, knots do like to migrate in huge flocks. Our friend here will undoubtedly meet up with others as it follows the standard knot migration route along the Atlantic Coast. In spring, en route north along the coast, nearly all of the North American knots arrive at Delaware Bay in huge flocks just when the horseshoe crabs lay their eggs. The knots gorge themselves on the eggs before continuing north."

Kevin has introduced hundreds of young students to birding over the years. The elementary school where he taught was adjacent to a large park with varied habitat, attractive to many species of birds. Kevin's field trips to the park were popular with the students, many of whom acquired a substantial interest in birds as a result.

Last year I took a memorable birding trip to Gambell, Alaska, on St. Lawrence Island in the Bering Sea, near Siberia. Our field ornithologist guide was Jeff Bouton, who had been introduced to birding by Kevin. One day, when Jeff and I were walking back to the Eskimo village, he told me how, as a fifth grader, he had come upon Kevin watching a snowy owl through his spotting scope near the school. Jeff took a look at the magnificent bird through the scope and was hooked on birding from that moment on.

We slowly moved closer to the group of peeps. They were busily pecking in the algae at the water's edge. I guessed they were either **semipalmated** or **least sandpipers**, the two most common peeps of the area. Just as I was about to ask Kevin which they were, I saw a similarly sized but much browner bird about ten feet farther down the beach. The color difference told me the first group was probably semipalmated sandpipers and the browner bird was a least sandpiper. Kevin verified my identification and added, "Both species become progressively grayer as they develop their winter plumage, but the semipalmated is always the grayer of the two." That bit of information made me wonder just how accurate my identification would be if I were looking at only one of them. It would be hard to know how far into its winter gray plumage it had advanced; was it a slightly advanced semipalmated or a more advanced least? Kevin gave me another hint. "Least sandpipers have light-colored legs; the semipalmated, black legs. Be careful, however; the leasts' legs can look dark if they are in a shadow or are caked with mud."

Then Kevin noticed a slightly larger bird among the semipalmateds. "Look at the well-defined buff-colored area on its breast and neck; see also that its wings project farther in back than the semipalmateds—a **Baird's sandpiper**! Baird's are rarely seen here in spring but are not unusual in the fall." I was still studying the Baird's, wondering if I would have noticed it without Kevin's help, when he noticed another bird and announced it might be a **Western sandpiper**. It looked very much like a semipalmated to me, but Kevin pointed out the differences. "It has a slight reddish wash on the back and what might be a slightly larger bill. What caught my attention was its being territorial, chasing away semipalmateds that came too close. The differences, however, are just not sufficient for me to say for sure that it is a Western." I found Kevin's unwillingness to make an identification revealing. It told me that there are situations when the subtle differences between two species, coupled with individual variations, make it impossible for even an experienced birder to make a positive identification. It takes a skilled birder to know when to call and when to fold.

As we walked on, Kevin told me about shorebirds' plumage. "Juvenile shorebirds typically have more white outlining their feathers, giving them a fresher look; they are, after all, brand-new feathers. The adults look a little tattered, for they are in the process of molting and have a mix of their old, worn breeding plumage and new winter feathers. The adults leave the breeding grounds first and the juveniles remain for a while before coming south. I think all the birds we saw this morning are adults. Keep an eye out for the differences over the next few weeks to see if you can detect when the juveniles come through." I was deep in thought. Pageant observation is getting to be strong stuff. I'm now into identifying age-differentiated migration.

Farther down the beach were two shorebirds slightly larger than the peeps. They ran down the beach with their short legs moving quickly along the water's edge, their black legs and bills contrasted sharply against their light-colored bodies—**sanderlings**. They are very common here. I told Kevin, "I remember reading about them and being impressed by their migration journeys. They nest in the high Arctic near the magnetic north pole, visit us here briefly, then continue on their way to winter along the Atlantic Coast." Kevin agreed and added, "The other shorebirds we have seen this morning follow similar migration routes—they nest in the Arctic too."

We stopped to watch the sanderlings play games with the waves—they would see how close they could follow a wave as it receded outward, then, when the next wave came in, they would retreat as little as possible without getting wet. Kevin said they do this to increase their chances of finding something to eat that has been brought in by the wave's action. Kevin and I had come too close; the sanderlings flew farther down the beach. "Notice the broad white stripe extending the length of their wings," Kevin said. "Other small shorebirds show white stripes on their wings in flight too, but the sanderlings' stripes are more prominent."

Farther away, we spotted a group of five **Bonaparte's gulls**. Three were in full adult breeding plumage—bright reddish-orange feet and black heads. "In a few weeks," Kevin said, "the black on their heads will be gone and only a small black spot behind their eyes will remain. This will be their winter plumage." Then he pointed to one of the other two Bonaparte's. "Its white head with the black spot behind the eye is the Bonaparte's winter plumage. Now compare its light-colored feet to the bright orange feet of the other two birds. It is a juvenile in its first plumage; it hatched just a few weeks ago. As you can see, a Bonaparte's first plumage is similar to an adult's winter plumage. That is why the two birds are not in the same plumage—the juvenile is already in winter plumage; the adults have not yet changed." Then Kevin pointed to the other bird in the group. "It is one year old—it has black on the head indicating it did not hatch this summer, but its legs are not yet bright orange. It takes Bonaparte's two years to acquire adult-colored legs." I remembered my recent discussion with Mike and Bill at Hamlin Beach, where we discussed two-, three-, and four-year gulls. With Kevin's help I had just seen all three appearances of a two-year gull: hatch year, one year, full adult. I was astonished by how much more of the Pageant I could experience when I could tell a bird's age!

Kevin regretted having to leave. He had errands that had to be done before noon, admitting that domestic responsibilities, at times, get in the way of birding.

14. More Early Stages of Fall Migration
(August 19)

It was 6:30 a.m., just after dawn. I was at Hamlin Beach State Park, twenty miles west of Rochester. I had my spotting scope on a high bank that provided a sweeping view of the Lake Ontario shoreline. The site attracts birders to come and see the diverse water-loving birds that use this large body of water. I was eager to see what part of Mother Nature's Pageant would take place this morning. What was on her script for today?

I did not have long to wait. Flowing westerly along the shoreline was a steady stream of swallows, in strung-out bunches just a few feet from shore, ten to twenty feet above the water. As they flew over the rock jetty, they would go up a few feet so as to maintain a constant altitude. They kept coming, a continuous flow. Turning my spotting scope far to the right, I could see the flow coming toward me in an uninterrupted stream for as far as I could see, nearly a mile. The parade surprised me; I was expecting gulls, shorebirds, or perhaps other waterbirds.

Most birds migrate at night, but swallows, as I was observing, migrate during the day, as do a few other species such as hawks, ducks, and blue jays. Swallows can migrate during the day because they can feed en route, almost without breaking stride—or wing beat. I hoped to see one take an extra dip or dart to catch an insect, but each seemed very intent on keeping up with the group.

I wondered about their part in the Pageant. Are they going west now along the lakeshore because insects are more plentiful near the lake? Where did they spend the summer? There were so many that they must have been drawn from a large geographical area. When will they turn south and head more directly to their wintering grounds in Central and South America? Only Mother Nature knows the Pageant's entire script, and the answers to my questions.

A car door slammed in the parking lot behind me. I recognized Bill Symonds' red truck. In a moment Bill was setting up his spotting scope in front of the park bench next to me.

He helped me identify the swallows. "The smaller ones are **bank swallows**, and there are a few **barn swallows** mixed in." After a minute or so he added, "Occasionally a **tree swallow** comes by, too." We sat watching the parade as it continued unabated. Bill gave me more hints for observing swallows. "After some practice, you won't need to use your scope or binoculars to identify bank swallows, even though they may be three or four hundred yards away. They give their short, dry trill persistently as they fly by, and they are noticeably smaller than the barn and tree swallows." I watched, carefully noting what Bill had said. I picked out the smaller banks, heard their buzzy trill, and tried to imprint the sights and sounds in my mind for future reference.

"Mid to late August and into September, there can be large flocks of swallows moving west along the lakeshore. It is not known if these are post-nesting dispersal movements or whether they are the beginnings of their migration southward," Bill offered. He then helped me identify the barn swallows.

"The barns are the ones with the long, pointed tails, especially the adults. The immatures have not yet developed their pointed tail feathers, but their tails are still deeply forked."

My next challenge was to differentiate tree swallows from barn swallows: both were noticeably larger and had more pointed wings than the banks. Bill helped me out. "The barn swallow has a more direct flight pattern than the more irregular-flying tree swallow." Suddenly the identification of the two species became easier. Bill's hint worked.

"We have a steady flow of **ring-billed gulls** flying east along the shore," Bill announced. "I've been watching them stream by for several minutes." I had noticed gulls flying across my binoculars' field of vision, but I had been paying too much attention to swallows to realize there was also a large gull movement. Now my attention shifted to the gulls. There were hundreds of gulls going by in the direction opposite to the swallows. The gulls were at a higher altitude, so the two flights didn't clash. Bill explained, "The gulls spend the night in large groups on the water several hundred yards offshore, where they will be safe from predators. At dawn they leave the communal spot and spread out along the shore, selecting a place to spend the day. What we are seeing is their morning, daily dispersal. They pick beaches, parking lots, or fields where they can find something to eat." As I watched, some of the gulls decided to stop at the beach in front of us, which had been empty when I first arrived. Now there were at least a hundred gulls on the beach below us. Over the next hour we watched at least a thousand gulls in their morning dispersal.

Bill is not one to overlook anything—the mark of an experienced birder. He carefully scanned the group of ring-billeds, looking for something different. "Two **Caspians terns** sitting at the water's edge," he announced. "Their caps are not as pure black as the adult breeding plumage. They could be either immatures or adults going into winter plumage." I was noticing the black caps when, as if they had been waiting for me to finish noticing their plumage, they flew off, following the shoreline down the beach. They each gave a high-pitched musical *see-ya* call. "That's the immature's call," Bill said. Then, probably in response to the immatures, we heard the adult's harsh, low note—*kowk*. We watched the immatures catch up to the adult, and together they flew farther down the beach and out of sight.

Three **cedar waxwings** had been flying back and forth between the two clumps of bushes beside us. They were consistently on the move, and so close that it was easy to study their flight characteristics. They would flap their wings rapidly several times, miss a beat, then repeat the several rapid beats. It was a unique manner of flight, useful for identification from a distance.

We sat for a few minutes, seeing nothing but an occasional ring-billed flying by. "Most bird activity takes place during the first three hours of daylight," Bill offered. I looked at my watch: it was 9:30, three hours since sunrise. Considering the slackened activity over the lake, we decided to look for shorebirds on the beach. Any migrating shorebirds stopping here at the beach to rest and feed would probably remain here for the remainder of the day.

We walked down the steep incline to the beach, then walked along the shore. A lone shorebird, larger and much plumper than a peep, was at the edge of the lapping waves. "A **ruddy turnstone** still in its spring plumage!" I called out. Its head and neck were bold scrolls of black on a white background, a unique pattern. Its back and wing were reddish brown with intervening black sections. What a colorful and most unusual appearance!

We walked on, skirting the turnstone so it would not feel the need to fly. Not far away was another shorebird, about midway in size between the turnstone and peeps. A distinctive large black patch covered most of its belly. A highlighting edge of white surrounded the patch, and rufous covered its back. "The best bird of the day," Bill said. "**Dunlins** don't usually arrive here until September. This one is quite early, and easy to identify in its spring plumage. The dunlins we will see later will be in their all gray, nondescript winter plumage."

I wanted to learn what part these two species were playing in the Pageant, so I checked their range maps in the manual. The dunlin had just come from the Arctic coast. The turnstone had nested even farther north, on one of the islands in the Arctic Ocean north of the coast. I was fascinated by the distances they were traveling, from the Arctic to the Atlantic Coast of the southern United States, and by the fact that their routes had brought them to this spot where we could see them so easily. The chances of anyone ever seeing them on their nesting grounds were remote for sure. I later discovered that these two species were circumpolar in their ranges, meaning they nest widely in the North American, European, and Asian Arctic, and migrate south through those continents. They can be seen in many parts of the northern hemisphere.

A far more slender shorebird had been standing just beyond the dunlin. Our movement caused it to fly to the large rocks near the water level at the far end of the jetty. As it walked among the algae-covered rocks it teetered back and forth as though it were having trouble balancing. "The teetering can be observed from a great distance. This is an easy way to identify a **spotted sandpiper**. Its willingness to search among the rocks is also indicative. Most other shorebirds avoid a rocky shoreline, preferring mudflats or a beach," Bill coached. "Did you notice when it flew that its wings appeared to go only from the body level downward, giving its flight a stiff, fluttering, bowed look?" he asked. When Bill referred to the manner of flight, I remembered seeing it; both the flight and teetering were valuable hints for identifying a spotty at a distance, and I salted them away for future use. "Most of the shorebirds we are seeing now are migrating. The spotty probably nested here at Hamlin Beach or nearby. Very often a pair will pick a small farm pond as their summer home," Bill added.

15. Some Late-Summer Discoveries

Raucous noises came from one of the lifeguard chairs on the beach. Two **crows** were perched on the lifeguard's seat; another was standing on the sand below. The three cawed excitedly as though they were giving instructions to bathers. They're playing lifeguard, I thought. Bill was thinking about crows too. "I often see them at the beach in the morning, looking for a dead fish that may have washed ashore, or something else they might like. Later they move to other locations to round out their menu." After walking a bit farther, Bill added, "There is an old saying: crows appear in threes. That is not always the case, of course, but three certainly is a typical number."

There is something about crows, I thought, that has always fascinated me, but I can't put my finger on what it is. Perhaps it is their versatility, for they thrive in a wide variety of habitats. I have seen them in urban areas and in remote wilderness; in the midst of a bitter winter storm, or a warm summer day. They eat insects, corn shoots in a farmer's field, road kill, fruits, almost anything. More than likely, it's their personality that appeals to me. They are raucous, fun-loving birds, always noisily talking back and forth with each other, or enjoying the excitement of harassing an owl or hawk. Summing it up, they are smart, creative, flexible survivors, with a flair for enjoying life with their buddies. How could I not enjoy and respect them for those laudable characteristics!

We reached the end of the beach, and turned to retrace our steps. I suggested we leave the beach and head back to our cars via the hiking path—a change of habitat.

In a small tree not far from the path were six **cedar waxwings**. They flew to a group of low bushes on the jetty, about two hundred yards away. They would flap their wings several times, skip a beat, and repeat the sequence that I had observed a few minutes before. At that distance they appeared to be a modest brown color, not particularly attractive. "I don't see any berries on the bushes," I ventured. "They must be finding insects."

Bill offered his experience. "Now that the breeding season is over, they are starting to band together. By the time winter gets here there will be at least twenty or even forty in the group. Throughout the winter they will search the countryside together looking for trees or bushes that have berries or other fruit. The group will remain together until nesting time in the spring." "I certainly know about that," I said. "Every year, about Thanksgiving time, a flock of waxwings discovers the crabapple trees that surround my patio. They work ceaselessly for an entire day eating all the fruit, with the help of a few wintering robins, then disappear. I may not see them again for the remainder of the winter."

While Bill and I were talking, the waxwings returned to the nearby tree. I was struck by how different they looked up close. One of the birds was turned so its colors were magnificently illuminated by the sunlight, transformed into a superb work of art! The warm brown head and throat phased into a bright yellow belly. The brown on its back blended into several shades of gray toward its rump. The red spots at the tip of its wings and a yellow band at the end of its tail added just the right amount of bright accents.

While I admired Mother Nature's artwork, the group communicated with each other in their thin, insect-like, buzzy *wheez*. It is the only form of utterance I have ever heard from them. I shared my assessment with Bill. "Their beauty is strictly visual; they certainly can't sing!" I have often heard groups of waxwings wheezing among themselves in high branches hidden by the foliage; I would never have known they were there if I had not been familiar with their meager little buzzy vocalizations.

We passed under a row of tall trees, then came out onto an open area where a single maple tree stood. Bill stopped, directing his binoculars toward a branch extending well out over a picnic table. A phoebe darted out, grabbed an insect, and returned to its lookout perch on the branch; typical phoebe behavior. It was dark gray above and light-colored below. "It has a yellow wash on its belly," I called out in surprise. I had never noticed that on a phoebe before. Bill provided the explanation. "In the fall, phoebes take on a slight yellowish color on their bellies. Many birders who do most of their birding in the spring have never noticed this subtle change in the phoebe's plumage."

Several warblers flitted among higher branches of the same tree. Their plumage was drab, dull, no visible distinguishing markings. I was frustrated in determining what they were. When one faced away, I saw its yellow rump. "A **yellow-rumped warbler**," I reported to Bill. He already knew; he was just waiting for me to discover it on my own. I explained my identification. "A **magnolia warbler** also has a yellow rump but it always shows more yellow underneath, even in the fall." The season of the "confusing fall warblers" was coming up; some warblers will be in duller colors and may totally lack a key characteristic that identifies them in spring. The Peterson field guide devotes two color plates to "confusing fall warblers."

As we crossed the open field, several **American goldfinches** flew along the bordering hedgerow singing their flight song, *potato-chip*. The field guides say it sounds like *per-chick-o-ree*. I guess you take your pick as to which representation is more accurate. Bill pointed out their undulating flight. "Goldfinches go up when their wings are spread and go down when they're closed. The resulting up-and-down flight pattern is distinctive, and when coupled with their usually given flight call, makes goldfinches easy to identify at great distances."

The swallow movement had ceased, the gulls had settled in for their naps, we had seen which shorebirds were on the beach, and had checked out the birds along the hiking path. It had been an instructive morning, including a number of signs that the Pageant was definitely speeding up after the summer doldrums.

As we parted, Bill gave me one more hint. "There have been several sightings of **black-crowned night herons** along the south shore of Long Pond. As you go by on the parkway, look for them standing at the water's edge among the cattails. Very few, if any, have nested here in recent years. Those being seen probably nested elsewhere and have dispersed into our area after the nesting season. This time of year they stand at the edge of the ponds in the mornings, their white breasts visible from long distances. Later in the day they hide out in the interior of the marsh."

Minutes later, on the drive home, I slowed down as I approached Long Pond, looking for white spots on the far shoreline. Sure enough, there were two, several hundred yards apart. I stopped on the shoulder of the road, and looked at one with my binoculars. Although five hundred yards away, the night heron's white chest, contrasting against the dark green foliage of the cattails, was easy to spot. The rest of its body was black and gray, so I could barely make out its outline, but I saw enough to verify what I was seeing. Thanks to Bill, the sighting—another entry in Mother Nature's script—was a fine conclusion to a pleasant morning.

16. The Nursery Is Closed; Dispersal Is Under Way (August 20)

Throughout the summer, I become increasingly pleased by my observations and awareness of the nursery's activities, especially seeing the young birds starting to come to the feeder.

Now, in late August, I was starting to notice changes: I no longer heard the song sparrow sing; the chickadees didn't come to the feeder nearly as often; the adult red-bellieds were seldom seen; the nuthatch didn't appear; and the robins, which had always been noticeable around the lawn since early spring, were absent. I really missed the chipping sparrows. They had a pleasant, sleek little presence that I admired so much. It was obvious that most of the birds I was used to seeing had left the area, leaving my mornings now relatively uneventful. The summer residents had almost totally dispersed, even though their official migration southward would not commence for several more weeks. Some of the permanent residents, such as the woodpeckers, were still represented, but I was seeing them much less frequently.

Earlier, I had seen a juvenile **downy** showing a small bit of a juvenile's red on the top of his head. Now there was the beginning of red on the back of his head, the emergence of adult male plumage. There were no juvenile-plumaged **hairys** either, only young ones in brightly black-and-white newly acquired adult plumage. A juvenile **red-bellied** was showing the beginnings of an outline of red over the nape of the neck, the start of molting into female adult plumage. These late sightings marked another point in the progress of the Pageant, the molting of juveniles into adult plumage.

With the young birds now grown to maturity, most of the adults and young had separated. They had left the site of the nursery to enjoy themselves in different surroundings. Ornithologists call it "dispersal," a significant event in the lives of many birds, their version of our summer vacation. It is believed by a number of experts that some of the young take this time to explore for nesting sites for next spring. Whatever the reason for it, dispersal was now clearly underway.

Having experienced such a pronounced lack of activity on the patio in the mornings, I found myself spending fewer early morning hours there. Now, I was exploring other nearby sites, expanding my sampling of the Pageant's dispersal phase.

17. A Grackle Colony's Morning Scatter (August 29)

Driving the circular on-ramp to enter the Lake Ontario Parkway, I first faced toward the still-dark northern sky. The ramp then curved toward the eastern horizon, where the sun was radiating from the morning's first light. Something blotted out the sun's first rays—a cloud, or shadow perhaps. Before I could make out what I was seeing, the ramp turned abruptly to the south. As I left the on-ramp and increased speed, I glanced to my right—north—and spotted the dark form again; it was not a cloud, but a huge flock, thousands of **common grackles**. They were flying parallel to the highway. I looked over my shoulder to see how far back the flock stretched. It appeared to be endless! The colossal number of birds covered the northern sky.

Thousands of birds were flying out of the cattails of the huge marsh that borders Lake Ontario, after having roosted there overnight. As I drove farther, the cloud dissipated. The birds were spreading out over the countryside to search for food.

I had heard about this phenomenon. After the nesting season is over, grackles gather into large numbers to roost at night, usually picking a site near water. By mid-November, they leave for points south to spend the winter together.

My morning's field trip had started with what I considered to be a footnote to Mother Nature's script.

18. Immature Plumages Provide Challenges and a Surprise

Having left the grackles behind, I parked at the lake's shoreline where it becomes the west spit of Braddock Bay. An immense willow dominates the site. South of the tree, a hedgerow separates an open field from the bay.

Local birders are very aware that on the right day this varied habitat can yield an impressive collection of birds in dispersal or migration.

When I opened the car door, about twenty swallows flew from the telephone wire above me. In a few seconds, after deciding I posed no threat, they returned, perching on the wire. Swallows are very common here; the lake, marsh, and adjacent fields provide a wealth of flying insects, their only diet. By stepping back a few feet for a better angle, I could see there were several different plumages represented. I had a perfect view of them all in a row on the wire, up close, sitting still, and facing me so I could see their identifying breast markings. I wondered if they knew how accommodating they were. How different it was from several days ago at Hamlin beach when Bill Symonds helped me identify migrating swallows that were too far away to be identified by their plumage. We had to distinguish them by their flight-call notes, manner of flight, and overall shape.

I first studied several adult **barn swallows**, noticing their blue backs and cinnamon throats. The long feathers on both sides of their tails emphasized their deeply forked tails, the chief characteristic of barn swallows.

Among the adult barns were three similar-looking swallows, but they were lighter underneath. When I saw a slight hint of cinnamon color on their throats, I knew they were young barns. The clincher, however, was their tails; although they had not yet acquired their long, protruding tail feathers, their tails were sufficiently forked to be barn swallows.

Perched farther down the wire was a group of swallows with brown backs and white bellies. Some had relatively clear breasts, while others had obviously dark breast bands—two more species for me to identify. The breast bands clearly indicated **bank swallows**. I was unsure what the others were until I saw two adult **tree swallows** sitting with them; they had bluish backs but lacked the barns' forked tails. I remembered that a young tree swallow has a brown back and gradually acquires the blue back throughout the fall. It took me awhile to sort out the three species of swallows. There were both adult and immature plumages to add complexity. [See plate 14]

I walked toward the hedgerow, eager for more challenges. Perhaps I would see more challenging immature plumages. The hedgerow took me away from the lake into a mixture of woodland and open fields. A distinctive call note, a short, metallic *eeek*, came from the high branches of an ash in the hedgerow. I recognized the call's unique characteristic as a **rose-breasted grosbeak**! I hoped it was a male and would honor me with its melodious song. Females don't sing; they only give the call note. The grosbeak psychically received my request. His song clearly echoed across the field, similar to a robin's, but a more musical rendition. When it was repeated, I listened carefully to be sure it was not a robin. I concluded it was very musical, so I was sure the bird was a grosbeak.

I scanned the tree, wanting very much to enjoy the grosbeak's striking beauty. The adult male has a large, triangular, bright rosy-red breast patch, framed in white and emphasized by the bird's black head, that attracts the eye. I looked in the song's direction. There it was. I could even see it singing. But I was startled by its totally unexpected appearance. The singing bird had a dull reddish-brown breast with considerable streaking. It did not look at all like a male rose-breasted grosbeak. Could it be an immature robin? The color and streaking certainly suggested it. Had I confused the similar-sounding songs, in spite of my being so careful on that very point? Then the mystery was solved; the bird turned its head just enough to show me its heavy bill, dark cheek patch, and eye line, all marks of a grosbeak. I checked the field guide for clarification. There was an exact illustration of the bird I was seeing—a first-fall male. Next spring it would have the bright red breast I had expected to see. I laughed; that young grosbeak sucked me in with his adult singing, then threw me for a loop with his unexpected plumage.

In the hedgerow, a small bird was working its way down a spindly tree. It had two interesting characteristics. It was going down the trunk head first, but it was not a nuthatch, the only other bird I could think of that did that. Also, its entire body was pure black and white, blotched and streaked, a color scheme that looked out of place, almost artificial, among the surrounding greens and browns. It was a **black-and-white warbler**. Expecting it to be a juvenile, I looked carefully for a wash of buff color on its sides. There was none. The black around his throat completed my identification—a handsome adult male. The fact that his throat was still black rather than white meant that he had not yet gone through his fall molt. My best guess is that he had nested in Canada and was now starting a leisurely trip to the Gulf Coast or South America. I wished he could tell me where he had nested and where he was going to spend the winter. I wanted to know what route he was taking and how long it would take. Unlike my encounter with the grosbeak, psychic communication did not work in this situation. I received no answers.

A little bird ducked into the roadside bushes. I assumed the bird was intent on hiding from me, thinking I would not find it amidst the dense growth. But there it was; it didn't hide as I thought it would. It had remained at the edge of the branches where I could see it, a magnificent display of beauty—a **blue-winged warbler**! I was delighted. I see few blue-wingeds in the spring and even fewer in the fall. Its bright yellow head and belly, contrasting blue-gray wings, and black eye line were as brilliantly colored as any I had seen in spring. It was an adult male. I wondered if it had nested here, the northern edge of its nesting range, or whether it was on a dispersal flight, before heading to southern Mexico.

There was a narrow break in the bushes with deer tracks in the mud at the bottom of the ditch. Using the deer's trail, I climbed onto the road. I looked around to survey the habitat; a tree about a hundred feet high was easily the tallest object around. Sitting on a dead snag near the tree's top were five orange-brown birds. Their size and shape verified they were **Baltimore orioles**. Immatures are full-sized this time of year, and their plumage is nearly identical to their mother's. Perhaps one of them was the mother.

Much farther down the road, a group of grayish birds were lined up on the telephone wire—fifteen of them—perched close together. The only characteristics I could see were faint grayish streaks on their breasts. I moved in for a closer look, slowly, so as not to frighten them. A hint of a crest on the top of their heads identified them, and a little yellow at the tip of their tails verified it—young **cedar waxwings** in juvenile plumage. In a few weeks they would molt into warm brown with a yellow belly, like their parents.

Walking back to the car, I wondered about the plumage of the young birds I had seen this morning. The field guide referred to some as juveniles, others immatures. Then there was the first fall male grosbeak. Was he an immature or a juvenile? What was the significance of these specific terms? It was important for me to know in order to understand the costumes the birds were wearing in the Pageant. When comfortably seated in the car, I opened the field guide again, this time to that part of the Introduction that describes plumage. Juvenile plumage is worn only for a few weeks. If it is replaced by plumage that still does not look like the adult, it is called immature plumage. The first-fall grosbeak plumage I saw was an immature plumage because it replaced juvenile plumage. If a bird takes more than a year to acquire adult plumage, as in the example of two-year and three-year gulls, the subsequent years' plumage is called sub-adult.

Mother Nature had certainly provided unexpected sightings today, as well as chances to investigate the Pageant's costume changes.

September

19. Fall Congregations and More Plumage Changes (September 12)

I was met by a serenade of sweet call notes, rising in pitch, *sweeee, sweeee,* coming from a large patch of wild blue asters coloring the side of the path. It was **goldfinches** flitting among the asters, chattering with each other, and pulling apart the fluffy seed pods of the spent flowers. When I approached, over a hundred finches flew into the nearby scrub growth. Their characteristic undulating up-and-down mode of flight, as a group, reminded me of rolling ocean waves. Some gave their flight call, *per-chick-a-ree,* while disappearing into the background foliage.

Now that the nesting season was over, the goldfinches could band together to satisfy their gregarious tendency, and to search for food more efficiently. I have seen them in moderate-sized groups before, but never one this large. Perhaps the extent of the aster patch had attracted birds from several bands.

I continued downhill toward a row of trees, beyond which was the cattail marsh that surrounded Buck Pond. With the sweet call notes behind me, it was now quiet—no wind, no singing. Most birds had stopped singing weeks ago. The complete silence seemed loud, playing tricks with my ears.

Then, as though the silence had prepared me for it, a lone sweet musical warble drifted across the field, breaking the silence. It was a familiar song, but several species have a similar call; I wasn't sure which one it was. It could be a house finch, possibly the similar-sounding purple finch, or a warbling vireo. There were even phrases that reminded me of a goldfinch. By tracing to the source of the singing, I spotted the gray and white songster, and watched it sing. It was perched in the top of a lone ash, in an otherwise open field. There was a hint of an eye line, which identified the bird as a **warbling vireo**. It was a typical warbling vireo sighting—heard first, then seen, perched high in a well-foliaged tree. Vireos move slowly and sparingly. These habits cause them to be easily overlooked, except that they frequently sing long, continuous presentations. It is such a common bird that I was about to turn away after a quick look, when something unusual caught my eye—yellow on its belly. I wasn't expecting yellow on a warbling vireo. Then I recalled the phoebe at Hamlin Beach three weeks ago; I hadn't expected to see yellow on it either. I recalled that both phoebes and warbling vireos add a little touch of yellow to their bellies in the fall. After studying the vireo's fall plumage, I moved on.

A little bird flitted among the weeds close to the ground at the edge of the path. It was dull gray with a hint of yellow under its tail. Its nondistinguished plumage did not help me identify it, but when it wagged its tail I knew: the small slender body, the hint of yellow, close to the ground—of course, was a **palm warbler**. In spring, palms show a lot of yellow, but like many other warblers, in fall they are quite drab. There was no way of telling from its plumage whether it was a male, female, or a recent hatchling. I did know, however, that it had recently changed into its fall plumage, left its nesting grounds in Canada, and was on its way south, possibly to the Caribbean—that was its part in the Pageant. It flew off into the underbrush.

I continued down the path to an expansive view of the large pond that extended almost a mile to a barrier bar at Lake Ontario. The water shimmered in the bright sunlight. Cattails outlined the shoreline. When I stopped to enjoy the view, as if my arrival was his cue, a **marsh wren** came forth with an abbreviated version of his call. He was just a few feet away, hidden in the cattails. There were the usual two introductory notes, but then the trill that normally follows ended prematurely. I listened carefully, expecting to hear a more complete song the next time, but the same unusual rendition was repeated several times. I decided it was a first-year bird, one that had hatched just a few weeks ago, and was practicing what he thought was the official marsh wren call. His problem may have been that no adults were singing for him to mimic. According to the reading I have done on how birds learn to sing the song of their species, a combination of instinct and practice is necessary. Most birds have a natural inclination to their species' song, but it must be developed and refined by imitating the adult birds they hear. The regional variations to a species' song are evidence of the importance of imitation.

As I walked farther, the cattails expanded into an ever-larger marsh, and correspondingly, the chorus of **red-winged blackbird** call notes became louder as I walked. I was seeing only a few of what was obviously a huge flock, so I stopped to investigate. With my binoculars, I slowly scanned the cattails, far to the right and then to the left. The careful look revealed hundreds of red-wingeds dispersed across the marsh. They were hard to see because of being partially concealed by the tall, slender, pointed leaves of the cattails. They were all boisterously talking to each other, their combined voices making it impossible to hear anything else. I focused on the few I could see well. They had red wing patches— males. The females had obviously congregated somewhere else. I was not surprised at that, because the males and females separate after their young are on their own.

Occasionally a red-winged would fly out of the cattails, dropping back into the marsh a short distance away. After seeing several of them fly, I realized they were molting, and missing part of their tails. Their new tails would come in before it was time for them to leave for the southern states. Over the next several weeks, I will see other flocks of red-wings here in the same marsh. Those that had nested farther north will be passing through on their way south. Mother Nature's orchestration of red-wings' migration is clearly in stages, with the more northern nesters coming later.

The morning's events had shown me some of the changes birds undergo during the fall as part of Mother Nature's plan—molting, plumage changes, young learning to vocalize, and preparations for migration.

20. Long-Distance Travelers That Favor Plowed Fields (September 26)

Mike Davids has been seeing migrating shorebirds, so I arranged to join him this morning. We met at dawn at the Town Line Road bridge over Brush Creek near the lakeshore. It is the same site where in June we found the Virginia rail and least bittern.

I arrived first. The colony of **wood ducks** we had seen in June were still there, several hundred yards upstream in a wide, placid area of the creek. In June they were all drab gray. But, since then, three adult males had completed their molt and had acquired stunningly beautiful plumage. The others, either females or the now full-sized immatures, remained a drab gray. I enjoyed the quiet, serene family scene.

One of the woodies took off, flew a short distance, and landed amidst another small group. In flight its dark color was silhouetted against the bright sky, clearly showing its distinctive profile—a wide, long tail, square-cut at the end—very different from the shorter, pointed tails of most other ducks.

While watching the woodies' activities in the wide waters of the stream, I became aware that there were two sizes of ducks swimming together. The smaller ones had to be **blue-winged teals**. My presumption was verified when one of them decided to stretch; as it flapped its wings, blue wing patches glistened in the sun.

I recognized Mike's white car as it came down the road, stopping at the pull-off by the bridge. For the next few minutes we searched without success for bitterns and rails. "Most of the rails and least bitterns have already gone. Our chances of seeing one now rapidly diminish each day," Mike explained.

Then I learned what Mike had in mind. "Yesterday, I found a number of plovers in a freshly plowed field just down the road from here. I think it would be worth checking the site again today." He drove off, and I followed. Within minutes we were parked at the intersection with Chase Road. We stood on the berm, looking out across a huge, freshly plowed field. Mike explained the site's attraction. "Some species of shorebirds have learned to feed on the insects, worms, and grubs that the farmers' fall plowing exposes. From mid-September until mid-October, I see **black-bellied plovers** and **American golden plovers** in the fields, sometimes in large flocks. The farmers' crop rotation system makes it necessary for birders to search out, each year, the current year's plowed fields that are attracting the plovers and other shorebirds.

"Yesterday," Mike continued, "the birds stayed in the southeast corner of the field even though it is nearest to the road junction and farm house." Now, four **killdeer** were searching the new furrows near where Mike had found the plovers yesterday. Killdeer, also members of the plover family, are by far our most common shorebird, probably because they thrive in a variety of habitats: farmers' fields, school athletic fields, mudflats, beaches, even parking lots.

"A **buff-breasted sandpiper**!" Mike called out excitedly. "It's at the far side of the field walking along a furrow." I was eager to see it, having never seen one before—a lifer for me. (The terms "lifer" and "life bird" refer to the first one sees a bird of a particular species.) With Mike's detailed directions I finally found the bird in my binoculars. I was elated, but also frustrated—it was so far away that I could not see any of the distinguishing characteristics of its plumage. Mike, aware of my annoyance for not being able to identify it myself, explained how he did it. "The buff-breasted walks continuously, while plovers walk quickly for a couple of seconds and then stop for a moment. This is a good way to alert yourself to a buff-breasted that is too far away to identify by plumage."

The bird was just a tiny speck in our binoculars, so we went to our cars for spotting scopes. Mike found the bird in his scope. "It is walking up and down the furrows, sometimes being hidden by the rolling terrain. Aah!" he said. I could sense the excitement in his voice. "It has turned to face us; its buff-colored breast is now unmistakable." The timing was perfect for me. I had just found the bird, and was still adjusting the focus, when it turned and showed its breast. The buff-colored breast and throat were conspicuous. Now I was satisfied. "My, but it's small," I said. Mike responded, "It is small. But notice that its neck is longer, and its bill shorter than most small shorebirds." Knowing I was interested in learning as much as possible about the bird, Mike told me about its migration. "Buff-breasteds nest on the Arctic coast and the high Arctic islands. Then, they fly to southern Argentina for the winter. What a trip: from the top of the world to the bottom! Can you imagine the effort and perils involved with that?"

Mike continued, "Their numbers, along with many other species of shorebirds, were drastically reduced during the nineteenth century. Professional hunters provided large numbers of them to meat markets in the large East Coast cities, where the meat was considered a delicacy. Although the numbers of some of the species have rebounded somewhat after hunting was banned in 1918, buff-breasteds are still seldom seen. We were darn lucky to see this one. It's about a week past the time they normally come through—the first three weeks of September."

Mike, always vigilant, continued to scan the field. I sensed delight in his voice again. "Here's a **golden plover**! I thought there might be one—buff-breasteds like the company of plovers." I stood behind Mike to align myself with the direction his scope was pointing; I pointed my scope in the same direction. As I focused on the plover, Mike explained his identification. "Both golden and black-bellied plovers can have similar plumage in the fall, depending upon the stage of their molt, but this individual is too slender to be a black-bellied." Mike continued, "Golden plovers were also brought to near extinction by hunters. Now, it's comforting to see flocks of golden plovers each year as they pass through in the fall." After a few minutes of silence, Mike added, "I've been looking for a flock of **American pipits.** They can be found in plowed fields now too, but apparently they are not here today."

As we collapsed the legs of our scopes' tripods preparing to put them away, Mike told me more about migrants in plowed fields. "Plovers, buff-breasteds, and pipits fly across Lake Ontario from their nesting grounds in Canada. When they reach land they are anxious to find a place to rest and feed. They usually look for plowed fields because they can easily find insects and worms in the freshly opened furrows. I check the plowed fields in the morning for the previous night's arrivals. But I have also learned to check again late in the afternoon because some of the birds fly across the lake during the day."

Mike suggested we go to Salmon Creek. "I've been watching the water level drop along the backwaters of the creek. The mudflats there along Manitou Road, about a mile upstream from where the creek empties into Braddock Bay, are getting larger, attracting more and more shorebirds."

While driving to Salmon Creek, I continued to think about what I had just seen and learned from Mike. On many occasions I have gone to mudflats and beaches to see migrating shorebirds, but I had never realized until this morning that plowed fields also attract migrating shorebirds. What I had just seen had very nearly been permanently removed from the Pageant's script by turn-of-the-century hunters. Fortunately, legislative action was taken just in time, saving the scene for posterity. Unfortunately, few of the species are as plentiful now as they had once been, and some of their numbers will remain dangerously low. We saw only one, lonely buff-breasted sandpiper today! It would have been much more satisfying to me, and certainly to the buff-breasted, if he could have been with a large flock of his brethren.

21. Shorebirds Cross Paths on Different Migration Routes

We stopped at a small parking lot at a fishermen's marina. As we walked to the water's edge, Mike gave me an overview of the area's shorebird habitat.

"Braddock Bay, including its shoreline, the surrounding adjacent fields, woods, and wetlands, is an outstanding habitat for many species of birds. It's one of the best birding areas in the country because of the influence of the Great Lakes. But what is lacking are large mudflats to attract numbers of migrating shorebirds. The beaches along the lakeshore provide only a narrow strip for the shorebirds to feed on insects and aquatic life. It's narrow, because the lake has no tide to distribute the food over a wider area of the beach like the ocean beach does. Consequently, shorebirds prefer broad mudflats, and search thoroughly for such feeding locations. In spring, they often use flooded spots in farmers' fields. I'm sure many choose to fly over the area to find a suitable habitat elsewhere."

We looked out over Salmon Creek, where at this point, the waters of Braddock Bay have extended up the creek, widening it to almost a half-mile across. In front of us, not far from shore, was a small mudflat—a few water-tolerant weeds had sprouted—but it was mostly devoid of vegetation.

Mike explained why he had suggested this site. "I have seen a number of shorebirds here over the last few weeks, but only when the winds are calm. It is my guess that on days with a brisk westerly wind the shorebirds find an area that is more sheltered. Today is calm, so they should be here, basking in the warm sun."

Possibly in response to our approach, two **killdeer** flew the length of the mudflat, giving their loud, shrill, *killdeer* call. After their noisy greeting, we noticed two more killdeer standing on the mud at the water's edge.

"There's a **semipalmated plover** too, poking along the water's edge," I said. Mike answered me with a perfunctory "yeah." He had apparently already seen it. Whenever I see a semipalmated plover, it strikes me that a beginning birder might wonder if it were a young killdeer. These two birds have the same color scheme—the semipalmated is smaller, and has one black stripe around its neck instead of the killdeer's two. Next to the semipalmated plover were two sandpipers. The brown streaking on their breasts ended abruptly, showing well-defined lines of demarcation with their clear white bellies. When I saw their yellow legs I called out, **"pectoral sandpipers."**

I wanted to learn more about the three species, so I looked at their range maps in the field guide. It revealed interesting insights! The three, here just a few feet apart, could hardly be more different in their annual routines. Pectorals nest along the Arctic coast, where few humans live. They then migrate all the way to the southern part of Argentina, another sparsely populated part of the world. The only chance for pectorals to see humans, or for humans to see them, is during one of their few migration stops, such as here at Salmon Creek. I wondered, am I the only human these two pectorals have seen? The killdeer are different. They spend their entire lives within the United States or southern Canada, not migrating far, if at all. It's almost as though they search out humans at golf courses, airports, athletic fields, or popular beaches. Semipalmated plovers live a compromise between the other two species.

Mother Nature's plan gathered the three diverse species and placed them together at Salmon Creek. We saw their diverse paths intersect this morning, and soon, they will again be thousands of miles from each other.

While scanning the edge of the cattails, a large gray form totally filled the field of vision in my binoculars, startling me. At the same time, I heard Mike. "Aha! Here's an adult **black-crowned night heron!**" It was so close I had to lower my binoculars. I could see it standing at the edge of the mudflat, no more than thirty yards away. Its stockiness was emphasized by the relatively short legs it had for a heron. Facing away from me, it showed its gray and black back, indicating it was an adult; a young bird would have been brown. It was standing perfectly still. It was resting, its head pulled close to its body, perhaps sleeping. Apparently, it had been standing there a long time without us noticing it. I was fascinated by its awesome presence because I had never been this close to a night heron before. After having nested somewhere in the Midwest or East, it was now traveling long distances on a summer vacation. Its wanderings, fortunately for us, have included Salmon Creek. Where did it come from? Where had it spent the summer? We didn't know.

While still watching the night heron, I was jolted by another event—a big fight! The troublemaker, a **Wilson's snipe**, was charging the pectorals with its wings spread, flapping them repeatedly. It was attempting to terrorize the pectorals, and to chase them away from its feeding site. But the pectorals paid little attention, ignoring the bully. The snipe, now even more incensed, charged again, brandishing its exceptionally long bill. Finally, the pectorals gave in to the snipe's demands and moved way. The boisterous snipe may have nested here, or it could be passing through on its way south from Canada.

As we walked back to our cars, I told Mike how grateful I was for his tutoring. He offered more. "What we saw today is nothing compared to what is coming. Millions of waterfowl will use Lake Ontario as a giant east-west corridor for migration. Next Saturday Bill Symonds and I will be at Hamlin Beach, one of the best vantage points for monitoring the migration. We'll see you there."

October

22. Lake Ontario, the Waterfowl Migration Thoroughfare (October 4)

It was early morning at Hamlin Beach State Park's area #4 picnic site, on a high promontory—a panoramic vista. I could see far out over the lake, and along the shoreline, both to the left and right; there were views of the lake for many miles. Bill and Mike were already there, sitting on the park's benches, scanning up and down the lake with their twenty-power spotting scopes, looking for waterfowl.

The site's broad view, substantial elevation, and protrusion out into Lake Ontario, has enabled routine monitoring of the waterfowl migration.

The waterfowl migration census at Hamlin Beach has been coordinated over the last few years by Brett Ewald, through the auspices of BBRR. An official counter, usually Brett or Bill, or one of several other volunteers, has been assigned for each day from September through December. Other interested birders, such as Mike, often come by to help out. Counts by species, hour of the day, and weather are carefully recorded. A database has been developed and will become even more valuable over the years for assessing shifts in populations and other migration changes.

Bill brought me up to date. "Over the last few days it has been warm, the lake calm, like a mill pond. Under such conditions waterfowl are not interested in migrating. But the cool wind today is different, and the ducks are active. You picked the right day to come." I sat down on the bench between Bill and Mike, and set up my spotting scope. Mike announced, "Fourteen **white-winged scoters** going west." I found them in my scope, plump and black, coming toward us, in a long line one after the other, about a half mile out from shore. They passed in front of us, then moved away, toward the left. The sun shone onto the upper surface of their wings, exposing their clear white wing patches. I described what I saw: "At first they looked all black, but after they passed, their white patches were obvious." Bill added, "Scoters can be tricky. If you don't see white patches, wait till they move by to another angle. If you still don't see patches, you may be seeing surf or black scoters. There will be more of them in a few more weeks; then I'll teach you how to tell the three scoters apart."

Every few seconds more **white-wingeds** flew by, long strung-out lines, low to the water. Mike explained what I was seeing. "Scoters fly efficiently, reducing wind resistance by keeping low to the water, so low that they may fly between the troughs of the waves. Also, they fly close behind the bird in front, in its wake, further reducing wind resistance. We are on a high bluff looking down on them. If we were standing on the beach at water level, the waves would mask our view of many of them."

"Where are they going?" I asked.

"Scoters spend the winter along the Atlantic coast, then go to their nesting grounds in western Canada. In spring, birders at Cape May, New Jersey, see hundreds of thousands of scoters going north, up to Delaware Bay toward Lake Ontario, then on to Hudson Bay. Their route keeps them on large bodies of water most of the way."

While watching more white-wingeds file by, I saw a flock of ducks. They were more slender than scoters, and were flying high, in a bunched-up cluster. Bill coached, "Don't assume they're all the same species. Look at each duck carefully." When they came closer, and we had excellent views, he continued tutoring. "They're mostly **mallards**, but look! Some are black. They're **black ducks**. Both species are large, robust ducks. At a distance the mallard doesn't have any standout markings, but the black duck is very dark with white under the wings. Oh, and look at this, toward the rear of the flock—a **green-winged teal**! It's easy to spot—nearly half the size of a mallard, brown, and showing no other markings that are visible from this distance. It is not unusual to find green-wingeds flying with larger ducks." Bill had clearly demonstrated his point: it is worthwhile to carefully search each flock, looking for different species within it.

Mike was busy too. "**Common loons** are coming through!" He explained how to look for them. "They fly solo, not gregarious like ducks. Here's one now! See its humped-back silhouette?" I saw it, flying alone, ten to twenty feet off the water, a quarter mile out from shore. "They are still in their summer plumage, black above and white below. In a few weeks they will change into winter plumage, gray above instead of black." Over the next few minutes I carefully studied about twenty loons as they came by, one at a time. I was becoming more confident in recognizing their characteristic shape, even when they were as far out as half a mile. I recognized their unique profile—their long necks and tails extended from the lower part of their bodies, and their backs had a pronounced hump. "We will be seeing red-throated loons appearing in another month. Until then, common loons will be increasing."

"I thought we were already seeing many loons. Will we see many more?"

"We will see thousands—first common loons, and then later in the season, red-throateds will be prevalent."

Every few seconds there was another sighting. Intensity was building as Mike and Bill worked to identify and record each bird as it came by. I watched how effectively they used their spotting scopes. They started looking far to the east, because most migrants were coming from the east going west. When they spotted something, they would track it in its westerly movement, as it came closer, until they had identified it. They would then scan the vast western part of the lake, searching for anything they had missed, before pivoting their scopes back to the east. I tried their routine, learning that starting far to the east maximized my time for tracking and studying a sighting. The number of flocks were coming faster, so when Bill announced he had a sighting, Mike would follow the next sighting, doubling the birds they could count and identify at one time. Bill recorded their counts by species.

Bill and Mike had been tracking other flocks and missed a group, so I helped. "Flock of ducks, straight out, high, going west!" There was a diagonal line, a one-sided wedge, of sixteen ducks several hundred feet above the water, at least five hundred yards away. Bill and Mike found them, deciding they were **pintails** because they lacked wing patches. Bill explained, "Both wigeons and pintails are similar in appearance—light brown, long slender necks, and slender pointed wings. They have different markings around the neck, but at this distance, the white patch on the leading edge of the wigeons' wings is about the only difference you can reliably see." Mike added, "Look at the slender, streamlined **pintails**! They are flying right by the plumper, slower flock of twelve mallards."

23. Jaeger: The Arctic Pirate

Mike was intently watching a large dark bird flying erratically far out over the lake. "I think it's a **jaeger**! It's darting back and forth among several ring-billed gulls, flying large circles as it repeatedly darts at the gulls—typical jaeger behavior." I found it in my scope. It was about the same size of the gulls. It looked like a first-year gull with its dark immature plumage, but it didn't behave like a gull; it was more powerful and athletic. With obvious excitement, Bill agreed. "It's a jaeger all right, my first one this fall." I was thrilled when I heard the word "jaeger." Not only had I never seen one before, but I knew practically nothing about jaegers. To me, they were mystery birds. Mike continued to narrate the jaeger's movements, "As it chases the ring-billeds using large swooping turns, it gets slightly closer, then farther away, then closer again." Bill coached me, "When it comes closer, look for the lighter-colored feathers at the wings' wrists." I focused intently. As the jaeger turned from one of its closer loops, its back facing the sun, I could barely make out the subtly lighter-colored feathers Bill mentioned, the only discernible markings on its plumage.

When I cheerfully announced that it was my first jaeger, a lifer, Bill told me more. "Jaegers are closely related to gulls, but are more powerful and agile. They often hunt for small birds and mammals like hawks do. You have seen a jaeger in its most typical behavior, pirating. It attacks a gull or tern, forcing it to drop the fish it had seized. The jaeger then catches the falling fish in midair." I looked up jaegers in my field guide and found that there are three species: the parasitic, pomarine, and long-tailed, all looking much alike. Bill continued, "This is probably a parasitic, the jaeger most commonly spotted here. As you see in your field guide, the parasitic and pomarine are differentiated in their adult plumage by the shape of their central tail feathers. Unfortunately, here at Lake Ontario, we usually see immatures that have not yet acquired their identifying tail feathers. Consequently, we find them almost impossible to tell apart. The only differences are subtle ones that only experienced jaeger observers can spot. The guess I make on this one is based on its agile manner of flight and relative size compared to the gulls.

"We see them only in the fall, mostly in September and October, as they migrate from the Arctic to the Atlantic Coast. We never see many, just a few. When we see them, they are usually well out from shore; consequently, our elevated location here is one of the better sites along the lakeshore to see them. They migrate south from Hudson Bay and James Bay, then to Lake Huron and to the west end of Lake Ontario. Soon after dawn, they start to move east along Lake Ontario, reaching here by midmorning, heading east on their way to the Atlantic Coast. Later in the fall, for reasons we don't understand, we occasionally see one going west."

24. Arrival of the Most Common Lake Duck, the Scaup

"The scaups are picking up in numbers," Mike remarked. "Here's another group, a large one." I had seen several other groups of scaup within the last few minutes, flying higher than loons and scoters, closely together in tight bunches. This flock consisted of more than a hundred. Focusing on several individuals, I noticed they had short, stubby necks—different from the long-necked mallards and pintails we had been seeing.

Mike suggested, "Here are two scaup for you to study. The lead bird, the brownish one, is a female **greater scaup**. The much darker one following is a male **lesser scaup**." I found them directly in front of us and not far away—stubby scaup profiles.

"I can see the distinct difference in color to tell the female from the male, but how did you distinguish the lesser from the greater?"

"The first bird, the greater scaup, has a white streak extending the length of each of the otherwise dark wings. The white streak flashes quite visibly with each of his wing beats. The lesser scaup has white wing streaks that are only half as long, hardly visible with its wing beats. To use proper terminology, the greater has a broad white streak through both its secondaries and primaries, while the lesser's wing streak is only on its secondaries. Secondaries are the flight feathers on the part of the wing closest to the body; primaries go from the bend in the wing to the tip."

Bill told me more. "The scaups we are seeing today are among the first to arrive this fall. About a third of them are lessers migrating to points farther south for the winter. By November most of the lessers will be gone. As the lessers leave, large numbers of greaters will be arriving from northern Canada. They choose large bodies of water like Lake Ontario because they are excellent underwater swimmers—they have shorter, more sturdy necks than do shallow-water feeding ducks like mallards. They survive by eating mollusks off the bottom, sometimes from great depths. We see them by the hundreds, or thousands sometimes, flying in bunches or sitting in huge rafts [a raft is a large flock of ducks huddled closely together sitting on the water, often one to two hundred yards off shore]. During the winter, I scan the rafts to see how many lessers have lingered with the greaters, rather than continuing south with their kin. On the average, no more than five percent are lessers. The greaters will be the most commonly seen duck on the lake throughout the winter. The white-winged scoter is believed to be the most abundant during migration."

I reviewed the morning thus far, for what I had seen and learned. Waterfowl migration along Lake Ontario is a well-orchestrated, ancient aspect of the Pageant. It is diversified, and at times, fast-paced. One never knows when an unusual sighting may appear. I had picked the right day, the right location, and the right mentors, Bill and Mike, to interpret it for me.

25. A Diversion; Migration Is Under Way in the Woods Too

We had been very busy for the past two hours. Now the number of ducks passing by tapered off to a lull. We needed a break. I checked my watch; 10:00 a.m. Bill must have read my mind. "We will be seeing fewer birds now, the sun has warmed, the wind has tapered off, a lazy, warm afternoon is starting. Waterfowl like to migrate in nasty weather."

I relaxed and had just poured coffee from the thermos when a man and his dog came by, walking the hiking path that parallels the beach. He stopped, asked what we had been seeing, and volunteered that he had just passed a number of small birds in the nearby clump of Scotch pines. He didn't know what they were; he wasn't a birder.

His comment caused me to realize I had been so caught up in the waterfowl migration lately that I had overlooked the fact that Mother Nature was also directing considerable migratory activity among land birds. I didn't want to miss any part of her Pageant, so I told Bill and Mike, "I'm going to take advantage of the lull and see what migrants are in the woods. It's only a hundred yards away. I won't be long. Give me a yell if anything happens." Mike was encouraging. "I saw some red-breasted nuthatches and kinglets there when I came in the first thing this morning. Maybe they're still there. If Walt Listman were here, he'd tell you that seeing large numbers of red-breasted nuthatches at this time of year is a good sign for an upcoming winter finch season."

I strolled along the path to the grove of tall Scotch pines. I heard waves lapping at the shoreline on the far side of the grove. Movement caught my eye, and then I saw several small birds in the lower pine branches, two **red-breasted nuthatches** and a **brown creeper**. One nuthatch was working its way down the trunk of one of the pines, inspecting the rough edges of the bark for insects or their eggs. Its toes were its means for securely holding to the bark as it went straight down the trunk head first. Occasionally it would bend its neck in an upward arch to look around from its upside-down position before it continued downward. (Nuthatches and black-and-white warblers are the only birds in this area that go down a tree trunk head first. In contrast, woodpeckers keep their heads up, using their sharp-pointed tails for additional support.)

The nuthatch reached the bottom of the closest trunk, then turned to look at me. Perhaps we were studying each other. It was much smaller than the white-breasted nuthatches that I see at my backyard feeder in winter. The black eye line was obvious, a characteristic not shared with the white-breasted species. The most obvious characteristic, however, was its orange-red breast and belly, indicating it was a male. A female would have shown only a hint of red.

In the next tree was the other red-breasted nuthatch. Its maneuvering of a horizontal branch was not as spectacular as its companion's vertical descent. All I could see was its back. I remembered my discussions with Betsy Brooks, the director of Braddock Bay Bird Observatory and a highly regarded bird bander. I learned from her that the red-breasteds' arrivals and departures are complex. We are geographically at the edge of both their year-round and wintering ranges. She said that some red-breasteds are summer residents, while others spend the winter. She also thought that some nesters decide they like the area and choose to spend the winter. I have seen them more frequently during migration than at other times of year, and asked her why. She said it could be the simultaneous coming and going of both summer and winter residents. A few may spend the winter farther south and visit here only briefly during migration, but she was unsure of how many that might be.

Betsy eagerly pointed out that the most characteristic aspect of their movements is that they are irruptive. She explained this special term used by ornithologists. During some winters, large numbers of a species will move south from their usual Canadian wintering areas; in other winters only a few will come. When they do come south, the extent of the area they cover is unpredictable. Species known for irruptive movements in this area in winter are **snowy owls, red-breasted nuthatches, chickadees, redpolls, pine and evening grosbeaks, pine siskins, crossbills, snow buntings, and Lapland longspurs**. Most species' irruptions are believed to be tied to their food source, most notably the conifer seed crop in Canada. The snowy owl irruption, however, depends on the population of lemmings (mouse-like rodents from the far north).

Because of the red-breasteds' dependence on conifer seeds in winter, I realized it was no accident that I had found the two nuthatches here in a clump of pines. Pines are their favorite kind of tree, even when they are looking for insects—their staple summer fare. I guessed that while they were looking for insects, they were probably also checking on the availability of pinecone seeds for winter. They arrive in this area much earlier than most other irruptive species, although more red-breasteds may arrive later. The number of early red-breasteds, compared to previous years, may be the basis for Walt's belief that an influx of red-breasteds in the fall is a harbinger of later winter finch irruptions.

My attention to the red-breasteds had run its course, then shifted to the **brown creeper** when it flew to the base of a pine's trunk. As soon as it landed I lost sight of it, its brown and white streaked plumage effectively camouflaged on the side of the trunk. I spotted it again when it started to work its way upward by spiraling around the trunk. Like the red-breasteds, it was looking for insects in the crevices of the bark. When it reached the smaller, upper branches, where there were fewer crevices, it flew to the bottom of the next tree. I watched it repeat its routine several times, spiraling upward, flying to the base of the next tree, then spiraling upward again. It would inch up the trunk by pressing its long, stiff, sharp pointed tail feathers against the trunk, the same supportive technique used by woodpeckers. In contrast, the nuthatches I had been watching worked their way down the trunk, not up. They didn't use tail feathers for support because their tails were too short. Although creepers and nuthatches search the same tree trunks for the same insects, they do so in different ways. Another major difference: creepers are year-round residents; they don't migrate and don't have irruptive movements. The nuthatches and creeper worked their way through the row of pines together, rarely far apart. I followed their progress down the path.

Thin, high-pitched call notes came from the top of the tall pines. I had fleeting glimpses of small, busy birds in the small twigs at the end of the high branches. They were difficult to see, and continually on the move in the heavy foliage. Finally, I had a good look—one of the tiny birds was fluttering in place, deciding where to land or possibly which insect to catch. The in-place flutter of such a tiny bird identified it—a **ruby-crowned kinglet**. I started seeing others, busily flitting among the branches, persistently communicating with each other by giving their call note, *ji–dit*.

The kinglets flew off, and I no longer saw the nuthatches nor the creeper. I reversed my steps, anxious to return to the waterfowl migration. I thought about what I had just seen in the last few minutes, a very predictable part of Mother Nature's script. Kinglets are usually seen in small groups, often with nuthatches and creepers, especially at this time of year. They all prefer to be among conifers, such as this grove of Scotch pine.

Bill and Mike were glued to their spotting scopes, pivoting them back and forth, scanning the horizon. They admitted that they hadn't seen anything noteworthy while I was gone. I was a little surprised, having expected them to have at least made up something to spark my jealousy. It occurred to me that the lack of activity over the lake while I was gone may have been lucky timing. Perhaps something special was now due.

26. A Spectacular Sight and Success Story: A Peregrine Falcon

There was excitement in Bill's voice. "Peregrine falcon straight out, coming this way!" I saw it. It was much larger than a kestrel, the small falcon I often see. Its long, slender, pointed, streamlined wings were beating rapidly, bringing it closer to us with incredible speed. It was brown, indicating that it was an immature. Adults are gray. "I'll bet it left Canada's north shore of Lake Ontario at about dawn and has taken several hours to fly across the lake." It quickly flew by the clump of pine trees near the picnic area, turned parallel to the shore, and was out of sight. The time from when Bill first saw it far out over the lake until it had reached shore and was out of sight was no more than five seconds. "Peregrines are the fastest birds in the world," explained Bill. "They can cruise at sixty miles per hour. Not only is the peregrine the fastest flying hawk, it is also the most agile, choosing to only take prey in midair. To capture prey in midair, they power-dive—their wings are closed, tightly held to their bodies. They can be going a hundred, silently. The prey never knows what hit them. A special hook on the peregrine's bill instantly severs the victim's spinal cord."

Mike explained their migration. "Most hawks depend on the buoyancy of thermals to help them migrate. Falcons, however, are 'active flyers.' They usually don't bother with thermals, flying directly across the lake, as we just saw, where there are no thermals. Falcons are about the only hawks we see migrating in the fall. Those hawks that use thermals to migrate, skirt the north shore of the lake in the fall."

I was very aware of why our peregrine sighting this morning was so special: they are on the endangered list. In the 1970s, pesticides such as DDT had totally extirpated them from the Eastern United States and they were rapidly disappearing in the West. After DDT and certain other pesticides were banned, the peregrines and eagles, who also were hit badly by DDT, started to come back. Thanks to the people who have conducted captive breeding/releasing programs, peregrines have been successfully reintroduced in the East.

Our local utility company here, Rochester Gas and Electric Corporation, has sponsored a program over several years to reintroduce peregrines. They obtained baby peregrines from a licensed company that hatched the chicks in captivity. The utility company then cared for them until they could be on their own. One year a nest was made on a very high ledge of the power plant in Rochester on the lakeshore— high cliffs are the peregrine's natural sites for nesting. Two chicks were fed daily until they were able to successfully hunt on their own. The feeding was done incognito so the chicks would not bond to the person providing the food. The young peregrines quickly learned to hunt, and eventually decimated the power plant's pigeon population. Several of us took turns watching their progress and safety each day for about a month. A spot of spray paint on their right wings enabled us to tell the two apart. When their survival skills were sufficient, they flew away and we never saw them again. One was later reported near Toronto, the other near Buffalo. Their paint marks have been replaced by new feathers, making it impossible to tell whether the peregrine we just saw was one that I had watched mature.

A three-noted whistle-like call came from the shoreline, as shorebirds took off from the beach below. Each had a large patch of white at the base of its tail, except one. Mike identified them: "Eleven **black-bellied plovers** and one **golden plover**." I admitted that in the fall I have trouble differentiating the two plovers. Mike helped me understand the differences between them. "These two species are difficult to tell apart in the fall, because the golden plover loses the gold on its back; both species become gray. There are two easy ways to tell them apart. The golden has a two-noted call, while the black-bellied has a three-noted call, the call we just heard. And, as we just saw, there is a white spot on the rump of the black-bellied plover, none on the golden plover. Also, the black axillaries (armpits) of the black-bellied are another way to tell them apart when they are flying." Bill chimed in, "They were smart to have stayed hunkered down until the peregrine had passed. A nice plump plover would have been a perfect lunch for the peregrine."

There was another lull. I found myself thinking, How could I describe what I had seen the last few hours? It was like a parade, a continuous, long flow of participants, only better. A human parade consists of units one expects to see—bands, firemen, veterans or national guard, politicians, and Boy Scouts, usually in that order, although sometimes the politicians move up closer to the front. What I saw this morning had too much diversity to be predictable; it was more exciting. As if Bill were reading my thoughts, he offered, "The anticipation, and then the excitement—when it happens—it's what we wait for. We must come out to see what happens, whenever we can." I thought, "Discovering what Mother Nature has orchestrated today is what is meaningful to me."

27. A Seldom-Seen Plumage (October 5)

The bird was facing me, showing its yellow breast and head. It was sitting motionless, high in a tall tree. The color first caused me to think it was a warbler, but its bill was not thin like a warbler's. Perhaps it was a yellow-throated vireo, which would have a heavier bill, and would be more apt to perch motionless. Then it turned slightly, showing its side: yellowish, a slight hint of olive, except for indicative black wings. It was a male scarlet tanager in winter plumage! The female looks similar all year around, but she does not have the obvious contrast with the black wings. I wondered why I could not remember seeing a winter-attired male before; checking my reference material, I discovered why. Throughout August, the predominantly bright red male gradually acquires increasingly more splotches of yellow, with the red disappearing. By the first of September, he is all yellow, except for the wings, which are all black. Then he leaves for South America. The bird I just saw was late in leaving the area, affording me the unlikely chance to see him in his newly acquired winter plumage.

28. Sampling Fall Migration

Over the past week, I had found permanent residents, such as an occasional cardinal, chickadee, jay, and crow; the only migrant was a robin. Perhaps the unseasonably warm weather had been the reason for the slow migration. Today was the first really cold day of the season; perhaps I could find a few migrants responding to the weather's reminder of the upcoming winter. I thought the owl trail at the west side of Braddock Bay would be a good place to find migrants. Finding the tanager when I first arrived may be a good omen.

Three-noted calls of golden-crowned kinglets came from several directions as I walked down the trail amid surrounding scrub growth. A gang of kinglets moved through the ash and pine branches at the edge of a more open area. The yellow crowns for which they are named were visible on several of them.

A similar-sounding call came from the other side of the path, as a brown creeper landed on the trunk of a tall, slender ash. It pressed closely to the trunk, and with its color nearly matching the bark, was almost impossible to see. Without its call to attract my attention, I would not have known it was there.

Every few steps brought me to one group after another of kinglets, most of their calls obviously that of golden-crowneds. I was pleased to find so many birds, after having taken the same walk several times in recent weeks, and hearing very little. Many birds must have been migrating last night.

Braddock Bay Raptor Research had cleared a small field of underbrush, providing an open feeding area for the saw-whet owls that migrate through the woods here in spring. In the fall, they migrate along the north shore of the lake, so we do not see them then. At the edge of the clearing was a grove of pines and mixed hardwoods, full of active, noisy kinglets. My eyes were drawn to movement in a large brush pile left by the clearing operation. A wren hopped around on the top of the pile. At this date, it could still be a house wren, who may have spent the summer here or in Canada, and had not yet flown to the South for the winter. Or, it could be a winter wren that had nested in Canada, and had not yet moved farther south for the winter. To decide which wren it was, I looked carefully at its tail. It was very short and stubby—a winter wren. Another wren was in the same brush pile, also with a short, stubby tail. Both were preoccupied with each other, not at all concerned by my presence. I thought that was unusual. Typically, when I try to see winter wrens they are skulking within the brush pile, deliberately avoiding me. Now both of the wrens were making themselves easy to study. In addition to the identifying tail, I noticed prominent barring on the flanks, where house wrens show only slight hints of barring. The two exchanged call notes that were more harsh than the calls of their cousin, the house wren.

The path forked, and I went left, continuing past more scrub, dotted with stands of tall ash. More and more kinglets crossed the trail, squads of ruby-crowneds, interspersed with golden-crowneds. It was like they were orchestrated—first one species, then the other paraded by. I also thought of how their parts in the Pageant are intertwined at this time of year. The rubys will be gone soon, to winter in the southern states. The goldens, with less distance to travel, will remain for a month longer, well into December. The rubys nest farther north than the goldens, and winter farther south. The greater migration distance causes rubys to leave earlier.

There were countless white-throated sparrows, either feeding among the recently dropped leaves on the ground, or moving through the undergrowth from one low branch to another. Some would scurry ahead of me to maintain a safe distance, repeatedly moving again as I continued my approach. Some, perhaps a bit smarter, or lazier, would fly away from the path into the deep recesses of the undergrowth, having to move but once. Some gave call notes as they flew. Call notes came from both sides of the path, and from varied distances—evidence that there were many more white-throateds than what I was seeing. Twice I heard an aborted attempt at their song. I wondered if the attempts were from juveniles, inexperienced at their song, *old-sam-peabody*, which I hear frequently in spring, seldom in fall.

The kinglets and sparrows had been low, but there was a bird high in the branches of an ash. After studying it, I decided it was a thrush. It was unusual for a thrush to be at that height. Its chest was not fully streaked like a wood thrush, but I was struck by how very bold the chest specks were. Its face was brown, not gray. So, although I couldn't see the color of its tail in order to be sure, I surmised it was a hermit.

The path took me to where the tall trees thinned, revealing large expanses of clear blue sky. A steady flow of blue jays were migrating easterly toward the spits across the bay. We see this jay movement in spring, but I was surprised to see them fly in the same direction in the fall. Most birds that choose not to fly across the lake follow the south shore in the spring. In the fall, they follow the lake's north shore, because of the northeasterly tip of the lake. It seems illogical that the jays would follow the same easterly path both in spring and in fall. I would love to read that part of Mother Nature's script for an explanation.

It had been a good day during fall migration. It was diverse and eventful, and it held surprises and presented mysteries for which Mother Nature has not yet revealed answers.

29. Feeding Frenzy and a Surprise from the High Arctic (October 15)

When I arrived, Brett Ewald, the coordinator of the waterfowl census, and Bill Symonds had been at the Hamlin Beach observation site since dawn. Bill pointed offshore to the right. "About fifty **ring-billed gulls**, and six **common loons**, are actively feeding where there is a school of fish." Many of the gulls were flying in circles over the school of fish, about a quarter mile from shore. Occasionally one would drop into the water for a fish. Other gulls, sitting on the water in a large circle, would lunge for a fish. Gulls don't dive; they go after fish near the surface. The loons had positioned themselves at the edge of the circle of gulls. They were actively fishing, diving, and swimming underwater—catching fish that were deeper than those available to the gulls.

A flock of about twenty **red-breasted mergansers** flying eastward along the shore saw the activity below and dropped in to see if the fishing was good. Also divers, they positioned themselves around the periphery of the activity so they, like the loons, could conveniently dive under the group of gulls and resurface on the other side. Brett commented about feeding frenzies: "There are so many gulls, loons, and mergansers feeding at such a fast pace that it really is a frenzy. I always watch a frenzy carefully, because it tends to attract even more birds, some of them more interested in the birds doing the fishing than the fish. Jaegers, for example, muggers of the seabird world, like to steal fish from gulls. A peregrine or merlin may be attracted by the frenzy also, and decide to make a meal of a gull, tern, or duck."

Our focus on the feeding frenzy was interrupted by a flock of twelve medium-sized shorebirds flying along the beach, disappearing behind the point of land to our left. They were too large to be peeps, and definitely not one of the larger, long-legged species. From our elevated site, we had looked down on them, so if there had been white markings on their wings or tails we would have seen them. By a process of elimination I guessed they were either pectorals or dunlins. Bill and Brett had tracked them with their scopes. Brett identified them: "**Pectoral sandpipers**." Bill agreed. "They had dark brown backs; dunlins have gray backs. In a couple of weeks we will no longer see pectorals. They will then be close to their wintering grounds in Peru, Chile, or Argentina. Any similarly appearing shorebirds we see here then will almost certainly be dunlins. By December, they too, will be gone, having arrived on their wintering grounds along the Atlantic coast." I wondered, Why would two similar species, both nesting along the Arctic coast, have been given such different wintering sites by Mother Nature? Do the pectorals' longer distances to travel explain their earlier departure time?

The excitement in Bill's voice said it all: "**Sabine's gull** over the feeding frenzy." A Sabine's is very rare here. I have never heard anyone say they had seen one. Bill helped me spot it. "It's much smaller than the ring-billeds. The wing markings are distinctive: black wedges at the wing tips, a large white triangle in the middle of the wing, a large gray triangle on the wing closer to the body." With my scope at twenty power I had no trouble finding the unique wing pattern among the larger gulls. The Sabine's circled over the frenzy, occasionally dropping down to the water to feed, then rising to circle again. It repeated the routine a number of times. Whenever it banked a turn, the spectacular wing pattern was beautifully displayed.

Bill explained the importance of our sighting. "They are a very rare fall migrant here, and never seen in spring. What makes this sighting doubly special is the black head, its breeding plumage. The several Sabine's I have seen before had mostly white on their heads, their winter plumage."

We watched the Sabine's actively participate in the frenzy for about five minutes, giving us many great views as it turned and flashed its wings. Then it flew east, out of sight—but in less than a minute, it returned and landed on the water among the other gulls. It rested with the group for half an hour before flying off to continue its journey.

While the Sabine's was around, I noticed Brett was watching it very intently, his eyes seemingly glued to his scope. I learned why as he ecstatically reported, "It was a lifer for me." For someone who has done as much birding as Brett, it was a definite thrill. I was excited, too; I had never seen one either.

I looked it up in the field guide—breeds in the high Arctic, and winters at sea off South America. We were lucky to see the Sabine's on its very long sojourn. It spends so much of the year in parts of the world where very few people can see it! Like so many water-loving species, it had made use of the Great Lakes as an integral part of its itinerary. Mother Nature had tucked away in her script for today a special occurrence. We were at the right place and time to see it take place.

30. More Travelers Use the Lake as a Highway

The school of fish dispersed, the gulls and loons slowly scattered. But many birds were still flying by, so Bill and Brett remained attentive for the possibility of another special sighting.

"**Horned grebe** flying west, halfway out at twelve o'clock." With Bill's directions, I saw it—small, flying low to the water, dark gray with a white patch on each wing. "It reminds me of a miniature loon—a hunched back, long slender neck, with noticeable trailing legs," I said. "Good analogy," Bill replied.

Brett continued to identify and count the birds flying by. Bill counted the grebes, which were well distributed within our view over the lake. "About every hour I scan the lake to see if I need to add to my grebe count," Bill said. "There are twenty-four now, three more than an hour ago. The count tends to increase throughout the morning." He pointed out several to our left not far from shore, and a few more straight ahead farther out. Others had remained at the spot of the feeding frenzy. "Notice that they don't like to be too close together. They need plenty of room to dive and swim after fish."

Bill continued, "It's surprising how my count increases during the morning without us seeing them arrive. They are sneaky little devils. We occasionally see one fly in, but they usually drift into view or swim, sometimes underwater. Once here, they typically stay for hours. They may change their position as a result of diving and swimming, but they usually remain in the general area. That makes it easy for me to count them and adjust my total on an hourly basis."

"What is the purpose of your daily counts of horned grebes?" I asked.

"Making comparisons over the years can give us valuable information on whether they are failing or thriving. They seem to be holding their own as far as I have seen, but there are reports in other parts of the country where their numbers are declining."

My interest in the flow of the Pageant prompted my next comment. "I assume you can tell when they start to arrive, and how their numbers build, then taper off."

"Yes, in early September they start to leave their nesting grounds in the Prairie Provinces. In October they pass through here in increasing numbers to the point where by the third week of the month, about a week from now, I may see up to two hundred on a day with optimum conditions. They taper off during November, and by December most have moved on to the Atlantic Coast for the winter. A few remain all winter."

It took me awhile, but I eventually found most of the grebes Bill had counted. I easily found the white front of the relatively long, upright neck of those facing me. I had to be more diligent to find those that were not facing me; their gray winter plumage blended in with the dark water as background. In my spotting scope I could see they had sharp, pointed bills like loons.

I was fascinated by their quick, athletic moves to launch a dive. From their sitting position on the surface of the water, a powerful kick from their lobed toes (they do not have webbed feet like ducks) would propel them upward, nearly out of the water; then, with their heads pointed downward, they would disappear below the surface. All this happened in a quick, smooth motion. I found myself playing a little game—whenever one would dive, I would guess where and when it would reappear. I always guessed wrong—they were probably chasing fish, and the direction of the escaping fish and the distance they had to chase it were unpredictable.

I conjured up in my mind's eye what Mother Nature had recorded in her script for the grebes. Perhaps she had written for them something like this—"If you had carefully followed my directive in the spring, especially the timing for laying eggs, by September your young will be sufficiently mature to leave the vicinity of Saskatchewan and start southeastward. As you cross the Great Lakes region in October you can take advantage of that large fishable area for providing a food supply for much of your extensive trip. A few of you who believe it will be a mild winter, or are hardy souls, may remain on the Great Lakes for the winter, but most of you will continue to the Coast for the winter." I wondered how much more Mother Nature had implanted into their brains—much, much more, I'm sure.

A shadow came from behind us, and passed overhead moving toward shore. We looked up and shouted in unison, "**brant!**" It was a group of about fifty, close together, very low. They flew out over the lake, then adjusted their course to follow the shoreline. At first they looked black, but as they turned east, the sun divulged a brownish shade to their backs.

Brett commented, "The brant are going to the coast, probably New Jersey."

I asked, "If they follow the lake to reach the coast, why did this group fly over us from land?"

"They may have been feeding in a nearby farmer's cornfield, and probably spent the night there," answered Brett. Bill added, "They are one of the few waterfowl species we see consistently flying east in the fall. Many of the other waterfowl predominantly fly west, some because they winter on Lake Erie or Ontario. Others may be following the southwestern tilt to the shoreline before turning south."

I checked the field guide. Brants belong to the goose family (the Canada goose's scientific name is *branta canadensis*; the brant's is *branta bernicia*). I noticed in the illustrations how much the brants' shape and coloration resemble Canada geese. But brants are much smaller. They are only slightly larger than mallards. They nest in the high Arctic, most going farther north than the magnetic north pole. I could visualize them swimming among the ice floes, even in summer, finding their way around the multiyear ice pack. Then I imagined trying to find things to eat on the tundra or in the shallows of the Arctic Ocean. I wondered why they choose such a distant, and in many ways inhospitable, location for raising their young.

We were getting ready to call it a day when Brett spotted something on the horizon. It was a good-sized sailboat nearly a mile away, coming from the east. "It might scare up a flock of scoters," he suggested. Sure enough, a narrow line of tiny black dots, barely visible in the distance, was rising from the boat as it moved in our direction. The trail of dots steadily lengthened and widened, expanding to the point where it looked like a stretched-out cloud. "There they are," said Brett, "probably **white-winged scoters**." The cloud-like mass expanded higher as well as longer. The scoters were now a series of dense flocks streaming westward and stretching out in front of us. By the time the sailboat passed, Bill had estimated that we had seen at least eight hundred birds put up by the sailboat's approach. Brett commented, "They had probably been sitting out there all morning far enough so that the curvature of the earth and the waves kept us from seeing them."

31. Thousands of Common Loons
(October 18)

It was dawn at Hamlin Beach. Brett was furiously counting and recording sightings. "A fantastic day for **common loons**," he said when I approached. Even without binoculars I could see them streaming by. Not wanting to miss any of the action, I quickly sat down on the bench next to Brett, extended the legs of my spotting scope's tripod, unzipped the cover, and took a look. Even though the twenty-power lens narrowed the field of vision considerably, I could see several loons at once, all going west. Most were about a half mile from shore.

"I can see some farther out, partially hidden by the fog. There are probably many more that I'm not seeing at all," I said.

"You're right," Brett said. "We're seeing only a fraction of the total flight. We'll just have to do the best we can. I hope the fog lifts soon."

We worked out a way to make it a team effort. Brett positioned his scope so he could see the birds passing from about a half-mile distance out to the horizon, or what could be seen of it. I would call out to him the loons and other species that were closer. Brett used a clicker to efficiently increment the count for each loon seen. At the end of each hour, he entered the clicker's total onto the data sheet. He also recorded the sightings of other species as they were seen. I also agreed to count the horned grebes once an hour.

Over the next two hours we remained busy—sighting, identifying, counting, and recording. The sky remained dark and foggy. Brett recorded the 9:00 a.m. data: "Twelve hundred common loons and nearly a thousand other migrants." The others consisted of many **red-breasted mergansers**, several large groups of **greater scaup**, plus an assortment of **mallards**, **wigeons**, **cormorants**, and many **white-winged scoters**. I made sure he included my count of twenty-two swimming and diving horned grebes.

A **red-necked grebe** flew by. as do horned grebes, It looked like a small loon—humped back, long extended neck, trailing legs. When it flew over a group of its cousins, horned grebes, it dropped down to visit them. Its decision must have been a hasty one, because its landing was so abrupt and awkward that it looked like it had fallen from the sky. I laughed so loudly at the hilarious performance that I had to explain to Brett what had happened. Perhaps it was feeling a little weary from a long stint of flying, so it took the opportunity to take a rest and appreciate some company. Red-necks are solitary migrants. Or, maybe it was hungry and knew that horned grebes fish in groups when they find a good food supply—both species have similar diets. Not only was it an opportunity for the red-necked, it was a chance for me too. I compared the two grebe species. The red-necked had the same long, upright neck as the horneds, but much larger.

There were many gulls on the beach. Nearly a hundred **ring-billeds** and a few **herrings** were clustered together. About twenty **great black-backed gulls** were at the water's edge. Occasionally, one would take a drink. More ring-billeds—airborne—were circling and patrolling the water in search of breakfast. Other ringed-billeds were flying by on a fast, direct westerly course, interspersed with migrating loons and ducks. "A lot of gulls are moving west; it looks like they are migrating," I said in a querying voice.

Brett answered, "Huge numbers of gulls winter on the Niagara River near Niagara Falls some fifty miles from here. It is a well-known site for congregating gulls during the winter. They must be attracted to an excellent food supply there—the fast-moving current keeps the water open for fishing. Birders frequently scan the Niagara River gorge in hopes of seeing a rare visiting gull such as a little, glaucous, or Iceland."

32. Red-Throated Loons, Winter Finches, and Swans Arrive

Many more common loons went by over the next hour. "That's eighteen hundred, their peak flight so far this year," Brett proclaimed. "Unless there is a drastic change in the weather within the next few hours, we could have one of the record high counts for a day's flight."

My knowledge of loons was about to take another major advance. It started when I detected an instructive hint to Brett's remark, "This loon looks like it has no head. Look at it carefully." It was far to the right coming toward us, giving me plenty of time to study its approach. I saw what Brett meant: its light-colored head blended in with the background of brightly illuminated waves and sky. I had seen many common loons recently and unconsciously stored a mental image of them. Consequently, I easily recognized what was different about this loon. Its back was a lighter gray. I thought it looked smaller too, but was unsure. Size comparison and distance are difficult to judge across the featureless water. When it was directly in front of us Brett helped me. "It's a **red-throated loon**. I wondered when one was going to show up." Brett gave me more characteristics for differentiating it from the common loon. "Note its faster wing beat and the way it flaps its noticeably pointed wings higher above its body."

Over the next few minutes a number of loons went by, one at a time. A few were red-throateds; most were commons. They gave me a perfect opportunity to study the characteristics Brett had told me about. As a loon approached, I would first note the color of its back, then check its wing shape and flap. If the background lighting was such that it appeared headless, the decision was easy. I usually had little difficulty deciding whether it was a common or red-throated. After making my decision, I would ask Brett for verification. I was usually right. His hints were working marvelously—I was gaining confidence. I remember one sighting in particular: about all I could see through the distant mist was a pointed and highly held wing tip. That was all I needed for the identification. I was thrilled by being able to identify a red-throated under such adverse conditions!

A common loon landed on the water in front of us. Brett announced, "Looner landing!" After landing, the loon looked about to became familiar with its surroundings, then dove, resurfacing at a totally unpredictable location. After several dives it rested awhile, taking a lunch break from its long flight into the wind. I checked the loons' range maps in the field guide and paraphrased my findings to Brett. "The common loon nests over most of Canada below the tree line. In contrast, the red-throated nests mostly north of the tree line, along the Arctic Ocean and the high Arctic islands."

Brett gave his observations on the timing of their migrations. "The commons become numerous by mid-October, their numbers increasing into mid-November, then decreasing throughout December. As the common loons decrease, the red-throateds increase. Their numbers build from mid-November through mid-December, then quickly taper off. A few of both species linger throughout the winter, but most are gone by late December."

"The range maps in the field guide for both species show that most of them winter along the Atlantic Coast. I can see why they come through here; the Great Lakes are an excellent food source en route," I said. "But why are we seeing them going west? If they were going to the coast, wouldn't they be going east?"

Brett answered, "It is known that a few common loons head for the southerly angled shoreline of Lake Erie, from where they follow river systems to the south. But no one seems to know where the bulk of this population goes. I haven't seen anything in the literature to explain it. It's a mystery!

"Red-throateds have different migratory habitats. After leaving their nesting grounds, many are seen in the Great Lakes. When we see them here, they are usually flying west. We don't know how they get to the East Coast after going west from here. That's a mystery too!"

I mulled over the mysteries Brett pointed out, and thought of other questions of my own. Why has Mother Nature orchestrated the timing of the two loons' migration so that the commons come first, then the red-throateds? Why didn't she send both species at the same time, or did she think they would be competing for the same food supply? I'm sure she had her reasons. I then thought how thrilling it would be to have an interview with Mother Nature, and ask her my questions. On second thought, I decided that by the time I reach the realm where I can talk with her, I would have the insight to answer the questions myself.

Brett looked up from his scope. "I hear **siskins**." A flock of about twenty flew east along the beach, and in seconds they were gone. Then he pointed directly overhead. "**Horned larks**. See the black under their tails? It's the surest way to identify them in flight."

"Are we going to have a good winter for wandering flocks?" I asked. "It has been several years since we have had one."

"We might. I heard **evening grosbeaks** flying over the parking lot as I came in this morning."

The phenomenon of winter finches (siskins, grosbeaks, crossbills, snow buntings, and redpolls, plus cedar and Bohemian waxwings and horned larks) is part of our winter experience. Brett can recognize them by their flight calls; the fast-moving flock is otherwise difficult to identify. However, if you come upon a flock when they are busily harvesting the fruit from a tree—a version of a feeding frenzy—you can leisurely watch them for several hours at close range. A flock of twenty to thirty of one of the wintering species quickly scours a large area searching for food, then moves on. Adding more to the intrigue, some years there are many flocks, and a variety of species. Other years there may be virtually none to see—either they have been able to stay farther north, or the lack of food forces them to move to other locations.

They were majestic—large, pure white, flying gracefully with a slow, steady wing beat. Two **mute swans** were in front of us going east, only a few hundred yards from shore. The mute is not native to North America. It was brought here from Europe to populate our parks and private estates. In recent years, escapees have established themselves in isolated sites around the Great Lakes and the East Coast. Several pairs live in the vicinity of Braddock Bay. The mute has an orange bill; our native **tundra swan** has a black bill.

After a short lull, the common loon flight resumed, and by 11:30 a.m. we had counted 650 more before the movement all but ceased. Brett added up the total for the morning—2,600! It was one of the highest counts ever recorded at Hamlin Beach. As I drove home, I thought about the incredible parade orchestrated by Mother Nature this morning. I wondered how many loons in total she had dispatched this morning, birds that we were unable to see due to distance and visibility.

33. An Array of Late Fall Species in the Hedgerows (October 30)

It had the feel of late fall—a crispness, a cool breeze. At Beatty Point, along the lane down to the water's edge, the wild asters were bright purple and the leaves on some of the oaks and maples were still brilliant red or orange. The goldenrod, however, had turned brown, and so had the cattails. Farther on, around the marshy end of Buck Pond, I had a distinct feeling of emptiness, and melancholy, as far as bird activity was concerned. All summer and fall I had walked this route hearing a variety of residents. Later came the less vociferous migrants. But now the trees, bushes, cattails, and fields were mostly empty, and quiet of birds. Only winter residents will remain to welcome the snow and cold. Unlike a few days ago, the calls of the white-throated sparrows were now absent. They had migrated south by now. The swallows were gone too, as were the red-wings.

A **song sparrow** flew ahead along the hedgerow, one of the last summer residents to leave. When it turned to look at me, I saw the buff-colored background to its breast streaks, indicating it had hatched this summer.

Several **juncos** twittered and fluttered in the hedgerow. I had walked the same route several times recently. If they had been there then, I certainly would have seen them in their favorite haunts. They had just arrived for the winter.

The three-noted calls of **golden-crowned kinglets** came from a large red oak. At first I couldn't see them—the oak is the last of the trees to drop its leaves. Then the kinglets moved to the less leafy branches, where I finally saw them. Black, white, and golden streaks on their heads identified them as the source of the calls. They flew to the next tree. How tiny they were! They weigh only a fraction of an ounce. At four inches long, they are the smallest of our birds after the hummingbird.

I stopped at the bridge where Larkin Creek empties into Buck Pond. The view of the marsh was expansive, mostly cattails with an open strip of water finding its way to the pond beyond. Throughout the summer, up to about a week ago, a dozen barn swallows would be here continuously flying over the marsh in search of mosquitoes. Their flights would often take them directly toward me, then under the bridge where I stood, to their colony's nests attached to the concrete walls. Also during the summer, there had been large numbers of red-winged blackbirds perched throughout the cattails, creating a ceaseless chorus of their varied calls. But now there was no movement, no singing. I turned back toward the car.

A group of ten birds was sitting in the upper branches of a tall dead tree, silhouetted against the overcast sky. They were the size and shape of red-wings. As one flew away, it revealed its red epaulet—at least one red-wing still remained. I moved closer to identify the other nine. They sounded similar to grackles, but their tails were too short. Stepping sideways so that what little daylight there was came from behind me, I could see rust-colored breasts and necks—**rusty blackbirds**. Two of the rustys turned to show their identifying yellow eyes. Red-wings have black eyes. The single red-wing that flew away had probably tired of being different from the other nine, and was hoping to find other red-wings.

This was typical habitat for rustys: just a short distance from a marsh and water. Perhaps they turn rusty because of their constant exposure to a damp habitat. The more authoritative opinion, however, is that in early fall they acquire new feathers with rust-colored tips. By spring, the tips have worn off, resulting in a sleek black or gray breeding plumage. Beyond the blackbirds came a sparrow's call note, a more raspy quality than the white-throateds' or song sparrows' songs I often hear. It was five feet off the ground in a hedgerow of low trees—a **fox sparrow**. It continued giving its call note as I admired its distinctiveness. Compared to other sparrows, it is much larger, and more brightly colored—reddish brown rather than gray brown. Fox sparrows migrate from the South to northern Canada and back again, earlier than most songbirds in spring (April), and later than most in fall (October).

November

34. Late Migration Changes Along the Lakeshore (November 10)

At the Lake Watch site, Bill and Brett were scanning the horizon and shoreline with their spotting scopes. I joined them, asking, "Where's Mike Davids? I saw his car in the parking lot." Bill answered, "He's searching the park for winter finches. He'll be by later to give us a report."

Brett gave the status of the waterfowl migration. "The early migrants are thinning out; the later migrants are picking up." Over the next few hours I would learn just how descriptive that short sentence was. He continued with details. "We're seeing only a few cormorants now—two weeks ago they were going by in large flocks. The counts of most early migrants, such as brant, geese, teal, pintail, wigeon, and terns, are smaller. Our winter residents, usually later arrivers, are increasing in numbers: **bufflehead**, **long-tailed ducks**, **white-winged scoters**, **common goldeneye**, and **greater scaup**. The scaup are collecting in larger and larger rafts." Bill chimed in, "Also, the ratio of **common loons** to **red-throated loons** has reversed, a key sign of migration's later stages. In October we saw mostly commons; now the majority is red-throated." "Yesterday I saw 1,700 red-throats and less than a hundred commons," Brett added.

I settled down to watch the parade of migrants. Every few seconds one or two golden-eyes flew by, as well as buffleheads. There was a constant flow of red-breasted mergansers, usually in small groups of ten or fifteen. Of course, loons, mostly red-throateds, but also a few commons, trickled by, one by one.

About a hundred **red-breasted mergansers** were swimming and diving within an elliptical-shaped area, apparently above a school of small fish. They were not in a tight raft, as resting scaup would be, but several feet apart, providing room for each bird to dive, pick off a fish, and surface again. We had been watching the number of red-breasteds increase steadily since early October. Now groups of over a hundred were common. I counted eight **buffleheads** feeding at the perimeter of the group. Along one side of the group were several **common loons**, also feeding. The activity was attracting an increasing number of **ring-billed gulls**, and two **Bonaparte's gulls** also arrived. Most of the gulls circled above the group; occasionally one would swoop down to pick off a snack near the surface. Other gulls remained on the surface, looking for food they could see.

Separate from all this activity was a raft of about three hundred **greater scaup**, several hundred yards to the right of the feeding group. Most were sleeping, heads tucked under their wings. Bill scanned the raft. "A few of them are holding their heads upright; two are **lesser scaup**, the ones with pointed or peaked heads. Greater scaups have rounded heads. Sometimes there are other ducks in the raft too, such as a gadwall or wigeon—but not today."

Bill finished searching the raft and returned to scanning the horizon. "There are many **scoters and long-tailed ducks** moving by at least a mile out, at almost the limit of visibility." I could see them too, but complained, "How can you identify those tiny dots at such a distance?"

Bill explained his technique for identifying distant long-taileds. "The identifying features pointed out in the field guides are generally not visible at a great distance. Far away, a flying long-tailed appears to be white in front, and rear; in the middle are the beating dark wings. This three-area pattern, white-dark-white, is noticeable from great distances in fall and winter. In spring, the male's head is black, changing the color pattern." After Bill pointed out several flocks of long-taileds, I realized how well noticing the alternating color pattern worked.

35. A Closer Study of the Family of Scoters

The other participants in the distant parade were scoters. I could differentiate the scoters—plump, stubby-winged, and black—from the long-taileds now. I couldn't differentiate the three species of scoters that Bill and Brett were finding. Several weeks ago Bill had told me that after white-wingeds pass by, seeing them at a different angle to the light, often makes the white on their wings more visible. I was seeing scoters that did not appear to have white in their wings, even after they had passed. Once again Bill helped me out.

"If I don't see patches either before or after they pass by, they could be black or surf scoters. I usually recognize a **black scoter** from a white-winged by its smaller and more compact body and shorter neck. These differences are very subtle, and discernible only because I have seen many thousands of scoters over the years and have each species' appearance imprinted in my mind."

Flocks of scoters continued to stream by. Bill pointed out mixed flocks containing both white-wingeds and blacks. Seeing both species together helped immensely in establishing the differences in my mind. After seeing a number of excellent comparisons, the differences became easier to recognize. Sometimes, depending upon the light, the two-toned underwings of the black scoter helped in the identification.

Some of the mixed flocks contained **surf scoters**, so Bill added them to my identification lesson. "The neck of the surf scoter is longer than the black's; this is often obvious to an experienced observer, and when it is, it's an easy way to make the identification. If the light is good, the female surf may show white on the belly. An immature black scoter, however, can also show white on its belly. At other times, the light, distance, or angle may prevent you from determining black from surf; then we just call them dark-wingeds." I continued to identify, or attempt to identify, flocks of scoters as they came by, checking with Bill or Brett to make sure. I was making progress. There were quite a few white-winged and blacks, but an insufficient number of surfs to give me the practice of identifying them.

36. An Unexpected Lake Traveler—A Short-Eared Owl

Brett called out, "**short-eared owl** coming across the lake!" It was still nearly a mile out when I found it in my scope, chocolate brown, floppy wing beats, with buff and black patches on the wrist of the wing. We watched it circle a few times as it tried to shake the harassment by several gulls. It then headed for shore, making land half a mile down the beach at a high bluff. Brett continued, "It probably saw the bluff from far out over the lake and decided to head for it. It nested in Canada and is coming south for the winter. Sometimes during the winter at dusk, their floppy wing-flapping over an open snowy field catches our attention as they hunt for mice. They even hunt during the day if it's cloudy."

I had heard about the owl migration along the lakeshore on spring nights, and had assumed that all owls migrated at night. Short-ears are an exception—since they sometimes hunt in the day, they can also migrate during the day. Another lesson.

37. A Shorebird That Likes to Swim: A Phalarope from the High Arctic

A few minutes later I heard Bill's excited voice: "A **phalarope** flying west about half a mile out." What I saw was a small brownish form scooting westerly, low over the waves. I could see no particular form or shape to distinguish it from other small shorebirds, so I asked, "How could you tell it was a phalarope from such a distance?"

"We are high enough above the water that looking down on it showed its key flight characteristic—slight zigzags as though it was having trouble holding a straight course. They're only very slight zigzags, but definitely noticeable."

For a while Bill was unsure which phalarope it was. "It's too late for the **Wilson's phalarope**—they are seen in August and early September. I'm trying to get a good look at its back. If it's darker gray with some streaks, it will be a **red-necked phalarope**. If it's plain gray, it's a **red phalarope**." Finally Bill had the look he needed, "It's a red-necked!" Brett and I applauded spontaneously. It was a natural response to Bill's skill in making such an impressive identification. Brett told me more about phalaropes. "They are different from most shorebirds in that they spend much of their time on the water, as though they were tiny ducks. After nesting in little ponds on the Arctic tundra, they spend the winter far at sea off the coast of South America. That's where this little bird is headed."

Three **tundra swans** flew by, about a hundred feet above the water.

They were close enough for us to hear the wind being pushed by their giant wings! They were beautiful, all white and very large. Their long stretched-out necks accentuated their great length. How gracefully and swiftly they flew, in a straight line, one behind the other. The calm of the cold water beneath reflected the dark gray overcast sky, giving an eerie contrast to their pure white bodies. An elegant picture! Could a camera capture such a scene and do it justice?

Their black bills indicated they were tundra swans, our North American native bird. They nest in the high Arctic, in places such as Baffin Island, and were on their way to the Atlantic Coast for the winter.

38. Rare Winter Nomads: Bohemian Waxwings

Mike was walking the beach, coming our way. He had been gone nearly two hours. If there were winter finches he would have had time to find them.

"There are several flocks of **evening grosbeaks**, a large flock of **common redpolls**, and some **pine siskins**. The big news is the **Bohemian waxwings**—there are thirty-three, with about forty **cedar waxwings**, harvesting the fruit from an autumn olive bush."

Mike was pleased with his finding. "Not only has it been several years since any Bohemians had been seen in the area, but it is an unusually large number to be seen together—there are usually only one or two in a large flock of cedars, which are common here all year."

Although waxwings are not finches, the Bohemians, rare winter visitants, are usually considered part of the winter finch phenomenon. They nest in western Canada, and winter in the northwestern United States. Some winters, very unpredictably, small numbers appear in the Great Lakes region and New England. They are usually found with flocks of their cousins, cedar waxwings. Both species are gregarious, especially in winter, when they are seen in flocks going from one fruit-bearing tree to another. They will eat all the fruit from a tree or bush and then fly off as a flock looking for another feeding site. It is in such flocks of cedars in the winter that we may see bohemian.

Brett and Bill were committed to stay with the waterfowl migration census until noon. I decided to leave immediately, thinking that if the waxwings had eaten all the fruit where Mike had seen them, they might leave to look for another tree to harvest. The sooner I left, the better were my chances. "Take the service road at the west end of the park, and follow it for several hundred yards. They are on the left in an open area," Mike told me.

I carried my spotting scope with me. I wanted the best look possible. As I started the twenty-minute walk, I looked at my field guide, refreshing my memory on differences between the bohemian and cedar. I passed through a grove of trees, then into the open area Mike had described. A flock of birds was sitting in a tall tree two hundred yards away—waxwings.

With binoculars I could see two sizes of waxwings. The larger ones were the bohemians! The cedars were noticeably smaller. I set up my scope, zoomed in at sixty power, and focused. A bohemian popped into clear view. The belly was a clear, light gray, where the cedar waxwing is yellow. The bohemian's dark gray back was outlined by the narrow edge of its folded black wings, which were adorned with yellow and white markings. Like the cedar waxwing's, the bohemian's rusty-brown face emphasized the black eye line. A crest completed its unique waxwing profile. It was a handsome color scheme! Even the rusty spot under the tail was very visible with the high magnification. I was glad I had carried my spotting scope.

There were about thirty of each species, most sitting in the tall isolated tree. Some were in the nearby autumn olive bush, harvesting its fruit. After one group had eaten, they returned to the tall tree; then another group flew to the bush to feed. First one group, then another. It was an orderly process.

I was sure I would never see as many Bohemian waxwings ever again. I soaked up the exhibition a few minutes longer.

39. Discovering the Exit Flight of Red-Throated Loons (November 27)

It was overcast and foggy, and just after dawn. What I was seeing far out over the lake astonished me: a continuous stream of **red-**

throated loons flying east, not west. On several occasions this fall Bill and Brett had commented that whenever we see red-throateds, they are traveling west.

A few minutes later Bill arrived. He watched intently for several minutes. "It's a major flight going east, that's for sure." It was tough to count them. Our view was obscured by fog, rain, low light, and distance. My pique came out. "I know we are not seeing the whole flight. There are many more farther out than we can see." Bill was quick to agree. In spite of the difficulties, over the next hour we counted over four hundred, an impressively large number, all going east. I knew we were witnessing something special, but was unprepared for Bill's next statement: "I think we are the first people to see, or at least to report, the exit flight from Lake Ontario of the red-throated loons; perhaps their exit flight is normally farther out from shore, so no one has seen it before." He added, "They are probably the same birds we have been seeing going west over the last few weeks." Then he told me about the red-throated loon mystery.

"It is well known that red-throated loons winter along the Atlantic Coast, but here, in late fall, we always see them going west rather than east toward the coast. The bird clubs at Buffalo and Niagara Falls typically report only a few of them at the west end of the lake. Why we see them going west, and then how they get to the coast, is a mystery!"

I had been wanting to learn as much as possible about Mother Nature's Pageant. Now, she was showing me a part of her Pageant's script that has been unknown. A secret!

By noon the flights had all but ceased: they tend not to migrate in the afternoon. Bill was counting the last few stragglers at the end of the flight. Incidentally, I told Brett about our discovery several days later. He said the exit flight had continued the next day. He had seen about as many loons as we did and under similar weather conditions. Because we observed such large flights over two successive days, it verified that our recording of the exit flight was very significant.

40. Another Irruptive Arrival—An Eerie Snowy Owl

As a last check before leaving, I scanned the raft of scaup accumulated between the jetties in front of us, on the outside chance that a different species had joined them. None had.

As I was finishing scanning the raft, my scope's field of vision filled with a white, bulky shape, sitting on a rock on the first jetty. It was a **snowy owl**! It was large—as large as a great-horned owl. It was an eerie, monochrome picture: white plumage, speckled with spots of gray, surrounded by gray rocks, with dark waters in the background. An owl was the last thing I had expected to see in such a setting—on the ground, in the wide open spaces of the jetty and surrounding water. Bill took a quick look. "It has a lot of dark spots. That makes it an immature."

I learned from the range map in the field guide that most snowys live year-round within a few miles of the Arctic Ocean. Bill told me more, interspersed with counting the last few loons. "They survive almost exclusively on lemmings. If the lemming population is in a down cycle, many snowys roam south in the winter looking for other food. That is when we see a few here, some years more than others. Most are immatures, and due to their poorly developed hunting skills, few survive their first year."

Then Bill explained why this is ideal habitat for the snowys. "Tundra is their natural habitat, so when we see them here it is on beaches or open fields, habitat familiar to them. We sometimes see them hunt during the day, because they are accustomed to hunting during the Arctic's perpetual summer daylight. They rarely see humans in the Arctic, so they show little fear when they see us."

41. Snowbirds, Lovers of Winter

I was collapsing the legs on my scope's tripod, preparing to leave, when a shadow came from behind us, and passed overhead. It was a tight flock, about a hundred sparrow-sized birds, mostly white—**snow**

buntings! They swooped down to the water's edge, wheeled to the right in a tight formation, and then moved along the beach to the jetty. They wheeled again, and quickly settled on the beach. Light splotches of tan on their backs added camouflage; Mother Nature had chosen a perfect color scheme to hide them on the windswept, snowy beaches and open fields where they feed.

Some people call them snowbirds, fascinated by how they burrow in deep snow for protection against cold temperatures. I, too, have been fascinated by their mystical qualities and have long wanted to study these unusual birds up close, when they make their unpredictable, irruptive visits. This was the first time I had my spotting scope handy. Focusing first on one and then another, I watched their restless habits. After landing at a patch of weeds the flock busily searched for the weeds' tiny seeds. All of a sudden they shot up into the air in unison, darting farther down the shore to another weedy site. They were soon back again, continuously communicating with each other in short buzzy twitters.

Bill explained why we were seeing them along the beach. "After having nested along the Arctic coast, in winter they move to southern Canada and northern U.S. They are used to the tundra, so when they arrive here they select beaches and fields, habitat that suggests the tundra they know in summer."

He added, "Whenever I see snow buntings I automatically scan the flock looking for a **Lapland longspur**, a dark nondescript bird obviously different from the mostly white buntings. This fall I have looked at a number of bunting flocks as they pivoted in front of me, and in two cases there were longspurs." We searched our flock for a longspur, but to no avail. The range maps of buntings and longspurs are similar, Arctic in summer, northern United States in winter, suggesting that when we see a longspur with buntings it may have been with the flock throughout its long travels.

42. Experiencing More of the Winter Finch Phenomenon

As I left, Bill made a suggestion. "For several days now, there have been pine grosbeaks at the park's entrance. They fly back and forth among the several tall ash trees in the median of the parking lot. It's hard to say how much longer they will stick around." I was chagrined that I might have driven by them this morning and not seen them. They are rarely seen members of the winter finch group—at least, rarely seen in this part of the country. It would be a lifer for me.

"Also, on the way in this morning, I saw common redpolls eating catkins among the birch and alders along the park road halfway from here to the entrance. There have been several flocks in the park recently; some years we don't see them at all."

I stopped when I reached the alder bushes and walked around the clump that hugged the stream next to the road. They were just as Bill had said. A flock of ten **common redpolls** busily pecked at the alder catkins; little birds, looking like miniature sparrows, but with a dark red spot on the forehead and a black chin. Their pleasant twittering sounded like goldfinches, high pitched and thin. They flew away in a tight formation. I hadn't seen redpolls for several years.

A group of birds was sitting in the tall trees near the entrance parking lot. They were about the size of grosbeaks. I quickly studied the plumage of grosbeaks in the field guide so I would be prepared. The range map showed that they spend the summer in northern Canada and winter in southern Canada. Some winters, they drift farther south.

I closed the car door quietly and walked closer. They didn't move, providing me with an excellent close look. They were **pine grosbeaks** for sure, eleven of them, dark gray with a little yellowish-gray showing on the top of the head, the female plumage. After a few minutes they flew to a nearby tree to feed on ash seeds. Occasionally, one would give a high-pitched, musical, three-noted call, sounding very much like the yellowlegs we see on the mudflats. I had another life bird.

While driving home I reviewed the morning's sightings. They followed a theme: Mother Nature was taking the steps necessary to preserve several Arctic species from the dangers of the oncoming winter! Buntings had moved to their normal winter range; loons were on the last leg of their annual journey. I found some of her actions startling. She had anticipated an unusually poor food supply in the North and moved the snowy owl, redpolls, and pine grosbeaks farther south than their typical winter range, even though they are well adapted for most northern winters.

December

43. A Sampling of Winter Residents
(December 22)

All fall I had watched the migration from Hamlin Beach State Park. Today I returned to the park to see what Mother Nature had programmed for winter.

It was overcast and freezing. Several inches of snow covered the ground. I walked the road that wound its way through the park's camping area, which In summer, is busy, sometimes noisy. Now it is deserted.

Chatty call notes came from several gossiping **chickadees**. Two flitted among branches of shrubbery closest to the road. Several others were nearby in the undergrowth. They congregate during the winter to better find food and enjoy each other's outgoing personality (which has little chance to come out during the busy nesting season).

Chickadees are considered irruptive, meaning that some winters they move farther south than usual to find better sources of food. Betsy Brooks, of the Braddock Bay Bird Observatory, told me her banding records show there are more chickadees here in winter about every four years. Reports from banders who have recaptured the same birds Betsy had banded indicate that the chickadees don't go far during their winter travels, probably a maximum of two hundred miles. They slowly move southwesterly in fall, and somewhat faster back to the northeast in spring.

Two chickadees along the road showed no fear, and even seemed interested in my presence. They probably wondered, "Why on such a cold, cloudy day, of all days, had this person come by? It has been weeks since we have seen a human."

Chickadees usually respond to spishing, especially in winter when they have more time to be curious. I approached slowly and spished. The two came even closer, giving their call notes in response to my spishing. I then imitated their *chick-a-dee-dee* song as best I could. One responded with the last half of its own song. One farther back in the bushes gave its two-noted phoebe whistle; I imitated it, also. It repeated its whistle so I could adjust the pitch; I had been a note too high. We exchanged a few more times; finally, I thought my imitation sounded believable. I wondered if he found it believable, too.

More members of the group came in to enjoy the excitement, busily flitting among the bushes. They were noisy. We had quite a powwow. The inter-language discussion continued. Some reacted to my imitation of their *chick-a-dee-dee* song; others responded to my two-noted whistle. Then, one by one, they moved away. Had they lost interest in me, or had they decided it necessary to search for more seeds or fruit? I wondered if they had been talking among themselves before I arrived, or if they had started to talk after seeing me coming?

In the background several crows were cawing. They seem to have more fun in winter, too. They have more time to socialize. They are a very social group.

The *peent-peent* of a **white-breasted nuthatch** came from a large stand of very tall oaks. I walked farther down the road toward the call. By paying attention to the direction and elevation of the nuthatch's coarse, nasal call, and searching close to the trunks and larger branches of the oaks, I spotted it, scrambling along a very high horizontal branch. It was the only nuthatch I heard or saw. (Unlike chickadees, nuthatches do not form winter scavenging groups).

It was a typical sighting of a white-breasted nuthatch. It was alone in tall, mature oaks. Nuthatches prefer oaks, and acorns become their favorite food in winter when their summer fare of insects is scarce. They seem to prefer this seasonal shift in diet, permitting them to avoid migration or irruptive movements. [See plate 7]

As I continued walking, the habitat changed to low scrubby growth with wide grassy areas bordering the road. A small troop of sparrows darted away from the open area and disappeared into the bushes, some giving their *dseet* call notes as they went. One remained, crouched among the short grass not far from the road. On its head, broad stripes of dark brown alternated with light tan. On its throat a distinct white patch explained its name, **white-throated sparrow**. Now that they had flown into the bushes, putting themselves at a safe distance, they were freely popping in and out of view. After looking at each one, I discovered that some had brown and tan head stripes, and others had distinctive black and white stripes—the two color phases of the species. I have heard that white-throateds tend to breed with the opposite phase, even though both phases consist of both males and females. A male tan phase may mate with a female white phase, or vice versa, verifying the old adage that opposites attract. It was a late date to see so many of them. Large flocks are common during migration, as they move from Canada to more southerly locations, but usually only the loners linger this late. [See plate 12]

Farther down the road, the grassy area widened to open terrain. There was another group of sparrows, more slender and too chocolate brown to be more white-throateds. I caught a close-up view with my binoculars. They had chestnut-colored patches on their heads and white wing bars— **American tree sparrows**. The closest was still in summer's bright rufous cap. The others had already molted into their duller winter plumage. They will brighten again in spring. Several faced me, each showing a clear gray breast with a black spot in the middle. Their call notes were noticeably thinner than those of the white-throateds. They were attracted to grass, weeds, and low bushes, similar to the flora of northern Canadian tundra where they nest. Mother Nature sends them here in winter to avoid the forty-below temperatures and the difficulty in finding food. We benefit too, for they are sleek, handsome additions to our feeders and winter walks.

The road took several tight turns as it weaved its way through the campground. I passed a number of campsites that must have looked very inviting to young families during the summer. The habitat changed, becoming more diverse: tall trees, bushes, and open grassy areas near a marsh. I expected to see a more diverse group of birds.

A boisterous **robin** called from the top of a tall spruce; other members of its small flock quietly harvested fruit among nearby bushes. They were not the same robins that nested here this summer—they had nested farther north. They are examples of partial migration: they move south in winter, but don't completely leave their species' nesting range. Some birders claim they can identify the northern race by its being larger and more richly colored. The songster that had attracted my attention was more vividly colored than many of our summer birds. The white around his eye was especially more noticeable. I was not convinced, however, that he was significantly different from the males I see here in summer. Of the other robins that I could see well, none had the duller coloration of our summer females. Could they all be males? Song sparrows, herring gulls, chickadees, and some flickers are also partial migrants. When one sees a species' range map, showing that the summer and year-round ranges are large and contiguous, it is a good bet that the species does partial migrants. Some species migrate segregated by sex, but I have never heard that about robins. In spring, most male warblers migrate several days ahead of the females. This is believed to provide the male with time to select and establish a nesting site.

Each spring, some morning in mid-March, I discover that the summer robins have arrived in the woods behind my house. They arrived overnight, and by morning are happy, noisy, and eager to start nesting and raising young. They will be my neighbors all summer. By late September most will have gone. The woods will be quiet, and I will miss their company. In late November I will see robins again, the northern group, gleaning the fruit from the numerous crabapples in the neighborhood. When they have eaten all the crabapples, they move on to another fruitful location.

This morning, Mother Nature has been showing me the different types of migration. She has assigned a migratory habit to each species depending upon its specialized methods of survival. Chickadees are a combination of irruptive (in winter they unpredictably move farther south than normal, in search of food) and partial migration (their summer and winter ranges overlap). Tree sparrows use total migration (their winter range is hundreds of miles south of where they nest.) White-breasted nuthatches need not migrate at all, as far as we know. Robins and white-throated sparrows use a special form of partial migration, in which their nesting and winter ranges overlap, so that some of them spend the entire year in the overlap region. In addition, I am suspicious that some robins may be practicing differential migration, which means that a group of females, or perhaps older birds, may migrate to different locations than do other groups of their species. I have read that juncos sometimes practice differential migration too, but I have seen both sexes at my feeder. For the remainder of my winter walk I would note what type of winter migration or movement I was seeing.

A small bird flew across the road, landing fairly high up in a white pine. Its manner of flight, body shape, and habit of crouching against the trunk told me it was a nuthatch. Because of its smaller size, I knew it was a **red-breasted nuthatch**. He gave his repeated *peent* call, more nasal than the white-breasted's. From my studying of red-breasteds earlier this fall, including discussing them with Braddock Bay Bird Observatory's Betsy

Brooks, I knew Mother Nature had assigned red-breasteds perhaps the most complex set of migratory types: total, partial, irruptive, and various combinations. A few individuals are permanent residents. Others are partial migrants; some migrate short distances, others much longer distances in spring and fall. Some are irruptive, perhaps not migrating far some years and greater distances other years, depending upon the food supply. They can be seen here throughout the year, but there are many more around in the spring and fall. How many come here from Canada to spend the winter varies considerably from year to year. Looking again at the little nuthatch as he scampered along a large horizontal limb, repeating his little tin horn–sounding call, I wondered if he knew he was of such complex heritage.

Another group of small birds was flitting back and forth between the shelter of a clump of osiers and the seeds in the nearby tall grasses and last summer's wildflowers. Some of the group were dark gray, others a brownish gray. As they flew, flashes of white in their outer tail feathers confirmed they were all **dark-eyed juncos**. They are common, welcome additions to our winter walks and feeders. In spring, they return to their nesting grounds in Canada.

Metallic-like chirps directed my attention to a male **cardinal** flying across the road, his bright red plumage resplendent against the snowy white background. A slow, low, loping flight method took him into a row of high-bush cranberries, perhaps where he intended to have breakfast. Continuing my theme to note the migratory niche of each species I saw this morning, I placed the cardinal among the permanent residents. Cardinals are not known to have winter wanderings of any significance. They do, however, have a dynamic history. I remember Walt Listman, one of our area's premier birders, telling me that when he started to bird as a kid in the 1930s, he rarely saw cardinals, but over several decades they expanded their southerly range northward till they became common residents here. Walt's comments about the cardinal reminded me that other species have adjusted their ranges over the years: house finches, Canada geese, and red-bellied woodpeckers are examples. In fact, most species' migrations and related habits have evolved considerably since the retreat of the ice ages. Then it struck me: the Pageant evolves slowly over time! "Oh no," I thought. Evolution of the Pageant is another complication to consider in my project. It was then that I made a decision: I would concentrate my efforts on movements and activities that I can personally observe. I would not undertake historical studies of the Pageant.

January

44. Close Winter-Long Friends (January 15)

One unavoidable aspect of birding, regardless of the time of year or the species I'm looking for, is that the sightings are quite hit-or-miss. For example, if I meet another birder who has arrived a few minutes earlier or later than I, or has been walking a few hundred yards away, he is likely to find birds that I have missed. He has experienced a different part of the Pageant than I. Consequently, I feel inadequate about sampling the Pageant.

Braddock Bay Bird Observatory once asked me to assist in a census of the species seen and heard where the observatory's mist nets were capturing birds for banding. When I completed my census, the species on my list were very different from what they had banded. I saw some species, such as those high in the trees that did not come down to the mist nets; likewise, I did not see many species that had been banded.

To improve my sampling of the Pageant in winter, I have put out feeders. There are birds that live in my neighborhood year-round, but are difficult to find when I go looking for them. In winter, however, I can encourage them to come to me. Their routine visits to the feeder tells me about how many there are of each species. I can study their habits too, learning far more than what I had been able to do without feeders. Watching my feeders has added a valuable dimension to understanding the Pageant, especially in winter. I had already learned how valuable feeders are in watching the hatchlings and parents in early summer.

I looked out my kitchen window toward the woodlot just twenty feet away. A **downy woodpecker**, a male, as indicated by the red spot on the back of his head, landed on one of the four basswood trunks, about ten feet above the container of suet. The downy inched down the trunk until he reached the suet, using his stiff, sharp-pointed tail feathers against the bark to support his position. He looked around to see if the way was clear, then pecked at the suet for several seconds. He slowly worked his way back up the trunk looking for insects in the bark, then flew away, in his loping style of flight.

I heard the **hairy woodpecker's** loud squawk as he took the downy's place next to the suet. He usually announces his arrival and departure, but downys normally do not. Being larger and more domineering, the hairy may have triggered the downy's departure. The hairy had a red spot on the back of his head as did the downy, indicating they were both males. The two species have almost identical plumage, so at those times when I am unsure which species I am seeing I look at their bills for verification: the hairy's bill is long and powerful compared to the downy's thin, short bill. [See plate 2]

Both species come and go throughout the day. I wish I could recognize each individual, perhaps give them names, so I could better track their activities. The best I can do is note their sex, and from that try to deduce individuals. I have seen two downy males at the same time, one eating, another waiting in the woods. I have seen two female downys, too—two pairs of downys. Usually a male comes. After he has had his fill, the female eats. As far as I can tell, there is only one pair of hairys.

A **red-bellied woodpecker** landed beside the suet, less than a foot from the hairy. Both were about the same size. She was gray on the forehead, where her mate would be red. The two woodpeckers squawked at each other a few times, jockeyed for position around the suet, and then the hairy flew off. The red-bellied vigorously attacked the suet, giving me an opportunity to see why it is called red-bellied: normally in the field the reddish tinge on the belly is not visible, but on this occasion, the closeness and the angle of the bird as it pecked at the suet showed the very subtle reddish tinge on the belly. The large white spot on her rump was conspicuous in her retreat to a high perch among the tall oaks.

While I had been watching the woodpeckers, a chickadee flew to the seed feeder, just two feet away from where the larger woodpeckers were working on the suet. The chickadee took a sunflower seed, flew to a nearby branch, cracked open the seed, ate it, and returned to the feeder for another. Three chickadees were now there, taking turns. One would fly in for a seed, while another ate a seed at a secluded branch. The third awaited its turn to return to the feeder. The feeding procedures were different between the species: the woodpeckers would linger over the suet for several seconds, sometimes longer, but the chickadees were in and gone in an instant.

Later in the morning the suet was visited by two **white-breasted nuthatches**. They approached the suet by walking down the trunk head first. Sometimes they would take a sunflower seed too. I knew this was a pair: the top of the female's head and nape of the neck was slate gray, and the male's was jet black. It had taken me several occasions of close observation over the last few weeks to detect this subtle distinction between male and female.

It was not unusual to see all three species of woodpeckers, often both sexes, plus both male and female nuthatches and up to five chickadees. Male and female chickadees are identical, as far as humans can visually determine, but apparently chickadees can tell the difference. A few ground-feeding birds—juncos, mourning doves, and cardinals—usually cleaned up the seeds spilled from the feeder above.

I noticed the hierarchy of feeding among the birds at the feeders. The larger bird dominates. A smaller bird will wait at a safe distance until the larger bird leaves. A red-bellied will chase away a hairy, even though they are about the same size, and a hairy chases away a downy. A downy will chase away a nuthatch. A nuthatch will chase away a chickadee.

Some days are busier than others. I tried to correlate activity to weather. The birds tended to eat more on cold days, but not necessarily. There were some cold days when they ate less than normal. What I discovered was that the birds anticipated a cold front moving in and increased their feeding the afternoon before. It was similar to what I had learned about waterfowl migration—the frequency of flights often accelerated in advance of a cold front. Mother nature has continued to amaze me throughout my studies: she even equips waterfowl, and the birds at my feeders, with barometers, and they are skilled in using them.

Frequently during the day, I would stop my usual activities in the house and watch for a few minutes to see how many hungry visitors appeared. For three days I didn't see the female red-bellied. She may have been feeding when I wasn't looking. But my concern was growing. I enjoyed seeing the glistening red, almost Chinese red, on the back of her head and neck. I needed her to produce babies for my enjoyment in future years. Finally, there she was again. I had another cup of coffee to celebrate my relief.

I considered the woodpeckers to be my friends. I see them several times nearly every day. They are guests at my home, and spend the winter with me.

February

45. Calling Owls (February 10)

The use of suet feeders attracted woodpeckers, permitting me to learn much about their presence. Now, by imitating owl calls, I hoped to discover more about those birds, too.

I had stayed up watching a late movie. With early obligations the next morning, I ended up with a short night's sleep. After lunch, a nap was inevitable. It was surprisingly intense, and two hours later I had great difficulty waking. After the nap, I completed my day's activities with renewed vitality; at 11:00 p.m. I turned out the light and dropped off to sleep. At 3:00 a.m. I awoke, not the least interested in sleep, undoubtedly due to the long afternoon nap. It was the perfect opportunity to go owl calling; it would fill an important gap in my sampling of the Pageant.

Owls are likely to reply if they hear your persistent attempts to imitate their calls. The most productive time to do this is just before dawn or after dusk. However, anytime during the night can be good.

The woods near where Brush Creek crosses Townline Road is a known home for owls. At about 3:15 a.m. I was on my way.

Some people use recorded owl calls on a tape player. I imitate them myself. I have been told it is important to call the smaller owl, the screech, first. Screech owls may be intimidated if they have recently heard a larger owl. I have also heard that persistence is important. The screech owl needs to be goaded into answering.

Standing on the shoulder of the road, facing the woods, I started my imitation of the screech owl's declining-pitched whinny sound. With a few short breaks, I kept it up for several minutes. No reply. Perhaps there were no screech owls near. I moved farther down the road and tried again. After several minutes, with my lips getting tired, I began to doubt my chances for success. After about ten more minutes of calling I gave up on the screech owl and tried for a great horned owl.

I had given just a few great horned owl hoots when I heard a screech owl answer far in the distance. So much for highly regarded technical advice. I took up the screech owl call again; it answered. As we carried on a conversation with each other, the owl moved closer. Its call was getting louder, easier to hear.

I wondered how close it would come. Would it be close enough to see? I remembered that Bob McKinney carries a strong flashlight when he calls owls. I was with him once when a screech owl came within thirty feet. Bob shined the light on him so we could get a good look. Now the calls from the screech owl were no longer getting closer. It was moving away, calling less frequently.

If this were an area where the **barred owl** was known to live I would have called it. Its call is easy to imitate: just call out *who-cooks-for-you-who-cooks-for-you-all* in a deep voice. I have called the barred owl successfully in the Adirondacks, where they are plentiful.

I called the great horned owl again, giving my deepest pitch to a series of five hoots, the second and third hoots being faster to give it a rhythm. After several series of hoots an answer came from far off—a farmer's dog from down the road. I continued to excite the dog, but no owls.

Another site known for owls is the southwest corner of Island Cottage Woods. In a few minutes I had pulled off the shoulder of Island Cottage Road, surrounded by woods and Buck Pond.

As I stepped out of the car, a flash of wings went across the road in the dark, disappearing into the woods. It was large; probably a great horned owl. I immediately heard a **great horned owl** hooting in the same woods. I hooted a reply. Another great horned hooted from a position closer than the first. They had a conversation between themselves. I tried to participate, but they ignored me in preference to their own conversation.

I decided to call a screech owl. Since the one earlier this morning was not intimidated by a great horned owl call, perhaps I could encourage one to answer now. After imitating a few screech owl whinny calls, a reply came, distant, coming closer as we talked to each other. Within a minute it was fairly close, just across the road, but too far to see in the thick woods. Apparently satisfied I was not a potential mate or a rival, it moved back into the woods, calling as it left.

It was a successful night, expanding my sample of the Pageant in such a unique way. It was time for a hearty breakfast, and perhaps another nap.

March

46. Early Signs of Spring (March 19)

If Mother Nature were to define a calendar, I think she would make March the first month of the year. Here in Western New York, March is the awakening of Nature. I have been watching snow drifts become smaller, and buds of early plants swell.

The sun was noticeably warm and bright. Chickadees, juncos, and cardinals in the woods behind my house were flitting about more than usual, singing more persistently than they had all winter. A flock of **Canada geese** honked loudly as they flew low in a large V formation.

Several pairs of **robins** chirped excitedly from the nearby woods and hedgerow. This was the first time I had heard them. Their frequent, loud chirping told me they were reveling in their joy for having just completed their long journey, and that they were looking forward to the nesting season.

A loud, air-piercing *killdeeer-killdeeer-killdeeer* call came from a **killdeer** across the street. I saw it circle the field, then flash the orange on its tail as it landed. I could see its typical plover profile (killdeer belong to the plover family): stout with a short bill. It was behaving like a plover, too: taking a few steps very quickly, then stopping briefly before darting on again. There was another killdeer nearby, scrunched down close to the ground. These were probably the same killdeer that I had heard calling late last night as I was drifting off to sleep. I thought at the time that they were the first killdeer I had heard this spring. They have a propensity to call at night, perhaps when someone walks by, or a marauding cat sneaks near, or maybe they have loud arguments. I think my neighborhood now has more killdeer than there were years ago. They like lawns, athletic fields, even gravel parking lots, and of course, beaches and mudflats.

Spring was evident in sights and sounds.

Large numbers of waterfowl have been using Lake Ontario as a highway as they migrate to their nesting grounds in the prairie states and provinces. Also, early migrating hawks were skirting around Lake Ontario (they don't like to fly over water) on their way to Canada. I wanted to see these two aspects of migration, so I drove to Braddock. On the way, an American flag in front of the town hall showed we were having southerly winds, a boost to migrants heading north.

As I passed the ponds and cattail marshes along the parkway, my anticipation was building. I knew this trip was the first of many I would take this spring. With each successive trip, the intensity of migration would build, until it reached a profound climax at the end of May. Spring migration is far more exciting than fall migration: the birds are in their most colorful plumage, the air is filled with the songbirds' singing (a necessary preparation for nesting), and because they must start nesting as soon as possible to ensure that the hatchlings will mature sufficiently before fall, the migration period is condensed into a shorter, much busier event than it is in the fall.

47. Bald Eagles

Braddock Bay is known to be one of the best spring raptor migration sites in the country, and also known for the Braddock Bay Raptor Research (BBRR) migrating hawk census as well as banding and educational programs.

"Raptor" is a collective term for eagles, hawks, and owls. It is common, however, for people here to use the words "hawk" and "raptor" interchangeably. In addition to raptors, or hawks, many waterfowl are attracted to the bay, and small birds such as finches, jays, and shorebirds also migrate along the shoreline.

I walked up the ramp to the Hawk Lookout observation platform, where one is provided a panoramic view of the bay and surrounding marsh. It is almost a mile across the marsh and bay to where a row of trees widens into a small woods. To the left is a large cattail marsh and to the right is the mouth of the bay, widening into Lake Ontario. Sand spits jut out into the mouth from both sides of the bay.

The bay was mostly ice-covered except where Buttonwood Creek flowed in from the southeast corner and Salmon Creek entered from the west. The current of Buttonwood Creek formed a narrow ribbon of open water in front of the observation platform. The current from both creeks flowed into the central part of the bay, carving a large area of open water moving to the mouth, where heavy wave action opened to the lake.

Brett Ewald was on duty at the observation platform identifying and counting all birds, especially raptors. Brett has been involved with BBRR for several years, including three years as the person responsible for counting and identifying every migrating hawk that passes by Braddock Bay. Prior to coming to BBRR he had similar responsibilities at Cape May, New Jersey, another noted site for hawk migration.

He greeted me with his usual grin and proudly pointed to the mouth of the bay. "Four **bald** eagles are sitting on the edge of the ice for you to see! Three are immatures, either second- or third-year birds."

It was easy to see their overall dark color, a contrast to the surrounding snow and ice. They had not yet developed the adult's white head and

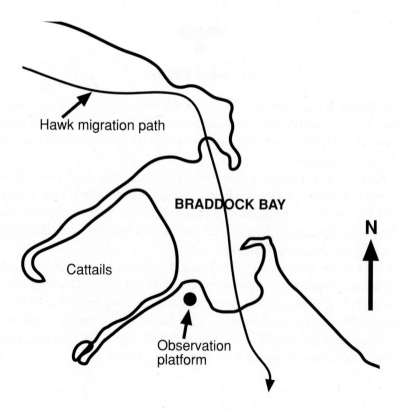

tail. Using Brett's twenty-power spotting scope, I could make out several small white patches on their bodies. First-year birds would be all dark.

"Here comes the adult!" announced Brett. It flew in large circles, and as it banked a turn, the bright sun reflected from its white head and tail, emphasizing the contrasting dark body. How magnificent was this large, powerful, and graceful bird! No wonder it had been chosen our national symbol.

"Notice how its long wings are the same width along their entire length. Most other raptors' wings show bulging or tapering to the wing outline."

The adult eagle then soared directly toward us. "Its wings are held perfectly flat the entire length of the wing. Most raptors bend the tips of the wings slightly up or down. The flat uniform shape from these two perspectives are why the bald eagle is sometimes referred to as the flying board." In a few seconds its powerful wings had taken it out of sight.

One of the immatures flew a short distance to feed on the carcass of a dead fish lying on the ice. About ten minutes later, the other two immatures joined in the meal. We watched them for about an hour as the immatures took turns picking at the fish. The adult was gone most of the time, but reappeared periodically to check on the young birds.

This is great, I thought. Not only was I observing the migration of eagles, but I was learning from Brett. The more I know, the more of the Pageant I can understand and appreciate.

48. Learning About the Life Cycle of Eagles from Frank Nicoletti

While Brett and I were watching the eagles, Frank Nicoletti arrived to find out what Brett had seen. Frank is considered to be one of the most skilled field identifiers of hawks in the country. Several recently published books on hawk identification list Frank in their acknowledgments section. He too had been a hawk census taker at Cape May, New Jersey, and here at Braddock Bay. He now does hawk banding at Braddock Bay in the spring and summer, and the hawk count in Minnesota in the fall. Several years ago he was asked by the Israeli Air Force to help solve a problem they had with hawks flying into jet engines and causing plane crashes. Frank observed the habits of the hawks at the air base and made a number of recommendations on how the air force could adjust flight plans to reduce the number of accidents.

At my urging, Frank started to talk about bald eagles. "The tidal pools along the Atlantic coast are great for eagles because the shallow water makes it easy for them to catch fish: eighty-five percent of their dives are successful in such locations. When they come inland to places such as Braddock Bay, there is less shallow water, because there are no tides. They have to make many more dives to capture the food they need. Consequently, we do not see the concentration of eagles here that we might along the coast."

Frank told me about the two distinct populations of bald eagles in the Eastern United States. "Some nest in the northern states and Canada; another population nests in the Gulf States and other parts of the South." He went on to describe their movements here at Braddock Bay. "In March, we see the adults, and a few of the immatures, of the northern population migrating north to their breeding grounds. The birds in front of us now are migrating northward. In April, we will see mostly northern population immatures coming through; they are later than the adults because they are too young to breed, and consequently need not be on the nesting sites any earlier."

Frank described the movements of the southern population. "In the South, bald eagles are able to nest in November, and by May the young are able to care for themselves. Consequently, here at Braddock Bay in May, we see the adults of the southern population coming through on a post-nesting dispersal flight— the movement of birds that occurs after the young are old enough to be on their own. It is definitely not a migration to wintering grounds. In fact, it is often in the opposite direction of that migration." I told Frank that it sounded like a summer vacation for birds. He agreed with my analogy. "They are no longer tied to the breeding site, so they just travel around for a while."

Frank described the immatures of the southern population. "We see the newly hatched southern birds on their post-nesting dispersal flights here in June, just a few weeks after their parents. These hatch-year birds (birds that were hatched earlier in the same year) are easy to spot because their first plumage is an overall dark color that we refer to as tawny-belly. I have seen five to ten tawny-bellies a day fly over here at the observation platform on a good southerly or westerly wind in June."

Frank mentioned that it is sometimes possible to identify a northern population bird from a southern bird.

"As is typical of most birds, those of the more northern populations are larger; the larger body mass is needed to cope with the colder temperatures. This is especially true of eagles. If you have seen large numbers of eagles from both populations, you can often tell by a bird's size where it is from, as it flies by the observation platform."

Frank then started to talk about the similarity of eagle and hawk behaviors.

"Much of what I have said about bald eagles is also true of hawks. The adult hawks migrate first, followed by the immatures; also, most hawks have some form of post-nesting dispersal flights. In spring migration and post-nesting dispersal, both the hawks and eagles seen here at Braddock Bay are flying east along the lake."

I asked Frank, "Where are the hawks coming from that pass by here?"

"The few birds we have captured here at our banding station that have been recently banded elsewhere have come from Ohio and Pennsylvania. They have been following the south shores of Lakes Erie and Ontario."

As Frank and I were talking, several **red-tailed hawks** flew by, each skirting the bay about a half mile to our south. Frank looked at each of them with his binoculars without interrupting his conversation with me. There was apparently nothing unusual about these birds, for neither Frank nor Brett said anything about them. I heard Brett's counter click as he saw each one. At the end of each hour he wrote the total from the counter onto his data sheet and reset the counter to zero. Every few minutes another red-tail came by. I asked, "How many red-tails have you counted?"

"I've seen sixteen so far today. That's good for this early in the spring."

Frank pointed out a **rough-legged hawk** to the south of us, following the same route as the red-tails. It was so far away that it was hardly more than a speck in the sky; I would have been hard-pressed to identify it on my own. Brett and Frank, I know, have great skills for identifying hawks at great distances. I can't help but think that their eyes must be sharper than mine, permitting them to see things on a bird that I can't.

Knowing my interest in how migration progresses, Brett offered, "Both red-tails and rough-leggeds are early migrants, so we will see many more of them over the next few weeks."

Brett and Frank continued to watch the sky for raptors. I knew they would let me know if something else of interest flew by, so I turned my attention to the ducks in front of us. Along the open water, where Buttonwood Creek flows into the bay, were two pairs of **red-breasted mergansers**. All four ducks were diving repeatedly in search of lunch. They have to be skilled and quick underwater swimmers to survive by catching fish. Sometimes they were under water for ten seconds or even longer, then reappeared ten or twenty yards farther down the channel. A male surfaced from a dive with his head turned so I could see the profile of his thin, narrow bill—a shape perfect for catching minnows and small fish. The bill gave him a look quite different from other species of ducks, whose broad bills are adapted for gathering vegetable matter.

Brett offered, "The red-breasteds started to arrive within the last week or two. They have been coming in such numbers that they are now the most numerous and easily seen ducks on the lake and nearby ponds." Then he added, "About two hundred yards to the right of the red-breasted mergansers, where the creek widens into the bay, are two pairs of **common mergansers**. We have been seeing commons frequently, but we will not be seeing as many as the red-breasteds. Commons arrive several weeks before the red-breasteds, and will also leave sooner." I took a few minutes to compare these two closely related species. The body of the male common merganser is predominantly white; the red-breasted's is dark gray. The females of both species, however, look much the same.

Closer in, near the immature eagles, were about thirty **ring-billed gulls** standing on the ice. Others were flying about overhead, perhaps hoping for a bite of the fish carcass. A large **great black-backed gull** stood at the edge of the ice not far from the eagles. Its black back and white head and tail caused me to look again to make sure it was not the adult bald eagle.

The eagles settled down for an after-meal siesta, and there was now only an occasional red-tail flying overhead. I thanked Frank and Brett for their assistance and drove east a few miles to Round Pond to sample more of the waterfowl migration.

49. Early Spring Waterfowl Migration

I stopped at the elevated overlook on the south side of Round Pond. The pond was about a quarter of a mile in diameter, and beyond it was a large cattail marsh extending another half mile. To my left, Round Pond Creek flowed into the south side of the pond. To my right, at the north end of the pond, the current entered a short, narrow outlet emptying into Lake Ontario.

The creek's current was sufficiently swift to make an ice-free path completely across the pond to the outlet. The open water had attracted early migrating waterfowl to feed on the accessible aquatic plants. Other nearby ponds were still completely frozen. Lake Ontario had considerable ice along the shore.

Far to the left, where Round Pond Creek entered the pond, were three pairs of **mallard**s and a pair of **American black ducks**. I wondered if they had spent the winter here, surviving by searching out open water to find food. The black ducks were especially visible because their dark bodies sharply contrasted to the snow and ice background. To the right of the ducks, along the stream, three **great blue herons** stood motionless about a hundred yards apart. It is conceivable that they too had wintered here, if they had found enough open water. More likely, however, they had been several hundred miles to the south, just recently moving north to Lake Ontario.

On the pond were two pairs of **buffleheads** and one male **common goldeneye**, eating aquatic plants in the shallows at the edge of the open water. Unlike the mergansers that I had just seen at Braddock Bay, with narrow bills for catching fish, these two species of ducks had wide bills adapted for eating plant material. I noticed, however, that their bills, although wide, were shorter than those of the mallards, who feed almost exclusively on plant material. The compromise in the shape of their bills allows a shift in diet for the buffleheads and goldeneyes. In winter, when the small ponds freeze over, these birds must move to Lake Ontario, where they dive for mollusks, crustaceans, and minnows. [See plate 8]

From a distance, the goldeneye's head appeared to be shaped like an equilateral triangle: the tip of the short bill is one corner, the bulge on the back of the neck another, and the pointed top of the head the third. I have never heard anyone describe it that way, nor does it look that way in the field guides, but it certainly does at a distance in the field.

At the far end of the pond, near the narrow outlet to Lake Ontario, there was a large open area in the ice. There were a number of ducks there, but they were too far away for identification. Curious to know what they were, and having seen what I could from the overlook, I drove to the north end of the pond, parking near the bridge over the outlet.

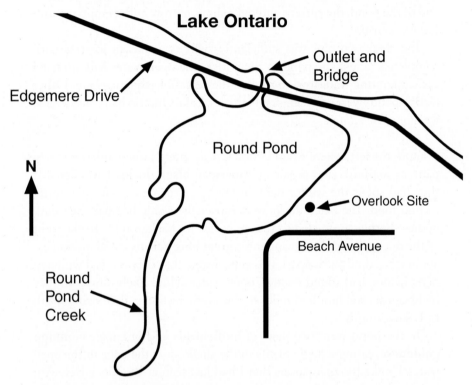

I walked onto the bridge. Under me flowed a mild current in a fifty-foot-wide channel. About a hundred black and white ducks were widely dispersed, slowly swimming about, periodically diving to search out something to eat. The outlet's channel is probably not a good place to find aquatic plants living on the bottom, so I guessed they were using their broad bills to filter out small crustaceans. The ducks looked somewhat like scaup, but the males had black backs; scaup have gray backs. The bright sunlight, made even brighter by reflections from the surrounding snow and ice, caused their jet-black heads and backs to glisten. Also very conspicuous, and important in identifying them, was a narrow, slightly curved, pure white line on their shoulders, which clearly separated the black neck from the gray side, confirming my identification: **ring-necked ducks**. The females had no noticeable characteristics; they were a nearly uniform grayish-brown. Ring-necks do not winter here, but had recently left the South and were on their way to nest in Canada.

Beyond the ring-necks were hundreds of ducks dispersed over the wide part the pond. Backlighted by the sun, I could not distinguish color in their plumage. Several, however, were positioned so the sun came partially from the side, enough so I saw red heads, making them either **redheads** or **canvasbacks**. The shape of the two species' heads are very different, making them easily differentiated by profile, even without seeing colors.

I discovered both species were there. On some, the front of their heads were slanted as though they had no foreheads—a classic profile of a canvasback. The other ducks had round heads with pronounced foreheads—redheads. It took me several minutes to look through the entire group to determine which species each duck was and to be sure there wasn't another species among them. I soon discovered that, in addition to the head shape, I could easily differentiate the two species by looking at the color of their backs, in spite of the lighting: the canvasback's is white and the redhead's is dark gray. They were probably migrating too, although both species occasionally winter here.

A little **pied-billed grebe** swam among the redheads. It too was a new arrival, having spent the winter in the South. Many pied-billeds nest here. This one might be planning to spend the summer, or it may go on to Canada to nest. Had Mother Nature told it to nest in New York, or Ontario? What were her criteria for deciding? The grebe was much smaller than the redheads, and it looked even smaller because it was partially submerged. Just a small portion of its back showed above the water. Pied-bills do this when they want to be less obvious. Why was it doing it now? Having been analyzing the shape of ducks' bills relative to their diet, I noticed the small, short chicken-like bill of the grebe, indicating it eats insects, small crustaceans, and probably not much vegetation. [See plate 6]

Four swans walked on the ice just to the left of the canvasbacks and redheads. How could I have overlooked them till now? My focus on identifying ducks had been even more intent than I had realized. I was especially pleased to see they had black bills, making them our native

North American **tundra swans**. They were large, all white, and majestic, as they strolled the edge of the ice. I was enchanted by the realization that they were going to be nesting on a pond on the tundra, or on an inlet of the Arctic Ocean.

This morning, Mother Nature had shown me several early participants in her annual Northeast waterfowl migration.

50. Owl Migration (March 28)

In recent years, the BBRR staff has been studying a little-known phenomenon: owls migrate at night along the lakeshore using a route similar to that which the hawks take during the day.

There are two owl species in particular that follow this route: the **northern saw-whet owl** and the **long-eared owl**. They fly at night because they are nocturnal birds with excellent night vision. They rest during the day. The spruce and pine woods on the west side of the bay, in what BBRR calls the Owl Woods, is a favorite daytime roosting spot for these two migrants.

It was eight in the morning when I arrived at the fishermen's parking lot across the road from the Owl Woods. John Bounds, BBRR's owl census taker, was just starting his daily count, so he invited me to join him.

He explained his task for the morning. "Owls migrate easterly along the lake shore during the night. Toward morning, they stop to hunt soon after finding this good habitat. At dawn they settle down to rest during the day. Every morning I count the owls that are roosting here in the owl woods."

We walked the path past numerous spruce and pines; osier bushes and silky dogwood filled in the gaps between the trees. As we came to each spruce tree, John searched for **saw-whet owls**.

"I look near the trunk on limbs six to ten feet off the ground. Saw-whets are almost always found sitting on a branch near the trunk at that height. I also look on the ground for fresh whitewash, indicating an owl has been sitting above."

We came to a clump of four spruce. John walked around them, looking at their trunks. He stopped and pointed out a little saw-whet sitting next to the trunk at eye level, just where John had predicted. It was only eight inches high, reddish brown, with small white patches and streaks. I walked to within three feet. The little ball of feathers showed no fear.

Seeing this wild, fearless, and very cute little bird was one of the most memorable experiences of my years of birding. Here we were in these quiet, snowy woods, face-to-face, just a few feet apart, looking intently into each other's eyes. I had the feeling that he was telling me who he is, and I was telling him who I am. I felt we were communicating in some mysterious way. I slowly backed off to leave the little migrant to rest for tonight's flight. I certainly did not want to cause it any stress. John said the saw-whet would be there all day, probably without moving unless disturbed. [See plate 10]

John could see I was infatuated by the owl. He offered a possible explanation: "Owls have a special appeal to people because their heads are flat, with both eyes in front, like a human's face."

We continued through the woods, looking among the pines.

"**Long-eared owls** prefer taller pines, rather than the spruces chosen by the saw-whets. Another difference between the two species is that long-eareds usually fly away when approached. The denseness of the trees they roost in makes it hard to get much of a look at them as they fly

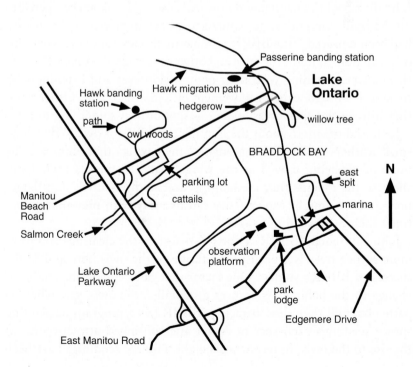

away. They are twice as big as saw-whets, but not nearly as big as great horned owls. "

He pointed higher into the trees, perhaps fifteen feet off the ground, as the place to look. We found no more owls, but seeing the one saw-whet made the trip worthwhile.

"John, how many owls do you see on these daily census rounds?"

"I often find one or two owls, but it varies. Many mornings I don't see any."

"Is finding owls as predictable by weather conditions as hawk migration?"

"Owl migration conditions are hard to figure out. Sometimes when I think there should have been a good flight, I find no owls. There have been times when I thought weather conditions would have not permitted flights, but I have found several birds. I hope further research will shed more light on the subject."

Probably because owls seem so mysterious, I liked learning about them, and was very much fascinated when actually seeing a very cute little migrant.

As we retraced our steps, heading for the path's exit from the woods, John discussed the habitat and how owls use it. "Look at the open area on the right," he said as he pointed to where an area of scrub growth had been removed. "The BBRR staff has made clearings here where the owls can hunt at night for mice and other rodents. Sometimes, the owls sit in a tree, watching with their night-vision eyes and listening with their very sensitive ears for movement by a mouse or vole. Other times they fly over the open areas hoping to spot or hear something to eat."

John told me more about the hunting capability of owls. "They have small feathers on the leading edge of their wings that eliminate the noise of air being moved as the wings beat. This makes their flight silent so the rodents they are hunting hear nothing. Owls hunt larger prey than one might expect. They can fly away with prey that is four times their own weight."

John continued, "BBRR's efforts to maintain the clearings and plant more spruce trees is crucial to the future of the owls here and to the success of BBRR's studies. One factor that can degrade the studies is change to the habitat. As spruces grow taller, the owls, saw-whets in particular, find them less attractive. BBRR has a program of planting spruce seedlings each year to ensure the continued attractiveness of the site to the owls. In recent years eight hundred seedlings have been planted." I mentioned that the stand of pines at the far end of the parking lot near the Hawk Lookout used to be a good site for owls. John answered that the pines have grown too tall, so owls are no longer found there.

John talked about the other owls that can be found in the area. "The **short-eared owl** migrates from Canada to spend the winter here, so we do not see a spring migration pattern. The **snowy owl** lives year-round in northern Canada on the tundra, but some winters a few snowys move south to find food. Their appearance here in winter is unpredictable. The other species of owls in the area, **eastern screech owl** and **great horned**, are permanent residents with no significant movement patterns during the year."

April

51. Hawk Banding Reveals More of the Pageant (April 4)

It was cool but sunny. Southerly winds promised a good day for raptor migration at Braddock Bay.

Along the Lake Ontario Parkway I noticed the antics of several groups of **red-breasted mergansers** cavorting near the shore on Long Pond. I pulled to the side of the road to watch. Five males were going through their courtship display of bobbing their heads up and down in a rhythmic fashion. The objects of their efforts were two nearby females. I could see the females' bills move slightly. Could they be making critical comments to each other about the dancers? The sun was highlighting the shaggy feathers on the back of the males' necks. It gave them a roguish appearance, appropriate to their courting behavior. Perhaps that was what the females liked.

I parked the car at the fishermen's parking lot on Manitou Beach Road and walked across the road. At the entrance to the owl woods is a sign: "This is a bird banding site operated by licensed personnel with federal and state permits. It is against the law to interfere with the operations or equipment." I walked down the path through the owl woods where a few days ago I had followed John Bounds on his owl census, passing some of the same spruce trees John had so carefully searched. I deliberately searched the tree where we had found the one saw-whet, but there were no saw-whets today.

I continued down the path to the hawk-banding blind. As the sign near the blind requests, I called out for clearance to approach. This is to ensure that one does not disturb a hawk overhead approaching one of the traps. Dave Tetlow, who is the bander today, had just arrived and was setting up for the day. He had unfurled the mist nets, set the traps, and was attaching a live starling to one of the lure lines. The line was tied to a harness that fits over the bird's shoulders. A live pigeon was attached to another lure line. Finishing the setup for the day, we entered the blind. The blind is a shack made of scrap lumber that gives a little shelter from the elements and hides people in the blind from the view of passing hawks. Dave sat on an inverted bucket in front of the observation slot, so he could see the traps, array of mist nets, and the likely approaches of hawks. I stood behind him, hoping to see a hawk banded.

The bow traps, each about four feet in diameter, were rigged so that when a hawk lands on them the bander can pull the trigger line, causing the net-draped bow to snap closed, trapping the hawk in the net. To attract a hawk to the trap, Dave pulled on a lure line attached to the pigeon's leather harness. The pulling action caused the pigeon to flutter awkwardly, so as to attract a hawk.

Dave saw a **sharp-shinned hawk** approaching about a quarter of a mile away. Apparently it was not hungry, because it flew by without hesitation. In less than a minute, Dave noticed movement off to the side near one of the mist nets. He pulled the line to the starling used as a lure for that part of the field. As the starling fluttered, an **American kestrel** swooped in, became entangled momentarily in the net, then flew away.

"Are the lure birds ever hurt when pounced upon by a hawk?" I asked.

"Only rarely, because I get to them in just a few seconds."

We sat waiting for a few more minutes while Dave described the weather conditions needed for a good day of hawk banding.

"Light winds and warm temperatures encourage hawks to ride thermals to higher elevations. Thermals are columns of rising currents of air caused by the warming effect of the sun. What we like for a good banding day is one warm enough to have thermals for migration, but not so warm as to cause strong thermals for the hawks to ride up too high. Strong winds help by breaking up the thermals, causing the birds to fly lower. When flying low, the hawks are more apt to be attracted to the bait birds."

A shadow passed overhead; Dave immediately recognized it as a **red-tailed hawk**. By the time I realized what was happening, the hawk had grabbed the bait pigeon, Dave had instantaneously pulled on the line to bring the bait bird and hawk onto the bow trap and pulled the trigger line; the red-tail was in the trap. In a flash, Dave dashed out, picked up the hawk by its legs, and holding both legs together in one hand, reset the trap. The bait bird was not hurt.

Bringing the bird into the blind, Dave placed it headfirst into an empty rolled oats carton. Although the carton was only half as long as the hawk, it was long enough to hold the head and wings securely. There were empty frozen orange juice cartons in the blind for holding smaller hawks.

With its head in the dark and its wings folded snugly, the hawk remained quiet while Dave organized his bands, scale, and log book, and prepared to process his captive. Picking out the appropriate-sized band for a red-tailed, Dave placed it on the bird's leg and secured it with a pair of pliers, with the bird still in the rolled oats carton. He then placed the bird and carton on the scales. He recorded the band number and weight, less that of the carton, in the log book.

Grasping its legs firmly, Dave finally removed the bird from the carton and measured its wing chord—the distance from the major joint in the middle of the wing to the tip. The measurement is used to determine the bird's sex. Male and female red-tails, like most hawks, have identical plumage, so determining their sex is not easy. Female hawks, however, are typically larger than males, so Dave uses a reference table for determining the sex based on the length of the wing chord. For each species of hawk, the table gives a female measurement and a male measurement. If the hawk's wing chord is greater than the female table entry, it is a female. If it is less than the male table entry, it is a male. If the wing chord measures between the two table entries, which was true for this bird, the sex cannot be determined by the bander. In the case of red-tails, there is considerable overlap in the size of the sexes, resulting in banders not being able to determine the sex of most of the birds. In contrast, the sex of sharp-shinned and Cooper's hawks can almost always be determined because the female is much larger.

Dave held the bird, free of its oatmeal carton, so I could have a great look. Its size, handsomeness, and obvious capability to kill in the field had me mesmerized. I will never forget the look in its eyes—the way it stared at Dave and then at me. It was accustomed to flying as high, as far, and as fast as it wished, but now it was being held captive in Dave's hands. Its wildness was evident by the movement of its eyes and head as it tried to make sense of the strange surroundings and happenings. We then went outside. Dave held the bird over his head and let go of its legs. The bird circled briefly, probably trying to understand what had occurred, and then flew away.

I asked, "How is the data you just collected used? What is learned from it?"

"Our data is combined with that collected by all the other hawk-banding stations in the country. When a hawk is later recaptured by another bander—or sometimes they are found dead and the band is turned in—the band number can be found in the database. We then know where and when it was banded relative to later recoveries. The data can give us valuable information on the bird's travels, and perhaps how old it was. One of the hawks I banded here was recovered in Minnesota, another in Virginia, and one on Prince Edward Island."

I remembered two weeks ago when Frank Nicoletti was telling me about the migration routes of hawks and eagles. Now I understand how that information became known. I realized that banding programs have given me information to better understand the Pageant.

Dave thought the winds were right for a good hawk flight, so I drove to the other side of the bay to the observation platform.

52. Early Migrating Hawks Funneled into a Narrow Route

It was about eleven o'clock when I arrived at the Hawk Lookout observation platform, about a mile east of the hawk banding station. There were already fifteen people on the platform, some seated on the bench, others standing along the railing. Most of them I recognized as regulars from past years, whom I hadn't seen since last spring.

Each time I go to the observation platform, I am struck by the scenery; it is beautiful, expansive, and serene. To the right is Braddock Bay, and beyond, Lake Ontario; to the left, an extensive cattail marsh. There is high ground on the far side of the bay where owl, hawk, and passerine banding take place.

The platform is at the optimum location for observing migrating hawks, vultures, and eagles. They migrate along the lakeshore, going east until they encounter the southerly turn of the shoreline at Braddock Bay. To avoid flying over water, which provides no rising air currents, they turn abruptly south to skirt the bay. The turn concentrates them into a narrower flight path, which often brings them near the observation platform. This is one of the several superb spring hawk migration monitoring sites in the United States; on a good migration day thousands of hawks may be seen from the platform.

Laura and Neil Moon were enthusiastic local birders with an especially strong interest in learning more about the hawk migrations at Braddock Bay. They knew this was an especially important site, so they (mostly Laura by herself, for Neil was still working) undertook an incredibly demanding project. Every spring day, all day, often alone, from 1977 through 1985, they conducted a diligent spring hawk count. They published detailed statistics in the local bird club's publication, *The Goshawk*, and summary statistics in the Federation of New York Bird Clubs' publication, *The Kingbird*. One of their difficulties in conducting the count was to find a satisfactory viewing site that was not obstructed by trees. Through Laura's efforts, a joint project between local and state officials was started to build the observation platform. It was dedicated

Every spring, thousands of migrating raptors fly around the bay, and pass by the strategically located observation platform.

in 1984. In 1985, Braddock Bay Raptor Research (BBRR) was formed under the leadership of Jeff Dodge to continue the study of hawk migration.

Today was one of the first good migration days this season. The temperature had warmed to the fifties, and was perfect for developing buoyant air masses for the hawks' flights. There were mild southwest winds, to the hawks' liking—they wanted to travel northeast.

Everyone on the platform was fascinated by the almost continuous flow of migrating **turkey vultures**. I joined in, scanning the horizon to spot the vultures when they first came into view. Looking west, we saw five tiny dots high in the sky at least a mile away. I patiently watched the five dots as they slowly became recognizable as vultures. My arms grew tired holding the binoculars to my eyes, but I wanted to continuously track their progress around the bay. Making use of the prevailing winds and the buoyancy of the warming air, they were able to continue easterly without having to flap their wings. (Mother Nature's aerodynamic design of the vultures' wings and bodies, plus the birds' skills, were impressive.) When they came within a half mile of the observation platform, their easterly course took them over the shoreline, which turned abruptly south at the entrance to the bay. Neither I nor the vultures I was tracking were prepared for what happened next.

Because the cold water surface of the bay did not sustain the warm air's buoyancy, the vultures had lost several hundred feet of altitude in just a few seconds and were flapping their wings rapidly only a few feet above the water. They immediately turned south to bring themselves over the cattail marsh, where some of the buoyancy was restored. When they reached the end of the bay, eager to maintain their intended direction, they promptly turned easterly again while only about fifty feet off the ground. They were still low and flapping aggressively to gain altitude when they flew directly over the observation platform. The very close view of these huge and graceful birds was dramatic! I was pleased to see that "my" birds had successfully maneuvered out of an unexpected and awkward situation.

In spring, and when the winds are favorable, huge numbers of vultures follow the lakeshore, going northeast. The range map in my field guide showed this to be near the northern limit of their breeding range. They did not have much farther to go, after having spent the winter in the South.

Two pairs of **northern harriers** flew over the cattails in front of us about a quarter mile away. We watched one pair go through their courtship antics, chasing each other in large vertical circles. The other pair methodically flew back and forth low over the marsh looking for frogs and mice. The male hunter, light gray with black wing tips, stopped abruptly, hovered, then plummeted to the ground, apparently to catch prey. The female, light brown in color, continued her search. Watching them in their typical habitat reminded me that harriers used to be called marsh hawks, before the American Ornithologists' Union officially changed their name to be consistent with the name used in Europe.

One of the hawk watchers said the harriers had arrived about a week ago and had been hunting the marsh in front of us every day. He said they would probably spend the summer; at least one pair nests here each year.

The observers on the platform began to pay more attention to the **Cooper's** and **sharp-shinned hawks** now continuously coming into view, one after another, every few seconds. Eager to learn more about what I was seeing, I moved closer to Brett Ewald, the hawk counter for BBRR for the last several years. Brett said, "These two species of hawks belong to the family known as accipiters, having short wings to facilitate hunting in woods and heavy vegetation. Telling these two species apart is one of the challenges in birding; their plumages are nearly identical."

I noticed that the main occupation of my fellow observers had become distinguishing the Cooper's from the sharp-shinneds. One observer would point out an approaching accipiter and then ask a friend which one it was. They would then discuss their conclusions, sometimes with a few good-natured barbs thrown in. Brett described the differences.

"The Cooper's hawk is thirty to forty percent larger than the sharp-shinned, but the females of both species can be thirty percent larger than the male. A female sharp-shinned, therefore, can be nearly as large as a male Cooper's. Since the relative difference in size is often indistinguishable, several other features are used to differentiate the two. Several years ago it was felt that the best way to distinguish them was by the squared-off end of the tail of the sharp-shinned versus the somewhat rounded tail of the Cooper's. Due to feather wear and individual variation, this is not always reliable. Today the shape of the wing and how this makes the head look are the preferred characteristics to look for. The leading edge of the Cooper's wings is nearly straight, making the head look more prominent. The sharp-shinned's leading edge curves backward near the head, causing the head to look less pronounced than the Cooper's.

Sharp-shinned

Cooper's

Also, the Cooper's head is larger than the sharp-shinned's. In making an identification, as many of these variable and relative characteristics as possible need to be noted."

Brett was calling out the accipiters: "Sharpie over the tree line!" or "Cooper's high overhead!" Most were just specks in the distance when first seen. Some came closer as they followed the shoreline; others turned south, detoured around the bay, and quickly disappeared from view.

I was amazed at how Brett was able to identify the two very similar accipiters from such distances. We talked about that for a while. "Sometimes," he said, "you can't tell a sharpie from a Cooper's until you get a good close look. However, there are several identifying characteristics, in addition to what I just mentioned about the leading edge of the wings, that can be seen at great distances."

I asked, "Are these special characteristics often visible, or only occasionally?"

"They are visible only when the bird is flying in a certain way, such as soaring, banking, or gliding. Some are visible only from a certain angle, such as head-on or from the side. For example, the sharpie's faster wing beat and the Cooper's stiffer wing stroke are good hints for identification. The more curved shape to the trailing edge of the sharpie's wing and the Cooper's longer tail are good points to look for, and often these characteristics can be seen from a considerable distance."

After watching Brett identify one accipiter after another, I came to realize that because he had seen many thousands of them, just the general appearance of the bird made his identification almost automatic. I mentioned this to Brett.

"The imprinted characteristics are difficult to describe," he acknowledged. "The mind recognizes them automatically. It is like identifying a friend from a distance by the way he or she walks and moves. In many cases we cannot describe verbally what it is about a friend's movement that we recognize."

Brett looked at his counts. "So far today there have been fifty-three Cooper's and thirty-eight sharpies," he reported. "In a few weeks the sharpies will be far more numerous; Cooper's tend to migrate earlier than the sharpies."What Brett said about the Cooper's coming through earlier seemed surprising when I looked at their range maps. In Canada, the Cooper's breed only in the southern areas; the sharpies breed throughout Canada, all the way up to the tree line. I thought the sharpies would have come first because they had farther to go.

There was almost always a **red-tailed hawk** in view as one by one they filtered by on their migratory route. One flew especially close overhead. Its pure white chest was framed by a dark band of streaking across its belly. I saw no red in the tail because it was folded; the bird was gliding. For identification I have always waited for the bird to spread its tail and show some red in the tail. Brett gave me a pointer. "Depending on red in the tail for identification is not reliable because it takes immatures two years to acquire a full red tail. The most reliable marks are the dark areas on the leading edge of the wings."

He talked more about red-tails. "We have been seeing red-tails coming from points south on their way to nest farther north. We have large numbers of permanent residents here too. It is common to see them soaring in large circles over open fields, looking for mice and other prey, while announcing their territory with a high-pitched scream-like call." Then Brett told how man has influenced the lives of red-tails. "It has been said that the interstate highway system has been a boon for the red-tailed by adding to their preferred habitat. We see them sitting in trees or on fence posts beside interstate highways, looking over the wide open area for their favorite prey, rodents."

He continued his tutorial. "Red-tails belong to the buteo family of hawks. Buteos are generally large, heavy-bodied hawks. With large, wide wings, they soar over open areas while hunting. In these respects, they are quite different from the accipiters we have been seeing."

"Which buteos do we see here at Braddock Bay?" I asked.

"We see the red-tailed, red-shouldered, broad-winged, and rough-legged. We have seen several rough-leggeds already today. We should be able to find one for you."

After a few minutes, just as Brett predicted, a **rough-legged hawk** was seen coming across the marsh. It flew almost directly overhead, only about two hundred feet above the ground. "Notice the large patches of black and white over its entire underside, the chief identifying characteristic of the rough-leg." Brett explained more about its plumage. "The degree of black versus white varies considerably by age, sex, and whether it is of the light-phase or dark-phase race. No other large buteo in the East is so distinctively marked underneath." He continued, "Rough-leggeds are early migrants. They winter throughout much of the United States, except the Deep South, and are now on their way to arctic Canada, north of the tree line. They will nest on the tundra near red-throated loons, snow buntings, and Lapland longspurs."

One of the hawk watchers called out, "rough-leg soaring high!" We all turned in the direction he was looking. I finally found it, but it was too high to see the identifying underside pattern. Brett, realizing I was not able to make the identification on my own, gave me some help. "Notice how its wings are longer and narrower than the red-tailed, giving them a more pointed look." Trying to relate what I was seeing to what Brett had said, I thought I could see his point. I was sure, however, that what I needed was to see several thousand more buteos for comparison.

Brett continued. "Because it is a buteo, the rough-leg has large wings for soaring on thermals. We are seeing it with its wings spread, circling, to achieve the maximum altitude from a thermal before gliding on to the next thermal. This flight technique contrasts with how the accipiters [Cooper's and sharp-shinneds] fly. Accipiters do not depend on thermals, but are active flyers. They flap their wings more, and travel a direct route rather than circling."

He discussed the effect of wind direction on accipiters' flight. "The wind direction affects them because they try to use the wind to their advantage. If the wind is from the south, they fly low across the bay, partially sheltered from the wind. If the wind is from the southwest they can make partial use of the wind and fly higher. A westerly wind permits them to ride the tailwind at a very high altitude."

53. The Variety of Waterfowl Increases—
An Eagle Snatches Lunch

There was nothing in the air. The question in everyone's mind was, "Will there be another flurry of activity?" A series of bad jokes filled some time. We waited a few more minutes. "Nine **Canada geese** flying west, fairly high," someone called out. It was easy spotting them crossing the southern part of the bay at a fast cruising speed. I had all nine of the dark-colored, long-necked Canadas in view when I noticed four smaller geese trailing the group of nine, all white except for black wing tips. Several people called out at once, "**snow geese**!" One of the more experienced birders on the platform, obviously very pleased with the sighting, announced that snow geese were uncommon at Braddock Bay. I continued to watch them as they flew farther and farther away. It seemed to me that the snows were trying their best to keep up with the pace of the larger Canadas.

Minutes later, Brett called out, "Six **pintails** directly overhead!" It was awkward to look straight up while holding binoculars. It was tiring to maintain that position for any more than a few seconds. Not being accustomed to seeing the underside of a pintail, I was struck by the curious silhouette I saw, a lanky duck with an extremely long slender neck and a long pointed tail. The long, pointed shape at both ends reminded me of the old Studebaker cars of the 1950s—cars known for looking the same coming or going.

We scanned the surface of the bay, finding several wigeons. The males' white foreheads were obvious even at the distance of a quarter mile. A large group of scaup were farther out in the middle of the bay, and next to them, an even larger group of ring-necked ducks. Later we spotted a lone hooded merganser and a pair of buffleheads.

Two pairs of small brown ducks flew along Buttonwood Creek in front of us. When they held their wings fully open to decelerate, the sun highlighted the green patch on their wings; they were **green-winged teals**. Every few minutes the teals flew around again, and settled down at another spot in the creek at the edge of the cattails. Each time they landed, I tried to see the green patch. Whether I could see it depended on their angle to the light.

I enjoyed the serene view and thought about the waterfowl. The ring-necks, wigeons, and hooded merganser had wintered along the Atlantic Coast and had recently flown over much of the East en route to nesting grounds in Canada. The snow geese had spent the winter near Chesapeake Bay, or the North Carolina coast, then traveled through several of the Eastern states, and were now headed for the high Arctic. The greater scaup and buffleheads could have spent the winter nearby, or they could have wintered along the Atlantic Coast and were just passing through. It would be interesting to ask them where they had spent the winter, and where they were going. The Canada geese are a real puzzle. They offer all the possibilities; they could have wintered anywhere in the eastern half of the country, including Braddock Bay. They could have been migrating to almost anywhere to the north, or they could be planning to stay here to nest. I decided that I knew little of what had led to the waterfowl's arrival here, and little of where they were going. How complex and mysterious the Pageant is!

Then it happened! Brett called our attention to a very large, dark bird about a mile to the west. It was coming our way with slow, steady wing beats. In contrast, a vulture would have been soaring much of the time. Also, the bird's wings were held perfectly flat rather than in the V shape of a vulture. As it came closer—still almost a mile away—it turned slightly, letting Brett see the size of its head. "A **bald eagle**," he announced. "The head is too large for a golden eagle." The bird quickly arrived at the far shoreline of the bay and then, while the people on the platform watched, it dropped down low, dove into the water, and then rose quickly. We could not tell if it had caught anything with that very quick maneuver. It crossed the bay to our right, flying over the east spit. Now we could see the white head and tail of a full adult.

Some of the observers saw the bird bring its feet up to its mouth. It was eating on the wing! We hadn't seen a duck where it dove, so its prey must have been a fish. The eagle circled several times, flying slowly as it continued to eat. After bringing its feet forward to its mouth one more time, it was out of sight far to the east.

Before leaving the platform, I talked with Trish Stanko, the owl bander with BBRR. She had been on the platform helping Brett record the totals from the day's hawk flight. I told her of my interest in seeing her operation and asked if I had to stay up all night to do so. She said that I should meet her and Jason Franz, her banding partner, about thirty minutes before dawn for their last round of the nets. I agreed to meet them the next morning.

54. Intimate Encounters with Migrating Owls (April 5)

It was 5:45 a.m. when I arrived at the owl woods. It had taken a very large cup of coffee for me to be there that early in the morning. It was here, several days ago, that I had met John Bounds taking his daily owl census. He would be along later this morning to count the owls.

Trish Stanko and Jason Franz were coming down the path to start their last round of the nets for the night—my time of arrival was perfect. As we walked up to the first net, Trish told me about the banding program.

"Braddock Bay Raptor Research has both federal and state permits to capture owls in the twenty-six mist nets we have set up along the path and nearby fields."

Jason showed me the nets. "They are woven from nylon string with a mesh of about an inch, are fifty feet long, and are stretched from about seven feet off the ground down to about a foot from the ground. Owls fly into the nets while hunting, becoming caught in the nylon mesh."

I asked, "How long do you run the program?" Trish replied, "We are here every night during March and April. By the first of May the number of owls drops off to where it is not worth continuing."

Jason told me more about their operation. "During the day we furl the nets so birds cannot get caught when no one is around to free them. We open the nets at dusk and check them every hour all night long. If it is raining, we check the nets more frequently so the owls do not suffer from exposure."

We were within twenty feet of the first net when I saw that something was caught in it. Trish ran to the net, immediately going to work. "It's a **long-eared owl**," she announced. I watched her work intently for at least a minute, manipulating the strings of the net to untangle the owl.

"When owls first hit the net they tend to spin around trying to get loose. The spinning gets them even more entangled. To get them out of the net, I have to reverse the twisting action. That's often quite tedious." Having finally freed the owl, Trish held it up for us to see. It even posed as it sat upright on her hand, while being firmly held by its feet. The very nervous owl was about fifteen inches tall, mostly brown, with orange in the large facial disk. Trish interpreted what I was seeing. "The disk-shaped face is designed to reflect sounds towards the real ears, which are hidden under feathers at the edge of the facial disk. Its visible 'ears,' which are not ears but tufts of feathers protruding from the top of its head, are about two inches long, and serve to camouflage the owl's outline. They are laid back now because it's excited." I was entranced by the large, round eyes intently watching me. Trish placed the owl head first into an empty orange juice container; its legs and tail stuck out of the open end. "This keeps the owl safe and quiet until I am ready to band it," she said.

We walked down the path to the next net. A **saw-whet owl** had completely wrapped itself in the netting and was hanging helplessly, needing Trish to come to its aid. Again, Trish had to work about a minute to get it untangled. She put it into another orange juice container. Farther down the path was another saw-whet in a net. Jason had gone ahead and had just finished freeing the owl when we arrived. We then took the three owls, in orange juice containers, back to Trish's truck, where she kept the banding equipment.

Sitting on the front seat of the truck, Jason and Trish attached official bands to the owls' legs. They then measured the owls' wing chords and the length of their bills and tails to determine their sex. They were all females. To obtain their weight, Trish put one owl at a time in a cloth bag and clipped the bag to the bottom of a spring scale. With all the data recorded by band number, on a form for submission to the Banding Laboratory of the U.S. Fish and Wildlife Service, she carried the owls to the edge of the woods, well away from the road, and released them.

Trish explained the value of monitoring owl populations and their activities. "Owls, like hawks, are at the top of the food chain. This makes them very sensitive to problems with the environment, pointing out dangers that have not yet affected humans. If we discover that something in the environment is harming owls, it could be an early warning for humans."

I thanked Trish and Jason for showing me their operation. While walking back to the parking lot, I thought about the morning's experience. It's amazing that we can predict when, where, and which species of owls will find their way to this small stand of spruce and pine. The owls' ancient migratory pattern has been discovered! This morning, with Trish's and Jason's help, I was able to see migrating long-eared and saw-whets fulfilling their destiny now.

55. Early Migrants Expand in Variety
(April 10)

The east spit protrudes out into the mouth of Braddock's Bay. At the spit's farthest point it hooks sharply to the left, creating a protected harbor for a marina. A footpath, used by birders and fishermen, runs the length of the spit. As I started down the path I realized how astute I was for having worn my winter jacket. The cold wind blowing off the lake felt more like winter than spring.

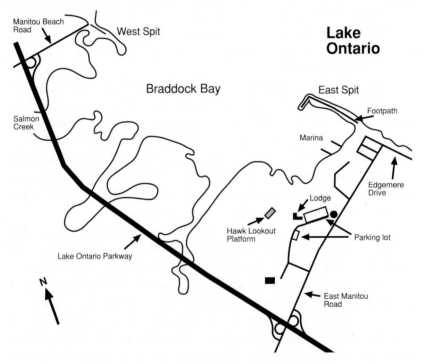

A small bird flew across the path. A sparrow with white wing bars, a touch of reddish brown on the top of its head, and a clear, light gray breast. With those field marks, it could be an **American tree sparrow**, which spends the winter here, and would be leaving for northern Canada in another few weeks. Or, it could be a field sparrow that might have just arrived from the southern states to spend the summer. A branch prevented me from seeing the middle of its breast. After I moved a few feet to the right for a definitive view, a distinctive black spot appeared in the center of its otherwise clear breast, the identifying mark of a tree sparrow. I wondered if it had spent the entire winter here, exposed to the cold winds off the lake. Perhaps it had stayed in a more sheltered spot nearby and only recently came to the spit in search of food.

A familiar song came from the scrub growth, three clear introductory notes followed by a jumble of several other notes—a **song sparrow**. It brought back fond memories. As a little boy, I walked along the hedgerows of my grandfather's farm in Ohio. One song sparrow after another would sing to me as I approached its territory. Since those early days, I have learned to associate hearing its song with the start of the songbird migration. Song sparrows arrive early in the spring, and sing profusely. Several more song sparrows sang. I had a contented feeling. Was it the memories of strolling my grandfather's fields in those long-ago innocent days, or was it recognition that once again, I had heard the song sparrow announcing the arrival of spring?

I turned away from the spit and toward the lake. Just off shore were about thirty **red-breasted mergansers**. A loose group, each had space to dive, cavort, and have a good time. Some of the antics were undoubtedly mating rituals. Several flew away, needing to run on the surface of the water a few feet to become airborne. Another flock, coming from the east, was flying parallel to the shoreline. They abruptly pivoted as a unit, took a closer look at their cousins on the water, then splashed down, joining the group. Mergansers have been common on the lake all winter, but in recent weeks they have been joined by "relatives" that had wintered along the Atlantic Coast. Now their numbers have grown dramatically all along the lakeshore and on adjacent ponds, becoming the most numerous ducks in the area.

I thought about their prominent increase and their impending conspicuous departure in a few weeks. I could imagine the script sent down from Mother Nature. "Upon my signal in late March, depending upon the weather, red-breasted mergansers will start to move northwest from the Atlantic coast to join their brethren that had wintered on the Great Lakes. After heavily congregating in the Great Lakes, about the first of May, they will disperse throughout Eastern Canada to find their nesting grounds."

I left the mergansers, walking farther along the path to where the spit widened into scrub growth and small trees. Perched on one of the bare-limbed trees hanging over the path were three male **red-winged blackbirds**. They flew without a sound. I concluded from their silence that they were still migrating. Males migrate separately from the females. If these males had intended to nest here, they would have separated and each would have established its own territory, which it would have loudly protected when I approached.

A **common grackle** was perched on a low branch at the edge of the path. It saw me, flew farther down the path, and then disappeared into the underbrush. It had identified itself as different from the red-wingeds by its long tail, wide at the end. I wondered just how much of an added effort it is for a grackle to "tow" its hefty "rudder" behind it. Red-wings and grackles like the same habitat—open and damp areas—and they arrive at approximately the same time in spring. It was no surprise seeing both of them here today.

The spit bends sharply to the left, making an area protected from the strong winds and waves of the lake. On the inside of the spit's elbow are shallow water and mudflats—habitat for dabbling ducks and shorebirds. Along the water's edge, an **American wigeon** searched for aquatic plants. I usually see drab wigeons at great distances, migrating well out over the lake in large flocks, on gray, overcast fall days. At close range, in bright sun, the richness of the wigeon's colors surprised me—its rusty breast bordered a gray neck, bright green streaked from the eye backward, and white covered the top of its head. I wondered if an artist could have conceived of a more handsome design, not knowing that in a moment, I was to see an even more impressive artist's design.

I was scanning the water's edge and mudflats when a large image of vivid colors caught my attention—bright, rufous red, highlighted in white. A glistening green head complemented the color scheme—a **northern shoveler**. Also noticeable because of the good light and short distance was its very long, wide bill—longer than its head—designed to sieve aquatic insects, worms, and small crustaceans from shallow water. I almost overlooked the female nearby, speckled brown, blending in with the mudflat background. It would be difficult to differentiate her from other female dabbling ducks were it not for her long bill.

Also on the mudflats was a large, slender shorebird, and, a third, a few feet beyond, busily poking their long bills into puddles looking for something to eat. All three looked identical: the same spotted gray plumage, slender bodies, long, narrow bills, and long, bright yellow legs. One was noticeably larger than the other two. With both sizes together, identification was easy—**greater yellowlegs** and **lesser yellowlegs**. When only one of the yellowlegs is present, it takes experience to judge by size whether it is a lesser or greater. When they take off, they usually give their flight call. The greater's call is at least three notes, the lesser's usually one or two. I could have made a commotion to persuade them to fly away to hear their call, but decided not to bother them. They should be free to refuel without being disturbed. They have flown a great distance recently, and have farther to go, traveling from the Atlantic Coast to northern Canada.

Across the bay, a large group of scaup swam among the marina's docks, heads down, sleeping. But several held their necks straight up, showing rounded heads—**greater scaups**. One pair of scaup was off by themselves. The male held his neck erect too, showing a slightly pointed shape to his head—a **lesser scaup**. Scaup are good divers and underwater swimmers, which is why they were in the deeper water around the marina, in contrast to the wigeon, dabbling in shallow water.

A red-breasted merganser flew in, landing near the greater scaups. This disturbed some of the greaters, so they took off. While they were circling and trying to decide where to land, I could see the white stripe extending the entire length of their wings. The stripes' flash of white was obvious with each wing beat. I have seen lessers in flight along Hamlin beach. Their wing stripe goes only half the length of the wing and is hardly visible at all in flight. How thoughtful it is of Mother Nature to provide the wing stripe for differentiating the two scaup from a distance, where the shape of the head is not discernible. The greaters landed a few hundred yards away from the merganser, apparently deciding he was not a threat after all.

I started to retrace my steps back along the path. A small bird flew ahead, abruptly landing on a low limb overhanging the path. Its perch provided a clear view of the surrounding area. A few seconds later, it flew out, snatched an insect in midair, and returned to its perch. It repeated the midair snatch several more times. Each time, after returning to its perch, it pumped its tail up and down as though it were having trouble keeping its balance—the indicative moves of an **Eastern phoebe**. This characteristic tail movement makes it easy to identify phoebes, even from a distance, without having to use binoculars. Phoebes are the first of the flycatchers seen in the spring. The others, such as pewees, least flycatchers, and kingbirds, don't arrive until May. I wondered if the later arrivers are more prudent. There couldn't be many flying insects out on a cold day like today. However, the little bird I had been watching appeared to be having success at finding lunch.

The short tour of the east spit revealed that the pace of the Pageant was accelerating. The spit's several habitats yielded newly arrived species from several different families: ducks, shorebirds, sparrows, blackbirds, gulls, and flycatchers. To sample another habitat, I drove to where Salmon Creek flows into the bay.

56. Migrants Attracted to Shallow Water

The Lake Ontario Parkway goes over a bridge where Salmon Creek flows into Braddock Bay. While driving over the bridge, I saw below a large number of ducks feeding in the shallow water where the creek widens into the bay. In a few days, fishing season would start, and the boat traffic going between the bay and creek would disperse the ducks to more secluded locations. I decided to take advantage of the ducks still being at this conveniently seen location.

From the fishermen's parking lot, I carried my spotting scope and binoculars down the path toward the ducks. A sparrow moved ahead of me, one bush at a time, as though it were leading the way. I stopped to identify it. A pink bill—a newly arrived **field sparrow**. I think of field sparrows as the summer replacements for our wintering American tree sparrows. They even prefer the same habitat—open fields and low bushes. The two species' plumages are nearly identical; the only obvious difference is the tree's black chest spot. Most of the time there is no chance of confusing them. They overlap in this area during late April, when the tree sparrows have not yet left for their Arctic nesting grounds and the field sparrows have already arrived to raise their young. They might meet again during the later half of October.

A high, thin call—distinctive and persistently given, but barely audible—came from the very large willow tree at the water's edge. Even though it was close, I still didn't see the bird until it moved. It was well camouflaged, brown and white streaked plumage, pressed close to the trunk—a **brown creeper**. Its bill was thin, delicate, and slightly curved—well adapted for dislodging insect eggs from the old tree's bark crevices.

Beyond the willow, well out on the bay, were two gray ducks with black rumps—male **gadwalls**. In any other light, they would be drab and uninteresting to look at, but the bright sun was shining directly on them, revealing the simplicity and elegance of the artistic combination of gray and black. They sat still—apparently not feeling an urgent need to feed—allowing me time to appreciate their genteel plumage. Another duck was close by, mottled brown, typical of most female dabbling ducks. If she had not been near the male gadwalls, I most likely would have dismissed her as a female mallard, the most common dabbler in the area. However, I saw a small white area on her folded wing, marking her as a gadwall. A female mallard would have shown blue at that spot, referred to by ornithologists as the speculum.

I moved for a closer look, but when the gadwalls saw me approach, they swam away. At the same time, just a few feet away at the water's edge, came an abrupt, loud flurry of splashing. A clump of weeds had at first hidden me from a pair of **green-winged teals**. Panicked by their sudden awareness of my nearness, they swam and partially flew their way out into the bay. After having reached a safe distance they stopped, catching their breath. The same bright sun that had so brilliantly displayed the plumage of the male gadwalls was now shining on the male teal. Its head was rich chestnut with a large streak of green. The female teal was the same nondescript brown as other female puddle ducks, but there was no mistaking her as a teal. She and her mate were little ducks, much smaller than the gadwalls.

Both teals and gadwalls winter in the South. Now they are on their way to the prairie states and provinces to nest in the many small ponds that dot that region. Some, however, may choose to nest here. Perhaps these two pairs will nest here in the ponds or at the edge of the bay.

Beyond the gadwalls were several **horned grebes**, diving, surfacing, and diving again. I watched how far they swam underwater—hundreds of feet—to catch fish. What a difference there is in the feeding behavior between grebes and the surface-feeding teals and gadwalls. I studied one of the closer grebes' breeding plumage. I am accustomed to seeing horned grebes in the fall, so I was struck by the profound plumage difference. It had a chestnut-colored neck, and near the top of its head were light-colored feathers protruding like horns, hence its name. In the fall they lose their bright colors and horns, changing both their color scheme and outline.

Far to the left—close to shore—was a duck in her brown female plumage, distinctive with an extra-long, slender, and erect neck. Near her was her mate, easily identified by the white streak running up the length of his long and slender neck. He was handsome—gray body trimmed in black, and his namesake long, pointed tail. They were **Northern pintails**.

I focused my spotting scope on the gadwalls, teals, grebes, and pintails to once again enjoy their beauty. I used twenty power, and with the help of the bright sun I saw, in these artistic combinations of bright colors and unique designs, what Mother Nature had created for each species. A beauty pageant, for sure!

57. Unexpected Weather—Unexpected Sightings

I returned the spotting scope to the car, then walked across the road to the owl woods. A few days ago I had watched Trish and Jason band saw-whet and long-eared owls. It was now about 2:00 p.m. The temperature had quickly and dramatically risen to the high 70s, unusually high for the date. Extra-strong southwest winds also developed. I was about to learn how these unusual climatic conditions can affect migrants. I passed between a growth of spruce on the left and pine on the right. Beyond a large open field was low scrub growth; no tall trees interrupted the landscape as I looked west.

An ambush! Three huge **turkey vultures** were hurtling directly toward me at terrific speed. They held their wings high in a V shape as they were pushed by strong, gusty tailwinds that rocked them side-to-side violently. Now they were directly overhead, so close that their nearly six-foot wing span looked huge! (Strong winds break up the thermals that vultures normally use to fly much higher). The sun penetrated their flight feathers, highlighting a two-toned wing pattern. The leading edge, or wing lining, was black; the trailing flight feathers were a translucent light gray. Having passed over me, they were now forced to flap their wings aggressively to clear the row of pines behind me. I had seen them for less than four seconds, and then they were gone. This is the northern limit of their breeding range. They must be anxious to end the long journey they had started in the southern states. I'm sure they were pleased to be whisked along their route at such a high speed.

Following closely behind the vultures were four large hawks. The buffeting wind was battering them back and forth sideways, and bobbing them up and down. They were having a more difficult time with the wind than were the vultures. The strong tailwind quickly brought them directly overhead, very low, providing a short but detailed look at their plumage. Their bodies and wing linings were rusty red. Their tails, spread wide for added stability in the wind, showed six or seven alternating black and white bands. They were **red-shouldered hawks**! It was the first time I had seen the red underparts of red-shouldereds. I usually see them at a distance, across the bay from the Hawk Lookout platform, and rely on the experts' experience with distant silhouettes to make the identification. It was an awesome view, made possible by the combination of several factors: it was early April, their prime migration time here; today's unusually warm winds from the southwest had triggered the group's flight; and the unusually strong winds were breaking up thermals, causing the birds to fly so low. Like many other hawks, they skirt the lake before turning north. If it had been a few weeks later, they would have already worked their way into New England or Canada. We rarely see them here, returning to their wintering grounds, because in fall, they follow the north lakeshore.

I walked farther down the path, enjoying more close-up views of red-shouldereds and vultures, and scanning the vegetation on both sides of the path for small birds. I had just a fraction of a second to see a little, stubby brown bird duck into a brush pile. Its tail was too short to be a house wren, and besides, house wrens wouldn't be in for another month yet. It had to be a **winter wren**!

The high-pitched, three-noted calls of **golden-crowned kinglets** came from a clump of spruce ahead. There were six, all within a few feet of each other—a charming little group enjoying each other's conversation. As they flitted among the ends of the branches, looking for insects or cone seeds, they were completely oblivious of my presence. They used their *zee-zee-zee* notes to stay close together while slowly working their way through the woods. Black and white edges encircled their golden crowns, enhancing their royal appearance. They were the first kinglets I had seen this spring, but I was not surprised; it was the time and place for them. They like spruce and pine, and although some spend the winter here, most arrive the first week in April. Golden-crowneds fascinate me. In spite of their size—they are our smallest birds except for hummingbirds—they are capable of caring for themselves in very cold temperatures. They arrive in mid-March when it can still be cold, and they often linger well into December. Mother Nature sends them into cold weather, confident in knowing they are well prepared.

Retracing my steps back to my car, I heard a **winter wren's** excited chatters and twitters coming from where I had seen him a few minutes before. His song is similar to a house wren's, with which I am very familiar because one lives in my backyard each summer. The winter wren's song is more musical, on a higher pitch, more intense, and of much longer duration. I listened to his protracted song until he finally stopped to catch his breath. I walked on, delighted by the tiny bird with a mighty song!

The kinglets and wren showed me that I was at the early stage of the spring songbird migration. Later stages are labeled by the arrival of the kinglets' and wren's cousin species. Golden-crowned kinglets will have moved to Canada, preparing to nest. In their place, ruby-crowned kinglets will be common for the remainder of the spring. A similar shift will happen among the wrens. By the first of May, when house wrens arrive to spend the summer, the winter wrens will be nesting in southern Canada or New England. Shifts such as these will help me identify advances through Mother Nature's script.

58. The Start of Spring's Songbird Migration (April 15)

The signs of spring were arriving with increasing speed: new shoots on the shrubs, greening of the lawns, and sounds of frogs at night. Temperatures drifted upward sufficiently so that I could leave my bedroom window open a bit to smell the fresh air and hear birds at dawn. I like to guess the potential of the day's birding by the calls I hear when awakening. If I hear a species I have not yet heard this spring, it had probably arrived during the night.

The sounds I heard in my backyard this morning suggested a good day. In addition to the usual background chirping of many robins and house sparrows, a different call echoed through the woods. I opened the patio door to hear it better. The leaves were not yet out, so the call carried well.

It was a distinctive *phee-bee*, raspy and given quickly, with the accent on the first syllable—an **eastern phoebe**. During the winter I heard **chickadees** calling *phee-bee*, but their call was higher pitched—the second note a long drawn-out clear whistle—not sounding anything like a phoebe. It was the first time I had heard a phoebe this spring, which meant he had arrived recently, perhaps flying in last night. Was he just passing through, or one of the phoebes that will nest here in the woods?

Another song came from the nearby hedgerow—musical, pleasant, distinctive. It started with several clear notes, like the song sparrow's initial notes. Then came several short trills—coarser than other sparrows' trills. I remembered hearing the song on audiotapes—a **fox sparrow**. If I had identified the call correctly, it would be a timely find. Fox sparrows come through in early spring, and are in northern Canada by the time most other small birds arrive. With the binoculars I keep on top of the refrigerator, I looked to that part of the hedgerow from where the song was coming.

Dead leaves were moving—a good sign. Fox sparrows are well known for scratching in dead leaves with both feet simultaneously to find insects and other small creatures to eat. Among the moving leaves—and partially hidden by them—was the bird I heard sing, crouched low to the ground, digging with its feet. It stopped, straightened up, erect and alert, to survey the area, and furnished me with an excellent view of a beautifully marked fox sparrow. It was vivid reddish brown, highlighting the warm gray on its head and neck. The colorful features looked even more bold because the fox is noticeably larger than other sparrows. This picture-perfect handsome bird had stopped in my backyard on his way to Hudson's Bay to spend the summer. Several days ago he had been in the South, possibly the Carolinas. I was elated! My knowledge of his song and habits had directed me to the exquisite sighting.

I sat down for coffee. When I opened the kitchen window I heard a **chipping sparrow**, also for the first time this spring. Its song—if you can call it that—was a boisterous rattle-type trill, on one pitch, lasting several seconds. It was searching the edge of the driveway for seeds. Again I reached for my binoculars. He was sleek, more slender than the common house sparrow. Noticeable were the clear gray breast and a reddish-brown cap, outlined by black and white eye stripes, which added just the right artistic touch to make him look quite spiffy in his sleekness. Chipping sparrows are dedicated suburbanites, preferring the lawns of suburbs to wilderness areas. They have obviously decided that suburbs are good places to raise their families. For several summers now, a pair has established its territory around my front yard. The male often sings as I drive out of the driveway and again as I return. I wondered if he sings because he views the car as an invasion of his territory. The thought occurred to me that if someone likes being greeted by a friendly creature when returning home, but doesn't own a dog, perhaps a chipping sparrow would be a good substitute during the summer.

From the newly arrived birds I had already found at home, I knew that the Pageant had progressed significantly overnight. So, after breakfast, I drove to Island Cottage Woods to discover what other species had arrived.

On the way, I listened to audiotapes of bird calls. Over the next few weeks the tape player would turn on automatically each time I started the car. I was still refining my call identification skills and needed all the help I could get.

59. Early Arrivals Drawn to a Lakefront Woodlot

Island Cottage Woods is just a few hundred yards from Lake Ontario. It has immensely large oak and beech trees, sections of younger scrub growth, and several small, shallow pools. It borders a cattail marsh that surrounds Round Pond. This diverse habitat attracts the many birds that must stop to rest and feed—or await more inviting weather—before flying across Lake Ontario.

On a weekend morning in mid-May, there may be thirty or more birders' cars in the parking lot at the edge of the woods. Across the road, a restaurant that's open for breakfast serves birders in need of nourishment or coffee. There were six cars when I arrived this weekday morning.

Recent rains made the trails muddy, so I pulled on my boots before leaving the car. The leaves were not yet out. Only a few plants had sent up green shoots, and the lack of foliage would make it easy to see early migrants. Slowly and alertly I walked the two-hundred-yard entrance path, along which many of the best sightings are often found.

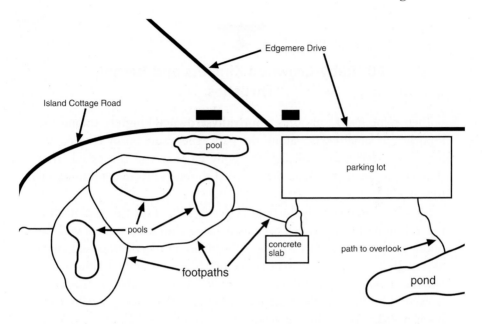

A **flicker** gave its *whirrr whirrr* call from back in the tall trees. I checked its call in the field guide to be sure. For reasons I cannot explain, I tend to confuse the flicker's call with the red-bellied's *churr-churr* call. They don't sound anything alike, but I seem to have a mental block regarding the two of them.

Another woodpecker was drilling, noisily hammering on a tree with its bill. The drilling had an uneven rhythm—several fast pecks followed by several slower ones. The unique rhythm identified it as a **yellow-bellied sapsucker**. I scanned the tree trunks in that direction, but the little bird must have been on the far side of one of them. I waited, hoping it would work its way around to the side of a tree facing me. No such luck. This was the first of several sapsuckers I hoped to find this spring. They are plentiful only during migration, unlike most of the woodpeckers we see, which are year-round residents.

60. Ruby-Crowned Kinglets and Hermit Thrushes

Then came *ji-dit* call notes from **ruby-crowned kinglets** among the branches of small bushes along the path. They were busily looking for insects and larvae to replenish the body fat they had consumed from their flight last night. Also, they needed to refuel before continuing on to Canada.

I moved closer to study the bouncy personality of the tiny bird nearest me as it moved from branch to branch, using chip notes to chat with its buddies. The little kinglet took a quick glance at me, then looked away, as though it were too busy to be concerned by my presence. I didn't know whether I was looking at a male or female. When a male ruby-crowned is excited he flips up the feathers on his crown, showing a red streak, his namesake. This ruby-crowned was composed, and I didn't see a red streak.

I came to the large concrete slab that had been the floor of a picnic shelter for clambakes many years ago. Only the slab remained, an open area in the midst of heavy growth. It was a perfect vantage point for observing birds, and a congregating spot for birders. I stopped to hear from other birders what species they had found this morning.

I was told that there were a number of **hermit thrushes**. The mature woods are an ideal habitat for them to rest in after a long flight, and to wait for favorable weather before going on to northern Canada. Because very few hermits had been seen prior to today, the presumption was that they had arrived with last night's south winds. Apparently, no one had seen anything else worthy of discussion, so the conversation moved on to other topics. I walked into the woods, looking forward to seeing my first hermit thrush of the season.

The main path leads from the concrete slab into the main part of the woods, then forks around both sides of a small pool. I took the left branch. On the path ahead was the **hermit thrush**, looking for earthworms along the damp path. The calm hermit didn't seem alarmed or afraid as we looked at each other for a few seconds. As I walked closer, it flew onto a low branch, looked back at me, and pumped its tail up and down a few times. I wondered if it was proudly calling my attention to its reddish-brown tail, which contrasted so sharply with the bird's olive gray back. After giving me ample time to appreciate its tail, it flew off, hoping to continue breakfast elsewhere without further disturbance. After a delicious, high-protein breakfast, it would find a safe spot in the underbrush to rest.

Another hermit farther back in the woods serenaded me with one of the most beautiful of North American bird songs. It starts with a long, mellow introductory note followed by a series of phrases repeated several times at varying pitches. I doubt that any bird can sound more like a flute than the hermit! The woods seemed enchanted by the song filtering through the trees. I was not the only person to have been enthralled by the hermit's beautiful song. President Theodore Roosevelt said of the hermit, "the purest natural melody to be heard in this or, perhaps, any land." Roosevelt spent much time in the Adirondacks in the summers of 1887–89. You can see his bird list by going to the Google search engine and entering *The Summer Birds of the Adirondacks.*

I spent the next few minutes walking through the woods. There were several robins, two more hermits, and a couple of crows noisily cawing as they flew over the treetops. The birding had been good this morning. I had found several new arrivals, indicating further advancement through Mother Nature's script—fox sparrow, ruby-crowned kinglet, phoebe, sapsucker, and hermit thrush.

61. Amorous Woodcocks at Dusk (April 17)

It was a warm evening with clear skies, and only a slight breeze. With such agreeable conditions I could not resist taking a pleasant stroll around Beatty Point.

The sun was sinking fast. I skirted the large marsh that surrounds Buck Pond, crossed the bridge where Larkin Creek empties into the pond, and walked up a slight grade, gradually leaving the marsh and pond farther behind. A large field was on my left. On my right were mature woods bordered by hedgerows and numerous wet ditches and muddy areas—ideal woodcock habitat. And, it was the time of year for their mating ritual. I hoped they would perform for me. It was in Mother Nature's script.

I was not to be kept in suspense. The male woodcocks' nasal *peent* calls echoed across the otherwise quiet evening air. Other calls came from different spots across the field, indicating each male had a portion of the field as his territory. I could not see them. Their habit is to sit low to the ground among tall grasses and weeds. As I walked along the lane, I counted fifteen woodcocks calling. I had come on an evening when many males were feeling romantic, and were calling to attract mates. I enjoyed their ardency.

Several years ago, I was lucky to see a male's courtship display flight. To impress a nearby female, the male flew nearly straight up into the air in a tight circular motion—at least a hundred feet high—and then in a swirling, tumbling dive, returned to the ground. After the flight, he resumed his *peent* calls. Tonight I was eager to see the acrobatic display again. I stopped, listened, and watched. Whenever I heard the distant twittering notes that the male gives during the flight, I scanned the field in that direction with my binoculars—but I could not see them in flight. The deepening darkness meant I was not to see the flight tonight. I was disappointed, but pleased to know they were there, and I had heard them.

I continued walking up the hill, awed by the number of *peeent* calls I was hearing from all directions. Then an instantaneous glimpse! A woodcock zipped across the lane just a few feet in front of me. It went by so fast that I was not aware of what had occurred until the bird was gone. It was the mental snapshot I took that instant that I later recalled. The bird was about the size of a robin, but it had no neck and practically no tail. It was a unique silhouette hurtling through the air about twenty feet above the ground. If there had been enough light to see its very long bill, I would have had a complete picture of its unique profile. Woodcocks have bills four inches long, and use them to probe muddy ground in search of earthworms.

I walked back down the hill, still listening to their calls. I was fascinated by the woodcocks' spring affairs. Why? Their secretive, nocturnal habits are certainly unusual. Observing their spring mating calls and flights is usually the only form of contact people have with woodcocks. The shy little birds are rarely seen because they sit quietly during the day and feed mainly at night. Their spring mating routine is so unique that once people see or hear it they feel compelled to witness the ritual again and again every year. What a great part the woodcocks have been given in Mother Nature's Great Pageant! [See plate 4]

62. More Species Use the Lake as a Migratory Highway (April 19)

There are three groups of birds we can see migrating now: waterfowl, hawks, and early songbirds. Where to sample the migration today depends upon which group has been most favored by the weather. Yesterday there were no recently arrived songbirds in the woods, and there were no southerly winds last night to foster new arrivals. Northwest winds today indicated that a hawk flight was unlikely. I decided to check on the waterfowl migration at Hamlin Beach.

Bill Symonds was already sitting on a bench in front of the park's area #4 picnic shelter when I arrived. This was our routine spot for watching waterfowl. The shoreline here protrudes farther out into the lake, and is higher in elevation, than the surrounding area, permitting us to see far out over the lake. It is an exceptionally wide, panoramic view, perfect for sampling the waterfowl migration. Bill lives nearby, and spends much time birding here. He is considered to be the person most knowledgeable of the park's birds—especially migrating waterfowl.

Bill was ecstatic! "One of the best days I've had—a huge movement of **common terns** and **Bonaparte's gulls**. They come from our right, pass directly in front of us, several hundred yards away, then pass out of sight to our left going west." I set up my spotting scope next to Bill. Almost immediately a Bonaparte's came by. "Notice the distinctive wedge of white that runs the length of its otherwise gray wing," Bill said. "You can see it prominently with each wing beat." Behind the first Bonaparte's was another, farther out, and another closer to shore. Then there were three more. Another gap and five more came by, one at a time. Even from a great distance, it was easy to see the wedge on the wing—the Bonaparte's distinctive appearance.

As if on cue, a common tern came into view. It was about the size of a Bonaparte's but the tern's wings were narrower, longer, and were a uniform light gray, almost white. The wing shape gave it a floppy appearance in flight. Several more terns followed in a loose group.

Every few minutes a dispersed group of common terns passed by. At about the same frequency, up to fifteen Bonaparte's would pass in a more scattered formation. At least a hundred yards separated the groups. Bill was keeping a running total of the two species. During the next two hours we saw over two hundred of each species.

As we watched gulls and terns streaming along the shoreline, Bill kept an eye farther out toward the horizon. "There are many large flocks of ducks flying west at least a half a mile out."

The first group I saw were **long-tailed ducks**. Bill's expert coaching helped me identify them.

"To identify a long-tailed that far out, note that the upstroke of the wing beat brings the wing very high above the body. The long, pointed shape of the wings accentuates the high wing beat."

After watching several flocks, I easily recognized their characteristic wing beat. Bill's coaching had helped me in long-distance identification, enhancing my sampling of the Pageant.

"There are scoters flying just above the horizon. Notice how blunt their wings are compared to the long-taileds. All of the scoters I have seen so far today have been white-winged scoters," said Bill.

"Where are they going?" I asked.

"Scoters spend the winter along the Atlantic coast, then go to their nesting grounds in northern Canada. The birders at Cape May, New Jersey, see hundreds of thousands of scoters in the spring as they move north along the coast before turning inland. Once they leave the coast, they head for the Great Lakes, then on to Hudson Bay. Their route keeps them on large bodies of water much of the way."

A few minutes later, Bill said, "Here's a line of **surf scoters**. See their white splotched face pattern?" I noticed the lack of wing patches.

A bird with an entirely different profile was also flying west, about twenty feet above the water, higher than the scoters. Unlike the distant scoters and long-taileds that I had been struggling to glimpse, this bird was close enough to see clearly. Bill announced, "A **common loon** in spring breeding plumage. See the humpbacked outline?"

Whenever I see a loon, I am reminded of years ago when I was canoe camping on remote Canadian lakes. Loons' eerie calls echoed across the water at night, sounding like a laugh, but with a sinister quality. The call is considered by many, including myself, to be the hallmark of the north woods. Each northern lake has its resident pair of loons; more than one pair, if the lake is large enough to provide sufficient fishing territory.

Over the next half hour we saw loons with increasing frequency, but only one at a time. At first, there was one every several minutes, and then they started to come with increasing frequency.

A loud, raspy squawk along the shore in front of us called our attention to a **Caspian tern** flying among a group of ring-billed gulls. If it had been silent, we might have overlooked it—at least I would have, because a Caspian is the same size and general color as a ring-billed gull. Knowing it was there, however, we easily spotted its large, bright orange, downward-pointing bill.

"**Little gull** straight ahead!" Bill called out excitedly. "They are rare here in the spring." Bill helped me find it. "There is a group of common terns and a group of Bonaparte's flying west just off shore about twenty feet above the water. The little gull is between the two groups."

"I see it! I see the black flash of its wings!" I reported to Bill. The tiny gull was all black on the undersurface of its wings, the upper surface light gray. As it flapped its wings, the alternating flashes of black and light gray were easy to spot, and most handsome. Comparing their sizes, I decided the little gull was slightly smaller than the common tern. How unusual, I thought, for a gull to be smaller than a tern.

Over the next half hour the number of scoters, loons, gulls, and terns definitely slowed down, and the interval between successive sightings lengthened. It was almost noon when a group of five ducks flew in from the east, splashing down in front of us. Two were very dark and three were medium brown. Bill looked at them in his scope: "Two **black ducks**, a **wigeon**, and two **pintails**." We guessed that they had been flying all morning and had decided to rest awhile.

A much colder wind started to blow. Bill thought it was a front moving in and that some of the movement of birds we had been seeing might have been in anticipation of the front. I decided that we had seen most of what we could see for the day and headed back to the parking lot and the trip home.

While driving home, I thought of the variety and numbers of migrating birds we saw this morning. Every spring millions of birds fly north following the Atlantic coast. When they reach the northern states they disperse inland, some following the Great Lakes westward and then dispersing throughout Canada. This route is known as the Atlantic flyway. Lake Ontario is a spur of the flyway that many ducks follow if they are going to the Canadian western provinces. This morning, Bill and I had sampled the flyway's traffic!

Atlantic Flyway

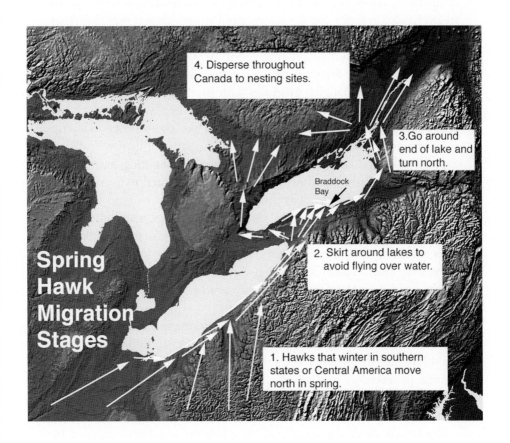

Spring Hawk Migration Stages

4. Disperse throughout Canada to nesting sites.

3. Go around end of lake and turn north.

Braddock Bay

2. Skirt around lakes to avoid flying over water.

1. Hawks that winter in southern states or Central America move north in spring.

63. Hawk Migration Picks Up as Weather Warms (April 24)

I knew it was going to be a good day at the Hawk Lookout. The temperature was to rise into the 70s, which would produce many thermals to aid hawks in flight. Strong winds from the southwest would further entice hawks to continue their northeasterly migration, and concentrate them along the lakeshore. It was about 10:00 a.m. when I arrived at the lookout. About forty people had gathered around the observation platform. After exchanging greetings with Brett Ewald and others from BBRR, I discovered that about half the people there were visitors from the Buffalo Ornithological Society. They make the seventy-mile trip each year at this time to observe the hawk migration. I listened to Brett explain to several visitors why this is such an outstanding location for seeing hawks. I have heard his talk before, but I wanted to hear it again, now that I have the Pageant as the context.

"The huge barrier of the five Great Lakes causes many northward migrating hawks to avoid flying over Lakes Erie and Ontario by following their southern shorelines in a northeasterly direction. When they reach the eastern end of Lake Ontario they disperse northward. Although most hawks use this route, a few find the narrow strip of land between the two lakes, at Niagara, and fly north from there.

"The large number of hawks and other raptors flying east along the Lake Ontario shore come upon Braddock Bay. In order to remain over land, they skirt the edge of the bay by making a sharp turn south. The abrupt change in direction concentrates them into a narrow flight path. The Hawk Lookout observation platform, where you now stand, is strategically located for observing the hawks flying this concentrated path."

The bench along the length of the platform was fully occupied by birders enjoying the attractive panoramic view of the bay as they waited for an interesting bird to be spotted. Those not accommodated on the bench were standing elsewhere on the platform or sitting below at picnic tables. Some of the birders, the most sharp-eyed and serious hawk watchers, continuously scanned the sky for tiny specks in the distance that might be an approaching hawk. Others waited to hear someone announce a sighting.

I listened to Brett define, for several beginning hawk watchers, two terms used in discussing broad-wingeds' migration. "A thermal is a column of sun-warmed, rising air within which hawks soar in circles to gain altitude. A group of soaring broad-wingeds circling in the same thermal is called a kettle. A large kettle can contain hundreds of broad-wingeds. Large kettles are common sights here at Hawk Lookout from the middle of April until the middle of May." Brett pointed out a broad-winged that had lost its thermal. "Watch! It is flying to where other broad-wingeds are soaring. That is how kettles form and grow—the hawks congregate to the most obvious thermal." [See plate 9]

It was the best time of year for hawk flights, late April, and the weather forecast was optimal. I could sense anticipation among the birders. It was as though each had a premonition that something spectacular was about to happen. Would it be a huge broad-winged flight consisting of many large kettles? A rare species? Maybe several special sightings!

I positioned myself near Brett, knowing if a raptor or any other kind of bird came by, he would see it and tell those within hearing where to look.

Everyone was watching ten **broad-winged hawks** gaining altitude by circling, and soaring, in a thermal, about a quarter mile west of us. As we continued to watch, I overheard Brett explain to visitors standing nearby what they were seeing.

"Notice that each broad-winged soars to gain altitude with its wings and tail spread wide for maximum lift." As I watched, either because the strong wind had broken up the thermal, or perhaps because the hawks had achieved their intended altitude, one by one, each turned and glided easterly to find another thermal. Brett continued, "When gliding, the broad-wingeds partially close their wings, setting them for maximum forward movement as they slowly lose altitude. By alternately soaring to gain altitude and gliding for forward progress, the broad-wingeds are able to migrate, almost effortlessly, in their intended direction. The hawks are lucky today—taking advantage of the warming sun–created thermals for gaining altitude, and tailwinds assisting in their easterly glides."

In less than a minute the broad-wingeds were out of sight. Over the next half hour, we watched several more groups of soaring broad-wingeds. Using the buoyancy of thermals, they would attain an altitude sufficient for gliding to the next thermal.

A buteo swooped low over the platform. It looked like a red-tailed hawk to me, but Brett said it was a broad-winged. I had been seeing so many broad-wingeds soaring at a distance with their wings and tails spread to the maximum; when I saw one glide, and at close range, it looked different. I resolved to study at home some evening soon, to sort out this problem.

Broad-wing Hawk

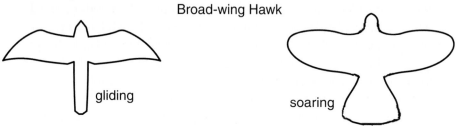

gliding

soaring

I was appreciative when another experienced hawk watcher volunteered to help me. "A red-tailed is larger than a broad-winged, but unless you see both species together, you need to use other characteristics for identification." There was consensus among the experienced hawk watchers standing nearby that the red-tail's belly stripe, visible from a considerable distance, is a reliable characteristic for identification. My tutor added, "An experienced eye can also detect the longer wings of the red-tailed in proportion to the rest of its body, as compared to the broad-winged, but this is difficult for a novice to do. It takes the experience of seeing thousands of both species to become familiar with the proportions of each." One of the hawk watchers pointed out that on a gliding broad-winged, the trailing edge of the wings were nearly a straight line. A red-tail's wing would be curved, showing bulges along the trailing edge.

From time to time, some of the more sharp-eyed BBRR experts spotted large kettles high and far to the south and west. Sometimes I could see a few tiny specks. Other times I saw nothing of the kettle being reported. I heard Brett's clicker adding to the count of broad-wingeds. It would be far more than what I had seen.

As time went on we saw an increasing number of broad-wingeds flying very low near the platform. Brett explained, "The wind has become stronger—partially breaking up the thermals and making it increasingly more difficult for the broad-wingeds to gain the necessary altitude. Consequently, some have decided to use the now brisk tailwind to take a direct easterly route, rather than circling in thermals. Here are some now," he said, as he pointed to four broad-wingeds only thirty feet above us. "Notice the fast, consistent wing beat. This is their active mode of flying, as opposed to their preferred passive mode using thermals." I was struck how the two modes of flying made broad-wingeds shape their wings so differently. They looked like two different species.

Several more broad-wingeds flew low enough for me to clearly see their plumage. The underside of their wings was white with a dark border around the edges. Their tails had alternating black and white bands.

At my urging, Brett explained how the broad-wingeds were fitting into the Pageant. "Broad-wingeds spend the winter in South America. In spring, many nest throughout the Eastern States. Those we are seeing today are going to Canada to nest. They will have had a long journey."

Due to the stronger wind, we were also seeing many **sharp-shinned hawks**—sharpies, as birders call them—flying low near the platform. Many were passing on either side of the platform not much higher than our eye level. As they zipped by, I had no trouble identifying them. They were much smaller than the broad-wingeds.

Someone called out, "**American kestrel!**" and pointed off to our right. It was only twenty yards away, less than twenty feet off the ground. I listened as Brett helped a young couple who were beginning birders. "A kestrel is a member of the falcon family and hence has a falcon's sharp-pointed wings. See how agile and buoyantly it flies. Compare its appearance to the similarly sized sharpies, which have wide, rounded wings."

Over the next few minutes I saw about a dozen kestrels and perhaps twice that many sharpies and broad-wingeds. There were several **red-tails** too, to provide variety. All were very low—close to our eye level—thanks to the strong winds and elevation of the observation platform. The strong tailwind brought them by very fast.

Whenever I saw a hawk, I would make a tentative identification in my mind and then wait for Brett or one of the other BBRR experts to announce what it was. I found this to be an effective way to improve my skills. Whenever a hawk flew in line with the sun, the color of its plumage disappeared in the backlighting. That forced me to identify it by shape, a challenge.

Brett called out loudly, "An immature **golden eagle** approaching from across the bay!" Almost immediately it was directly over the platform, very low—a perfect but brief close-up view. The wingspread was nearly seven feet. The combination of immense wingspread, slow wing beat, and amazing speed demonstrated how incredibly powerful it was. It came within twenty feet of us. Huge! Awesome! A large white patch toward the tip of each wing, and a large white area on the base of the tail, were a contrast to the mostly dark body. Brett said that the presence of the white patches was why he had called it an immature—an adult would have been all dark. In just a few seconds, the eagle was out of sight. The view was as short as it was magnificent.

There were many "oohs" and "ahs" as the birders on the platform absorbed the impressive appearance. Everyone enthusiastically discussed their impressions and excitement. The eagle was the special sighting people were hoping for, although they did not know what species it was to be until it happened. There was consensus that strong winds were responsible for such a close, although short look at the eagle. I silently reflected on the fact that the eagle was here today because it was playing its assigned part in the Pageant. It was less than a year old and was migrating north to Canada for its first time, not comprehending why, but feeling it was compelled to do so.

64. Late April Brings a Diversity of Land Birds (April 26)

Warm, fresh air was coming through the bedroom window. Anxious to see if the warming weather had brought a new wave of migrants, I quickly dressed. I downed a cup of coffee and drove to Island Cottage Woods. I was still waking up as I walked into the woods.

A thin, high-pitched, wheezy song came from along the entrance path—that of the tiny **blue-gray gnatcatcher**. It was my first gnatcatcher this spring. It had probably arrived just this morning. Looking in the direction of the call, I saw that there were two gnatcatchers flitting among the lower branches of maple and ash trees. Hungry after last night's flight, they busily hopped from one small branch to another, looking for insects. The closest one, just a few feet away, looked at me, then acknowledged my presence with its thin, raspy attempt to vocalize. Half its length consisted of an amazingly long tail kept cocked in an upright position—a distinctive profile easily seen from a distance. I walked farther into the woods, hearing other gnatcatchers' wheezy songs from several different locations. There must have been a large flight of gnatcatchers last night.

This part of the woods has three small, shallow pools, adding greatly to the scenery and serenity of the woods and attracting many species of birds, animals, and insects. Secluded pools in deep woods are especially attractive to the habitat-particular northern waterthrushes. For as many years as I can remember, I have found a northern waterthrush near one of the pools. This is the time of year waterthrushes start to arrive, so I carefully scanned the perimeter of the first pool. No luck.

The second pool was about fifty feet to my right; I scanned its water's edge. On the far side of the pool, a log extended into the water. A small brown bird walked, rather than hopped, along the log, its tail bobbing up and down as though it were teetering for balance. A **northern waterthrush**! Its dark brown back and white-speckled breast suggested a miniature thrush, hence its name, but it belongs to the warbler family. Its plumage remains the same throughout the year, which is unusual among warblers. Even immatures are identical to adults.

Their specialized habitat, and the limited time when they migrate through this area, limits the opportunities to see them. I was delighted. It was my first waterthrush of the season. This is the southern limit of their nesting range; there are a few sites in the area where they have been known to nest, but most continue farther north to New England and Canada.

Several other birders soon joined me in watching the waterthrush walk along the log and edge of the pool looking for insects. We were quiet so we wouldn't disturb it. Then, a clear song echoed through the woods— several clear notes followed by a slur. It was a northern waterthrush singing from the first pool. Had the bird been standing so still or been so hidden by a branch that I had overlooked it? He repeated the song several times so everyone had a chance to hear and study the notes. The bird we had been watching appeared to be excited by the singing; it started to jump up and down repeatedly. Then it sang in response. Perhaps it didn't like another male so close. They each sang several more times before becoming silent. The waterthrush in front of us continued its walk along the edge of the water until it was hidden by overhanging branches. I followed the path farther into the woods.

A **hermit thrush** in the middle of the path turned to show its red tail. I spotted another hermit. Then a third. Walking deeper into the woods, I saw—one at a time—at least a dozen hermits on or near the ground.

Some were scratching in last fall's dead leaves looking for insects. Most stopped their search for breakfast and eyed me suspiciously, perhaps wondering who or what I was before flying off.

Except for robins, hermits are the first thrushes to arrive in spring. Mother Nature's plan for thrush migration is well orchestrated. We see hermits in April. In May, the **Swainson's thrushes** pass through. Then, the **wood thrushes** and **veerys** arrive here to nest. **Gray-cheeked thrushes** are the last to pass through. They nest on the tundra, so they must wait for spring to arrive in the Arctic to complete their migration. Consequently, when I see them, it is near the end of the songbird spring migration.

In addition to hermits, there were many other small birds, everywhere—near the ground, high in the trees, in front of me, and behind me. They all appeared to be **yellow-rumped warblers**, but I looked at each one carefully to be sure I wasn't overlooking another species. If the bird was facing away, I could easily see its identifying yellow rump. If it was facing me, elongated dark streaking clearly outlined both sides of its breast. Both identifying characteristics were easily seen from a distance, often without binoculars.

Thinking back over the years, there have been many mornings here in spring when it seemed like 90 percent of all the birds in the woods were yellow-rumps. Because they are here from the beginning until the end of warbler migration and are seen in a wide variety of situations, it has often seemed like they are wherever and whenever I am looking for other species of warblers.

Their song was coming repeatedly from all directions. It was a musical trill ending with several notes on a higher pitch. Reacquainting myself with the yellow-rump's song will help me to differentiate the songs of less-common birds.

A song clearly not a yellow-rumped's was coming from a clump of trees near the path—the *fee-bee* song of a **chickadee**. A slow whistle-like call with the first note higher-pitched than the second, it sounds not at all like the phoebe's quick, harsh vocalization of the same syllables. It was the territorial and mating call that the male chickadee sings beginning in late winter, when he is pointing out his territory to other males. He continues the call until he finds a mate.

I first learned the chickadee's *fee-bee* call while skiing—the chairlift went past a stand of mature trees where a chickadee was calling. He was easy to imitate, although it was so cold that I had difficulty in shaping my lips. On successive trips up the chairlift I practiced the same syllables, adjusting my pitch to exactly match his. He answered me and we carried on a little conversation.

I spotted a woodpecker clinging to the side of a large tree trunk. The woodpecker's shape and size suggested a **yellow-bellied sapsucker**, but I needed to see a distinguishing characteristic of its plumage to be sure. It was partially hidden behind the trunk, but as it spiraled its way upward, it came into clear view. There were the face streaks and the white wing patch of a sapsucker, but yet it did not look like the typical sapsucker to me. It had no red on its head. The field guide explained the situation. First-year birds, those hatched nearly a year ago, have not yet acquired red markings.

A small olive-backed bird caught my eye. It had yellow on its throat, breast, and around its eye. There were distinct wing bars. Those distinctive characteristics meant it could be either a pine warbler or a **yellow-throated vireo**, both excellent sightings and hard to tell apart.

It was prime time to see the pine warbler, an early migrant. The vireo, however, comes later, in mid-May. I wanted a certain identification, rather than just going with the odds based on the date. Their calls are different. The pine warbler's call is a rattle-type call similar to a dark-eyed junco or a chipping sparrow. The yellow-throated vireo song has three-note phrases similar to other vireos. I watched and listened, but it did not sing. Then it turned, showing faint breast streaks—a **pine warbler**! Of our early migrating warblers—pine, yellow-rump, palm, black-and-white, and northern waterthrush—the pine warbler is the least seen. I had been pleased to find the waterthrush; now, with the sighting of the pine warbler, even more pleased.

Song sparrows had been singing in the tangle of bushes off to my right, three introductory notes with a trill at the end. Then a **white-throated sparrow** sang—*Old Sam Peabody, Peabody, Peabody*. Ever since I read about that interpretation of its song I have had no difficulty recognizing it. The different songs of the two sparrows reminded me of how different they are in other aspects as well. I see migrating white-throats in small groups of five to ten; they are in Canada by the end of May. Song sparrows, however, I see all summer long, individually or in pairs, as they go about their tasks of nest building and raising their young.

A twittering, rattle-type call came from a **dark-eyed junco** as it dashed into the bushes, flicking its tail from side to side, revealing flashes of white feathers on either side of its gray tail.

There was movement on the side of a tree trunk. Searching the spot, I saw a **brown creeper's** camouflaged plumage pressed close to the similarly colored bark. It crept upward on the trunk, flew down to the base of another tree, and worked its way upward again.

The birds I had seen over the last few minutes each played very different roles in the Pageant: creepers are year-round residents, juncos winter residents, song sparrows summer residents; white-throateds and warblers are migrants. In spite of their different roles throughout the year, it was as though their paths coinciding had been choreographed just for my enjoyment this morning.

A **black-and-white warbler** easily caught my eye, sporting bold, distinctive splotches of black and white. I wish all birds' names were so descriptive. It looked very much out of context here among the brown, olive, and gray colors of its surroundings. It scampered down the trunk of a large beech headfirst, another characteristic that sets it apart. Other warbler species would not try such an upside-down, nuthatch-like maneuver. It was searching the bark's crevices for dormant insects, eggs, and larvae. That is how it survives as an early migrant when most flying insects have not yet hatched.

I was thoroughly enjoying the morning, appreciating the recently arrived migrants that I had not seen for some time. What factors within the overall scenario of the Pageant had brought them here today? There is the presence of Lake Ontario just a few hundred yards away. It has temporarily blocked the birds' northerly flight until they feel rested and ready to proceed. There is the ideal habitat of the woods at the edge of the lake, where they can rest and feed. There were the previous night's warm, southerly winds, which had triggered the birds' northerly flight to this site. The time of year, of course, is key; everything was happening according to the Pageant's timetable.

From a thicket of low bushes tangled with grape vines came a song that sounded somewhat like that of the **Carolina wren's** *tea-kettle, tea-kettle, tea-kettle.* The note quality also carried as loudly as the Carolina's, but the song had two upward-slurred notes, unlike the Carolina wren's three-noted phrases. I decided that it was not a Carolina, but wondered what it was. The only birds I could see were several **ruby-crowned kinglets** flitting around in the bushes. As I focused on one of the kinglets with my binoculars, the bird opened its mouth and sang the song that had been puzzling me. Mystery solved.

Coming toward me on the path was a skilled and frequent birder here at Island Cottage Woods. I shared with her my mystery and lucky solution. "I agree," she said, "kinglets' songs can be very confusing." She added, "Kinglets also have a thin, weak call suggestive of the **blue-gray gnatcatcher**." She moved on, eager to see as much as possible in the short time she had before going to work.

As I walked past the kinglets I heard their gnatcatcher-like thin, wheezy call. I decided that the gnatcatcher's is raspier. I remained among the kinglets, studying their different calls. It added to my consternation with them when I discovered that they also have a long, rambling song similar to a **house wren**. I had learned a valuable lesson: when the versatile kinglets are around, don't identify a gnatcatcher or wren by sound without other verification.

The woods suddenly became silent. Dead silent. A shadow swept across the upper canopy; a **sharp-shinned hawk** flew low among the treetops. No wonder the woods became quiet. The many birds that had been singing a few seconds ago did not want to become the hawk's lunch. Sharp-shinneds, as members of the accipiter family of hawks, have short, stout wings designed to chase down prey among the branches of trees and undergrowth. This sharpie could pick off a warbler or thrush here in the woods without any trouble at all. Thinking about the sharpies' lunch reminded me that I had not yet had breakfast. I had been having too much fun to think about my empty stomach.

Heading back to the parking lot and out into the open again, I saw several **brown-headed cowbirds** sitting together in the top of a dead tree. They were talking to each other via short, bubbly, liquid-sounding notes. Not only do I find cowbirds plain and unattractive, but consider them to be the low-life of the bird world: they lay their eggs in other birds' nests, especially those of warblers and song sparrows. The baby cowbirds monopolize the food brought to the nest by the foster mother because cowbirds are larger, reducing the chances of the legitimate babies' survival. Whenever I see an adult cowbird relaxing and having a good time during the nesting season, I know why it is doing so. It irritates me to think its pleasure is at the expense of one of the species I am especially fond of. [See plate 3]

As I was about to leave the woods, a clear, sweet warble came from the upper branches of a tall tree. The singing bird had the general appearance of a sparrow, but its beautiful song indicated that it was definitely not a sparrow. Its bill was substantially heavier than a sparrow's. A dark patch on its face was outlined in white, suggesting a much smaller version of a female rose-breasted grosbeak. It was a **purple finch**! Unlike many other female songbird species, female purple finches do sing. Or, it could be a first-year male, for it takes a year for them to acquire the adult male raspberry color.

I had a quick lunch at the restaurant across the road from the woods, then left for Braddock Bay. It was warming up considerably, and there was a moderate breeze from the south—perfect conditions for a hawk flight.

The road from Island Cottage Woods to Braddock Bay is on a narrow piece of land that geologists call a barrier bar. Lake Ontario is on the right, and a series of large ponds are on the left. Several narrow channels provide the ponds with outlets to the lake. The ponds are excellent habitat for a number of birds such as black-crowned night herons, black terns, swallows, and especially our largest swallow, the purple martin.

A **purple martin** apartment house had been erected where the road comes close to the shore of Long Pond. A small colony of martins has occupied the house for the many years that I remember. As I drove by, a martin sat near the entrance of one of the apartments, and another on the roof. Because I saw just two birds, I guessed that the remainder of the colony would arrive in a day or two.

I recalled that this was the week the colony returns from South America. When I was a young boy, our next-door neighbor had a martin house that housed a colony of about twenty birds. In early spring, he lowered the house and cleaned out the old nests. Then he recorded on the garage door jamb their arrival date, which varied only by a day or two from year to year. I have fond memories of the martins flying low around our houses catching mosquitoes, serenading with their gurgling-sounding call, and entertaining us with their group antics and activities all summer long.

65. Favorable Winds, Thousands of Broad-Winged Hawks

When I arrived at the Hawk Lookout platform, Jerry Liguori, one of the official hawk counters for BBRR this year, was on duty. He filled me in on what was happening.

"Over the past hour, **turkey vultures** have been increasing in numbers. They come from the west. Reaching the bay, they turn south to stay over land, remaining at least a mile from us. A few **red-tails** and **sharp-shinneds** are among them."

I watched the continuous parade of vultures, but they stayed far off, turning south while still well to the west. More and more broad-wingeds were following the same route, but I had trouble seeing them on my own. Jerry pointed them out, just specks in the sky.

"It is not nearly as warm here on the observation platform as it had been at Island Cottage Woods a few hours ago," I said.

Jerry replied, "What you feel is the cool onshore breeze that has just come in off the lake; it lowered the temperature by about ten degrees in a matter of seconds." He explained further, "It takes at least a ten- to fifteen-mile-per-hour wind from the south to keep the onshore breeze from coming inland. If the southerly wind dies down, the cold air from the lake moves in.

"When a cool onshore breeze hits a warm southerly breeze, the cool air stays close to the ground and the warmer air goes over it, forming an 'atmospheric ridge,' running generally west to east, parallel to the shoreline. The hawks, wanting to travel east, will seek out and ride the ridge's air current. They generally avoid the center of the ridge, however, where the air can be turbulent." I remembered Frank Nicoletti telling me how **golden eagles** love to fly in the turbulent air, while the **broad-wingeds** choose to fly on the calmer sides of the atmospheric ridge. I now have a better understanding of Frank's explanation.

"The challenge for us hawk counters, census takers," Jerry said, "is to find the atmospheric ridge. Sometimes it will be only one mile inland; other times it can be two or three."

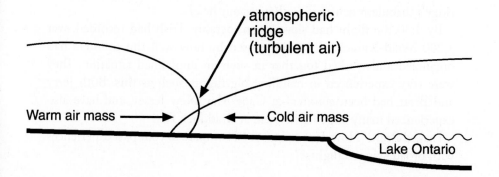

atmospheric ridge (turbulent air)

Warm air mass ——→   ←—— Cold air mass

Lake Ontario

"Brett Ewald had anticipated the onshore breeze, and about thirty minutes ago he left me, and went to the inland site that we use in such situations; it is about three miles south on Manitou Road. It looks like the kettles we are seeing off in the distance are near where Brett is located."

About that time we heard a car with its horn blowing. It was Brett. He jumped out, ran to the platform, and told Jerry to grab his equipment and move inland, where there were numerous kettles, each with hundreds of hawks going by.

In a few minutes we had moved several miles to the southwest, in a small parking area underneath the atmospheric ridge, getting set for plenty of action.

In addition to Jerry and Brett, there were two other qualified hawk counters, plus Trish Stanko, the owl bander, who was preparing to record the data. The four counters divided the sky into four sectors, permitting each to count independently. They had clickers to keep running totals of the broad-wingeds as they came by. I could hear their clickers madly totaling the **broad-wingeds**. But, if one of the team would see another species—there were a few **turkey vultures**, **red-tails**, **sharp-shinneds**, and an occasional something else—they would call to Trish to record the sighting. Totals were being kept for each species on an hourly basis. We had arrived at 2:50 p.m. In ten minutes the counters gave Trish their three o'clock totals for broad-wings, and reset their clickers to zero.

There were large groups of broad-wingeds all around us, moving in an easterly or southeasterly direction. There seemed to be two continuous streams of hawks, one flowing by just in front of us and another just behind us. They kept coming! There were at least fifty birds in view at any point in time in each of the two streams. I interpreted the two streams as being on either side of the atmospheric ridge, with the ridge's turbulent center directly over our heads.

By 3:30 the flight had slowed considerably. Trish had recorded over 1,200 broad-wingeds. I was impressed by how well the counters had organized and worked together in such an unplanned situation. They were very experienced in handling big flights such as this. Both Jerry and Brett had been counters at Cape May, New Jersey, and have also experienced many large flights here at Braddock Bay.

I asked Brett, "How does today's total compare to your past experiences with broad-winged flights?"

"During its short duration, this ranked with some of the other great flights I remember." He then recalled, "There was a huge flight here several years ago. What made it so spectacular was that the winds remained favorable all day. There was hardly a minute when there was not a continuous flow of hawks filling the sky. By the end of the day I had counted 17,000 hawks. I had trouble sleeping that night even though I was exhausted; I couldn't stop mentally clicking my clicker. Counting hawks is no substitute for counting sheep."

That evening I was preoccupied with the thought of what I had experienced. The part of the annual spring broad-winged migration I had seen today, hawks concentrating to skirt the Great Lakes, is the most impressive part of the Pageant I had seen so far. The broad-wingeds were near the end of their long journey. Most broad-wingeds, some of which I saw today, spend the winter in South America, take the land route through Central America, and flood the south Texas Gulf Coast before fanning out across the Eastern United States.

May

66. May Arrives; Cold Weather Delays Migration (May 6)

If a large portion of the northerly migration route is covered by warm southerly winds on a given night, a large flight will most certainly develop. But if desirable conditions do not develop, migration is greatly delayed or reduced. Over the past week, cold northerly winds have been blowing persistently. Frustrated birders have become anxious for the warbler season to proceed. I saw more warblers during the last week of April than in the first week in May. What few species of warblers I had seen were in unusually low numbers.

It was sunny and cool as I entered Island Cottage woods. Cold northerly winds again the previous night did not foster an incoming flight from the south. But Mother Nature's timetable is the overriding factor. It will proceed without large concentrated flights.

I was walking the entrance path into the woods when a small brown bird darted into a pile of branches that was left by those pruning back a wider trail. I eventually saw enough of a protruding tail to determine that it was my first **house wren** this spring. After I passed its hiding spot, I heard its long-winded song of excited, jumbled notes, expressing its bubbly personality. I assumed it was saying, "I'm sure glad the long trip from the Gulf Coast is over, and I'm eager to start nesting." It was a long distance for such a little bird to travel! No wonder he is relieved and happy.

I was well down the path when I heard what I thought was a **blue-gray gnatcatcher's** high-pitched, thin notes. But after my recent experience listening to the **ruby-crowned kinglet's** imitation of the gnatcatcher's voice, I wasn't sure. Then, I saw the singing bird. It was small, blue-gray, and had a very long erect tail.

Both sight and sound are important when birding: if I had not been alerted by the gnatcatcher's call, I may not have looked in its direction and seen it. Watching it sing further imprinted in my mind how to differentiate between the gnatcatcher and kinglet calls.

As usual, I went on to the concrete slab. Its openness—covering about fifty by a hundred feet—makes it convenient to scan surrounding trees and bushes, listen for calls, and assess how many birds have arrived.

Leaves moved on a branch hanging low over the edge of the concrete. Adjusting my binoculars for close range, a dazzling close-up picture popped into view: a male **black-throated blue warbler**. The direct, bright sun caused an explosion of rich, deep blue on his back, the jet black on his throat, and the contrasting pure white breast.

There is a special place in my heart for black-throated blues. As a boy of fourteen, not yet a birder, I looked out the window of our scout troop's cabin and saw a black-throated blue just a few feet away in the hedgerow. I had never seen such beauty! It was totally unexpected. I didn't even know what it was. Later, I found it in the field guide. I have since thought that if beginning birders were lucky enough to see a male black-throated blue up close, as I had experienced those years ago, even a very quick view would hook them on birding as a pastime. Perhaps that short event in my young life is why I am a birder today. Sometimes we appreciate the beauty of a bird more if we don't often see that species, but my enjoyment in seeing a male black-throated blue never wanes, in spite of its being common.

I wondered if a female was nearby. She would be much harder to see in her dull olive plumage; a small white spot on her side is the only feature that she has in common with her mate's plumage. As is often the case, the male was easy to spot, but there was no sign of a female. Over the years, I would guess, at least 75 percent of the black-throated blues I have seen have been males. My ability to sample the Pageant is limited, because some birds are easier to spot than others.

I left the concrete slab, and walked into the woods. Several **palm warblers** were in low bushes near the path; others were on the ground at the edge of the underbrush. Their brownish backs and yellow, streaked breasts, combined with their habits of constantly wagging their tails and staying close to the ground, made them easy to identify from a distance. Farther along the path, I started seeing so many palms that it seemed like a group of them was following me. Their being here today was predictable. This is the week most palms are expected to arrive, and this is their preferred habitat—low, moist shrubs and small trees. The birds I was seeing must be hardy souls, migrating in spite of poor conditions. They came from the Caribbean, having spent the winter among palm trees.

A **northern flicker** crouched on the path. Unlike most woodpeckers, flickers are as likely to be on a muddy path as clinging to a high trunk. He was poking his bill into the ground along the well-worn path. I couldn't see what he was eating, but it could have been ants, his favorite food. I moved slowly, stopping intermittently so as not to alarm him. I approached close enough to see the artistic design of his head: light gray, red, and buff, with a mark that looked like a black mustache. The females don't have mustaches. When he flew away, most of what I saw was his large white rump patch.

I was finding more birds than I had expected, thanks more to the calendar than the weather.

I walked on, crossed a wet spot by balancing on some logs, then moved deeper into the woods. To the left of the path, on a well-decayed log, a **hermit thrush** hopped into the air to catch an insect. Another hermit landed on the other side of the path. It turned its back to show its reddish tail. Then it flew into the underbrush.

From grape vines that hung from a tall oak tree came varied but familiar phrases from a small warbler. He was bright orange and black, which meant he was an adult male **American redstart**. Nearby was a first-year male. He still looked much like his mother, yellow where his father was orange, and gray instead of black, but he had a small hint of male orange on his shoulder, indicating he was within a few weeks of being one year old. Later in the year he would develop the full adult male plumage. Both redstarts took turns singing, rarely interrupting each other. It was a useful introduction to the numerous redstart serenades I would hear over the next few weeks. A great many redstarts nest here among our woods and scrub growths, and they sing a lot. Recognizing their songs, however, can be a challenge, for they have a diverse repertoire. I would watch each one intently while imprinting the melody on my mind. Today, they were singing a short song, several notes increasing in volume and pitch, and ending abruptly.

Large patches of the ground were covered by mayapple plants, early spring vegetation that had just recently shot up from the damp, rich woods soil. Among the mayapple's wide-spreading leaves I glimpsed a little bird that was walking, not hopping. I saw it for only a second before it disappeared under the cover of the foliage. It was olive-brown and had a white breast streaked with dark brown spots. It was an **ovenbird**. It resembled a waterthrush, which also is a warbler, in that they both stay close to the ground, walk rather than hop, and have plumage suggestive of a miniature thrush.

Mayapples have large multi-fingered leaves, each a foot in diameter, at the top of a foot-high stalk. A white flower, hidden under the leaf close to the stalk, appears in the spring and later develops into a small, green, apple-like fruit. The plants grow in large patches, closely spaced in just such a way that their leaves do not overlap, forming a canopy about a foot above the ground, mimicking the larger canopy some sixty feet above. A small opening in the mayapple canopy permitted me to see the ovenbird for just an instant, as it walked into cover again. Other ovenbirds were singing from at least four locations, *tee-CHER, tee-CHER, tea-CHER.* The volume, increasing with each phrase, clearly echoed through the woods. There was no doubt that the ovenbirds had arrived. The overlapping branches of the canopy high above cuts out most of the light to the ground, so little undergrowth exists. The floor's openness is why the songs' loudness reverberates so well. Preferring that habitat, ovenbirds spend most of their time on the ground, and in the shade. They even nest on the ground.

The path circled back to the entrance. As I approached the parking lot, I could hear noisy twittering calls overhead. Now out into the open, I could see four noisy **chimney swifts** streaking high above me, making short, jerky, bat-like movements, snatching insects in midair. The swifts were backlighted, so all I could see were their silhouettes. But that is all there is to see on a swift; there are no markings on their totally dark, gray bodies. Their long, narrow, pointed wings were swept backward. Their lack of a tail made them look like cigars with wings, the common description for their unique shape. They had wintered in Peru, and had just arrived to nest here, or were on their way to southern Canada.

Swifts fly for hours, usually at great heights, catching insects on the wing. I once told Brett Ewald how surprised I was that swifts fly so high looking for insects. I think of insects being close to the ground. He told me that some insects form swarms that rise in thermals of warm air to great heights. Swifts sense the thermals and search out a swarm for lunch.

I wanted to see which marsh-loving migrants had arrived, so from the parking lot at the edge of the woods I took a short walk to a panoramic view of the expansive marsh. In the foreground, six feet below me, a neck of Round Pond extended from the main body of the pond on the left to as far as I could see to the right. Beyond was a huge cattail marsh. The cattails were brown from having endured the winter, but over the next few weeks there would be new growth to color the marsh green again.

Many **common grackles** and **red-winged blackbirds** were clinging to the brown tops of last year's cattails. Lower among the marsh's growth were many, perhaps thousands, of grackles and red-wingeds loudly singing. It was a boisterous chorus reverberating from many locations in the marsh, in rich stereo. The grackles' part of the chorus was a continuous repetition of their coarse, toneless, raspy notes. The red-wings contributed a more varied selection of notes, also raspy, including their typical trill-ending *kon-ka-ree*. Accenting the chorus were several **swamp sparrows** offering their rattle-like songs.

Two pairs of **blue-winged teals** nibbled on the fresh green shoots of cattails. I wondered if they were enjoying the concert, or were oblivious to its overwhelming loudness.

Six **tree swallows** patrolled back and forth. They flew far to left, then far to the right, passing in front of me on each of their trips. From the high ground where I stood, I looked almost directly down onto the swallows' brilliant blue backs as they flew low over the water, catching insects.

These sights and sounds of the marsh in spring were totally engrossing. The short walk to get there, from where I had been in the woods, had provided a very different presentation of the Pageant. It was a change in scenery, of course, but also featured different music, choreography, costumes, and actors, which had traveled many miles for their part here today.

From the water's edge came the *whichity-whichity-whichity* call of a **common yellowthroat**. The little brown and yellow warbler was hopping among the branches of an osier bush, its roots precariously clinging to the steep bank. Two **yellow warblers**, their yellow bodies flashing in the sun, chased each other into the scrubby growth back from the water's edge. One landed, clung precariously to a thin vertical twig, and turned to look at me. It was a male; there were dull reddish streaks on his bright yellow breast. Then it sang the same clear, thin song I have heard many times, hearing it again for the first time this year: *sweet-sweet-sweet-I'm-so-sweet*.

Considering the date, I could have foretold finding these two species here in their respective habitats: the yellowthroat peeking out from low underbrush near water, and yellow warblers several feet off the ground among upland bushes.

From near the yellow warblers came a series of high-pitched, thin, rising notes, *sweee-sweee-sweee*. The **American goldfinch** has a number of songs and variations, but the call I just heard is nearly always included in its repertoire. I watched and listened to a male sing several different songs. He was perched on the top of a bush, showing off his newly acquired bright yellow spring breeding plumage, pleased he had discarded his dull olive-gray winter coat.

Moving away from the marsh, farther into upland habitat, I heard another distinctive song: *drink-your-tea-eee*—a **rufous-sided towhee**. I looked all around in that direction, on the ground, in the underbrush. Although he was a good-sized bird, I couldn't see him.

Another familiar song, a **house finch's**, was long, extended, and consisted of many varied phrases. It was similar to the warbling of the purple finch and warbling vireo, but there were harsh, raspy identifying notes intermixed throughout the song. He was sitting high in a tree yet to leaf out, showing off his reddish-orange breast.

House finches used to be strictly Western birds. Until twenty years ago I had never seen one in the East. Now I see them frequently, their having become widely distributed throughout the East. My very old field guides for eastern birds make no mention of the house finch.

It had been a brief walk from the parking lot to the overlook and back. In just a few minutes I had found both marsh and upland birds to add to the species I had found in the woods. It was a reminder that I must sample the Pageant continuously, and visit different habitats.

67. More Migrants Arrive (May 8)

We have had cold northerly winds for so long now that even a hint of a change in conditions brings hope that a few new migrants will arrive. Finally, last night, the temperature warmed. I had a quick breakfast and drove to Island Cottage Woods to see the results of the change in the weather.

As usual, I went directly to the concrete slab near the entrance. I use its open views into the surrounding habitat to assess the day's birding potential. Several **yellow-rumped warblers**, our most common migrant warbler, were busily scouring leafless branches at the edge of the slab. Some studies suggest that they have been increasing in numbers, because they winter in the United States, while other warbler species have been declining due to the use of pesticides and destruction of their winter habitat in Central and South America.

The sun activated a flash of the most brilliant color—it was a male **Blackburnian warbler**! He was close, in the open, at eye level. The bright sun shimmered on his flame-colored throat as if it were on fire! I usually see Blackburnians high in the upper canopy by straining my neck and back to get a limited view of them. Today's easy and full sighting was a treat. It was my first Blackburnian sighting this spring, undoubtedly one of the previous night's arrivals, now near the end of his two-month, three-thousand-mile trip from the Andes. When rested, and with inviting weather, he will fly over Lake Ontario to nest in the Canadian forests. Blackburnians certainly have a demanding role to play in the Pageant. They leave the Andes in Colombia or Venezuela, fly across the expanse of the Caribbean, then work their way across the United States (reaching the southern states in late April; the northern in early to mid-May) . Yellow-rumps, in comparison, have it relatively easy with their much shorter and safer route.

Considering the Blackburnian a good omen, I entered the woods, where very large oaks and beeches towered above, to see what other species had arrived. High in the canopy, two **flickers** were having a very loud conversation. *Wick-wick-wick-wick* calls pierced the air. Two days ago I saw a flicker here, feeding on the ground. Perhaps the same one was now either having a dispute over a very high nesting site, or was trying to impress a potential mate. They were too far away for me to see if both were males.

A chorus of harsh, raspy calls came from farther down the trail. A band of **rusty blackbirds** was congregated in low bushes at the edge of one of the woods' shallow pools. All were males in shiny spring plumage: glossy black bodies glistened in the sunlight, accentuating bright yellow eyes. Their mates would follow in a few days. The jovial group was busily talking among themselves, possibly discussing male bonding topics. Perhaps they were talking about their leisurely trip, from a few hundred miles south of here, where they had wintered. Or maybe they were plotting the completion of their trip to the wet woods of Canada, where they would disperse, meet up with their mates, and nest.

The path left the high canopy and damp habitat, then entered sparse woods mixed with scrub growth. A clear, sweet song wafted through the woods: *wheata-wheata-wheata-wheatcha*. My playing and replaying over the past week of the tape of warblers' songs had paid off—I easily recognized the call as a **magnolia warbler's**. I wanted to see this colorful beauty, but he was hidden by heavy growth. Mother Nature must have read my mind: magically appearing close by, near the path, low to the ground, was another magnolia, in stunningly bright yellow, black, and white plumage. Magnolias are one of our most numerous migrants, contributing much to our enjoyment of spring, through their melodious song and very colorful plumage.

A **house wren**, securely hidden in heavy underbrush, also sang. His was a busy, intent, and jumbled song. A **gnatcatche**r gave its wheezy, weak call while flitting among leafless branches. Even though he was some distance away, his long, cocked tail clearly identified him.

I heard a **Baltimore oriole's** distinctive whistle. It was clear, somewhat harsh, very easily heard, and unmistakable. Then I saw his brilliant orange and jet-black plumage. He was thirty feet up in a maple, characteristically hanging upside down from a small twig, searching tree buds for food. On the other side of the tree was a second male. The two probably came in last night, because I had heard no reports of orioles prior to today, and they are easy to spot and hear. We are close to the northern edge of their breeding range, so if they don't stay here to nest, they will not have much farther to go.

Many **white-throated sparrows** were calling nearby. Several, close by, were scratching among dead leaves looking for insects. Their call note, *dseet*, identified them. They use the frequently given call notes to keep the group together. Large stripes of dark and light tan covered the top of their heads, indicating the tan-striped color phase of the species. The other color phase is the white-striped, identified by black and white stripes on the head. Individuals of both color phases (also described in the entry for December 22) frequent the woods here during migration.

More palm warblers wagged their tails up and down as I proceeded down the path. Several **black-capped chickadees** sang their *chickadee-dee-dee* song.

The farther I walked, the more birds I found—some along the path, others farther into the heavy growth. Singing increased until it became difficult to separate and identify the songs of several species singing simultaneously. There were many birds in all directions.

The increasing activity has heightened my excitement and anticipation. I wanted to find every species Mother Nature had sent my way this morning. I checked each movement, and listened to each song and call note.

More small bands of white-throated sparrows rustled in last summer's leaves. Several chickadees were flitting from one tree to another. That was a good sign, for chickadees often attract other birds by their busyness.

A **black-throated blue warbler** appeared from behind a large branch, and a **black-throated green warbler** sang *trees-trees-murmuring-trees*. A **redstart** called, then showed itself. A **gray catbird** that was standing on the path hopped into a bush when it saw me. All these birds were low in trees or bushes not far from each other. I had found a pocket!

The word "pocket" refers to a phenomenon well known to experienced birders. This description is used when a number of small birds of several species are found close together, perhaps within a hundred feet of each other. The birds may be attracted by the presence of insects or something else of mutual interest. Sometimes, I believe, they come together because they find the activity of the other birds exciting. Whatever the reason for the gathering, birders enjoy pockets.

The pocket was a busy place: another oriole came through, more chickadees came by, the call notes of white-throats monopolized the underbrush, a **cardinal** streaked across the path, there was another black-throated blue, and several **yellow warblers** made appearances.

I would identify every movement or call, then check the next movement or sound. It was difficult to do when several birds sang at once. I had to separate their songs and concentrate on only one at a time. Many of the sights and sounds were species I had already found. Some, I guessed, were even the same bird again. I verified each carefully, so as not to overlook a different species.

By the time I had sorted through all the birds in the pocket, it was dispersing. Pockets typically do not stay in one area for very long. In the past, I have sometimes followed the pocket as it moved toward insects or moved in another desired direction. This time, the birds were dispersing in many directions. On some days, I found that if I stood in one spot, birds would come by me in waves, a series of pockets. Those are the days I think about in the bleak wintertime.

68. Broadening the Pageant's Sample—The Banding Station (May 9)

The Braddock Bay Bird Observatory (BBBO) bands nearly 10,000 birds a year during spring and fall migrations. The banding station is on the west side of the bay just a few hundred yards from the Lake Ontario shore. BBBO is part of a nationwide program to determine migration habits, longevity, and other facts about birds that we may not otherwise learn. The national program was started back in the 1920s to learn more about migratory game birds for the purpose of setting hunting regulations. Since then it has expanded to all birds and is coordinated by the U.S. Fish and Wildlife Service's Bird Banding Laboratory in Laurel, Maryland. The many licensed banders nationwide submit their data, including the unique band number on each banded bird, to the Bird Banding Laboratory. If a band is found and returned to the laboratory, the date and location of where the bird was banded, and possibly its age, can be found in the database. Only a small percentage of the bands are ever recovered, by either recapturing the bird or finding it dead. A great deal of information is learned from the program, in spite of the small percentage of recoveries.

I wanted to visit the station to compare the species they were capturing with the species I was observing on my hikes. The number and species of birds captured during a day at the station is always far more diversified than I would expect from my birding in the area. There are many aspects of the Pageant that I can learn at the banding station. For example, the arrival and departure dates and relative abundance of each species is much more evident from their data.

Things were really humming at the BBBO banding station when I arrived, for weather conditions the night before had favored a large migration. The several banders and their assistants were busy, so I just stood back and observed. There was much to see.

About a dozen finely meshed nets, each forty feet long and six feet high, are used to capture the birds. The netting consists of thin, black, nearly invisible threads woven into a one-inch mesh. Some nets are placed among the brush to capture sparrows and warblers. Other nets are in more mature woods for wrens and thrushes. Others are at the edge of fields for variation in habitat and species.

Every half hour, banders—or trained interns—remove birds caught in nets and take them in small, mesh transfer bags to the central work station. There the banders identify, measure, and weigh each bird, determine age and sex if possible, assess physical condition, and place a numbered band on one of the legs. When all the data is recorded on log sheets for submission to the U.S. Department of Interior's national database, the birds are released unharmed.

The length of the wing chord (from the bend in the middle of the wing to the tip of the longest wing feather) is measured on each bird. In some species, the length of the wing chord is the only way to determine the sex of the bird. For example, if a junco's wing chord measures more than 78 millimeters, it's a male; if less than 72 millimeters, it's a female. Between 72 and 78 millimeters, the sex cannot be determined. There are about ten other species for which wing chord measurements are used to determine sex.

"Fat class" is an assessment of how much fat the bird is carrying. The bander makes the assessment by blowing on a drinking straw pointed at the middle of the bird's breast. The blown air parts the feathers over a spot where the bird accumulates fat. If the bird has just arrived from a long migration flight, there will be a slight depression at the spot, indicating no fat. If the bird has been resting and feeding for a few days, the depression is filled with fat that has a yellowish color, while the surrounding skin color is white. The bander is trained to assign a class based on the amount of fat on the bird.

The station starts operating one hour before dawn each day, and on the same days each year. The number of captures by species can be compared from year to year to identify trends in populations. A difficult part of the program is keeping the habitat the same from year to year. There is a tree- and shrub-trimming program under way to accomplish this.

The species of birds captured during a day at the station is always different from what I would expect from my birding through the area on the same day. Consequently, I often visit the station to learn which birds I have overlooked in my sample, and to see, up close, their beautiful plumage.

I went with Betsy Brooks, the president of BBBO and an experienced bander, to check the nets. As we walked along, she called my attention to two **winter wrens** and a **house wren** calling from well-hidden spots in the thick underbrush.

While skillfully removing birds from a net, she stopped, pointed to a captured bird, and said, "Here is a quiz for you: what bird is this?" It was slightly larger than a sparrow—a dull olive color above, and a somewhat brighter yellow color underneath. I saw no other identifying markings. I ruled out several possibilities. The color was similar to several warblers, but this bird was larger and its bill heavier than a warbler's. The color and bill differed from a female oriole. It was not a female evening grosbeak, and not a yellow-bellied flycatcher, or a yellow-throated vireo. I sensed her curiosity in how well I would respond to the challenge. Many birds look different in the bander's hand compared to their appearance fifty feet away through binoculars. Some markings are more noticeable up close, while others are more prominently seen at a distance. Having been careful not to jump to conclusions, I finally gave Betsy my best guess—a female **scarlet tanager**—the secretive, inconspicuous mate of its eye-catching male. I think we were both relieved when she said that I was correct.

Back at the banding work table, Betsy and the other banders hurriedly processed the many birds just collected. There were several of each of the following species: yellowthroats, yellow-rumps, yellow warblers, white-throated sparrows, chickadees, and palm warblers. There were single birds of these species: house wren, junco, black-throated green warbler, black-throated blue warbler, Canada warbler, swamp sparrow, cardinal, redstart, Wilson's warbler, Swainson's thrush, and an ovenbird. It was an exciting, revealing display of one of the Pageant's peak days. It suggested the magnitude and diversity of last night's flight. Millions of birds, perhaps hundreds of different species, must have traveled northward across the Northeast last night, to have resulted in this many of them spending the day at BBBO's small sampling site.

It was most revealing that there were few species in common between what was being banded and what I had found birding nearby a few hours earlier. I had seen hundreds of migrating blue jays flying overhead, a flicker flew across the field, and a vulture glided by heading east—parallel to the lakeshore. None of these species were caught in the nets. I saw or heard redstart, yellow, and yellow-rump warblers—but did not find the other warblers being banded. I had not seen a wren or sparrow. The birds banded were from habitats where they could be more secretive, and less likely to be found by just walking by. I closely studied the migrants, staring into their questioning, wild eyes. There were hints of what they had been enduring. Most had come from as far as South America. They had spanned a sea or mountains, had been challenged by variable weather, strong winds, and long distances, and had to find food in unfamiliar locations. I developed an intimate, almost eerie feeling for what the Pageant had demanded of each of them. They were following the same route prescribed for their species, and enduring the same difficulties that their ancestors had repeated for thousands of years, to perpetuate their species.

69. Southwest Winds Inspire Migrants (May 10)

Moderate southwest winds covered much of the Northeast last night, providing favorable conditions for a large flight. I hoped that many of the birds that had flown in from points south had chosen to stop at Island Cottage Woods for a rest before crossing the expanse of Lake Ontario.

Several birders were in the parking lot, about to leave. They enthusiastically described how they had thoroughly birded the woods over the past hour, finding many warblers and a wide variety of other species. They were about to explore other nearby birding sites to determine the extent of last night's migration.

An **Eastern screech owl** was one of their more noteworthy findings. Because of their camouflage and motionless daytime habits, screech owls are rarely seen, but we know they are common because they often respond to someone mimicking their call in the woods at night. They are not migrants; this one was probably a permanent resident of the woods.

One of the birders was kind enough to delay his departure to show the owl to me. We took the path a short distance to a slender oak tree. He pointed to a spot about thirty feet up into the tree. "Look just to the right of the trunk, where a major branch protrudes." I followed his directions, found the branch he described, and stared at the spot. I didn't see the owl. Was I looking in the wrong spot? Then, as if by magic, the outline of an owl appeared where I had been staring. It was like one of those pictures designed to play tricks on the eyes. The owl's gray, streaked plumage exactly matched the color of the tree bark; the ear-shaped feathers on top of its head broke up the curved outline. It was perfectly camouflaged! It was small, only about the size of a fat robin.

"You had shown me exactly where it was, but I still had trouble seeing it; I can't imagine how you could have spotted it." My guide explained how. "We noticed several chickadees flocking noisily and persistently around the spot high in the tree. Remembering that chickadees, as well as crows, love to harass owls, we knew where to look and what to look for. 'Mobbing,' the term for this behavior of many species of birds, is done to point out to others the presence of a predator, and to possibly discourage the predator."

My guide left with his friends, and I joined several other birders on the concrete slab. We listened to yellow, yellow-rumped, and **palm warblers** singing nearby. Farther away we heard red-wings, grackles, a blue jay, and robins. The song-filled woods verified that many birds had arrived during the previous night's flight.

The most numerous calls and sightings were palm warblers. One of us would spot a palm and point out its location; then someone else would show us another, then another. Their calls were coming from all directions, repetitious buzzy notes all on one pitch.

A **least flycatcher** kept repeating his coarse, emphatic, *chebeck* call from underbrush off the edge of the slab. Another least called from his perch in full view off the opposite end of the slab. The leasts were the first I had found this season, marking another step in the progress of the Pageant. Leasts arrive the second week of May from Central America, after early warblers have been seen, and when the second group of warblers begins to trickle northward.

"A male **scarlet tanager** perched high in a tree about fifty yards away!" someone excitedly shouted. The brilliant red plumage glistened in the sun, contrasting with the dull, gray background of the still-leafless trees. For at least a minute he did not move—typical deliberate tanager behavior—allowing us to savor his beauty. There was another male tanager, this one closer but partially hidden by twigs. Knowing that females migrate with the males, I searched for one of the females. She would be harder to spot because her olive plumage blends well with the habitat, and like the males, her infrequent, slow movements tend not to catch the eye. Yesterday's study of the female's plumage told me exactly what to look for, but I was not successful.

Encouraged by the many sightings and sounds, I took the path farther into the woods, searching for other birds from last night's flight. Two birders farther along the path pointed to a **black-and-white warbler**, clinging close to the side of a tree trunk like a nuthatch. It flew to another trunk, and while descending headfirst it sang *wheee-seee-wheee-seee*. He repeated the high, thin notes in a rhythmic way, often described as a squeaky wheel rotating around an axle.

The birders spotting the black-and-white took the path's branch to the right; following my often flawed male intuition, I went left. After every few steps I stopped, listened carefully for singing, and watched for movement in the branches.

An **American redstart** was perched low in a large beech tree. Redstarts' songs are among the most commonly heard in our woods, hedgerows, and scrub growth throughout the spring and early summer. I watched this handsome adult male open his mouth and fill the woods with song. I paid close attention to what I was hearing, figuring that if I could recognize a redstart's song, it would help me sort out the calls of other species.

A huge oak dominated the area. In its top were two **Blackburnian warblers**. Unlike the easy and close views I had been enjoying, these migrants were high in the branches of the canopy. All I could see were their bellies and brief identifying glimpses of their orange throats.

My eyes were drawn to a point with bright colors: richly colored chestnut sides contrasted with a pure white belly; a yellow cap was edged with black. A handsome male **chestnut-sided warbler**! As though he felt an obligation to be officially noted for my sample of the Pageant, he posed, then raised his head and sang. I wanted to remember his song, too, for future reference. He sounded very much like a yellow warbler, but he ended on a down-turned note; a yellow ends on an upturned note. The role chestnut-sideds play in the Pageant is arduous. They winter in Honduras or Costa Rica; in spring they fly over the Gulf of Mexico, migrate across the Eastern United States, then disperse to nesting sites after reaching the Great Lakes.

A **Blackburnian warbler** sang. I spotted the female, and near her was the singing male. Had they traveled together from South America? Were they already paired in preparation for nesting in Canada? I wanted to ask them, if only they could answer. We know very little about these aspects of their lives, so significant to them.

From the lower branches of the same tree came a **blue-gray gnatcatcher's** high, thin, almost insect-sounding call. Well back in the woods sang a **black-throated green warbler**. Closer, but still out of sight, I heard a **black-throated blue warbler** sing. **Palm warblers** were still singing from all directions.

Over the last few minutes, my sense of awe had been building. Hundreds of birds of many species were within a few feet of me, having recently traveled thousands of miles across the Americas to be here on this day—an infinitely ancient, vast, diverse, beautiful phenomenon. I was now alone in the woods, with no one else in sight. It seemed as though these many players of the Pageant were all performing their roles for my personal pleasure.

In a larger sense, however, I was not alone. This morning, across the entire Eastern United States, there was a large, informal army scouting woods, hedgerows, parks, and backyards, hoping to be charmed by the beauty of chestnut-sideds, Blackburnians, or other warblers and migrants. I felt the comradeship of the legion. I wonder if the birds felt the comradeship among each other. Most had come from Central America, starting several weeks earlier. They may have joined with those from South America and the Caribbean Islands as they moved north across the eastern United States. Perhaps some of the birds I saw this morning had been traveling together for thousands of miles!

Sweet notes came wafting through the trees from high in the canopy— they were the unmistakable, repeated phrases of a vireo, "*here-I-am, where-are-you*." Compared to the notes of the very common red-eyed vireo, this song was thinner, higher pitched, slower, and more musical. The singer was not visible from its high, densely foliaged perch, but its musicality labeled it. A **blue-headed vireo,** as always, had arrived from the South a week before its more numerous cousins, the red-eyeds. From almost anywhere in the East, a lucky and alert birder can hear a blue-headed's pleasant song, as it migrates to New England or Canadian nesting grounds.

This bird has not always been known as a blue-headed. My 1947 Peterson's field guide lists the blue-headed vireo. Then the American Ornithologists' Union (AOU) considered blue-headed to be the same species as the western races, Cassin's and Plumbeous, so the AOU gave the combined species the name of solitary vireo. Recently the AOU reverted: the little bird I saw this morning once again has its own species name—blue-headed. I enjoyed the soft, pleasant chorus of many warblers and other small birds happily fulfilling their spring ritual.

The tranquility of the woods was disturbed by a very loud, contentious squawk, raspy, with a rising inflection. There was no mistaking a **great crested flycatcher**. The large bird was surveying his domain from a commanding position on an exposed branch at the top of a tall oak. He was declaring his dominance of the area by his wise-guy-sounding call. With an erect posture, he showed off his handsome slate gray breast, which emphasized a bright yellow belly. When great cresteds have arrived in spring, they let us know it, in no uncertain terms!

A **white-crowned sparrow** showed itself briefly among the tangle of grapevines near the ground. Its colors and patterns were much the same as the white-throated sparrows I had been seeing recently. But in spite of those similarities, the white-crowned presented an appearance remarkably different from that of the white-throateds. I studied the white-crowned, hoping to discern why it looked so dissimilar. There was the white-throat's obvious white throat, and the white-crowned's pink bill. However, those small markings did not account for the broad difference in their appearance. Watching the white-crowned work its way among the leaves and grapevines, and studying its aspect and deportment, I decided that its characteristic posture was what made the major difference in appearance. The white-crowned held its neck in a vertical position, an erect posture, while white-throateds maintain a more horizontal position as they huddle over the leaves they are inspecting. The overall appearance of people can be noticeably different because of their posture, so why not sparrows? A comparison of the nesting ranges of the two species of sparrows suggests a possible explanation for their different postures. The white-throateds nest and feed in the undergrowth of forests; white-crowneds spend the summer among low growth of the tundra, where their view is open and panoramic, allowing them to scan for approaching predators. [See plate 11]

The birds I have been seeing have been in a grove of very tall beech trees, some approaching a hundred feet high. From the top of the tallest of the trees came the *churr-churr-churr* conversation of two **red-bellied woodpeckers**. Looking up, I saw flashes of black and white on a steep, upward, inclining flight to a barkless, dead section of a tree trunk. Together the two birds were chipping away at the trunk, preparing a nest cavity. Good, I thought! Future red-bellieds for me to enjoy in years to come.

A thrush flew to a low limb overhanging the path. **Hermit thrushes** had been numerous recently, so I expected this to be one too. Facing away from me, I clearly saw that it did not have a hermit's reddish tail. When it turned to look at me, it showed a buff-colored cheek and eye ring. This was my first **Swainson's thrush** of the season. I should have expected a Swainson's thrush. By the second week in May most hermits have moved on to Canada, and Swainson's start to arrive. Hermits being replaced by Swainson's was another point in the progress of the Pageant. The two species' arrival dates probably differ because of where they winter. Most hermits spend the winter in the southern states, and arrive here in the North first; Swainson's have farther to travel from South America, and consequently arrive later. Their nesting ranges, however, are similar: they both nest throughout Canada, except in the northern tundra area.

Not far from the thrush, a sparrow darted into a brush pile. A brief glimpse of its gray face patch and striped chest revealed it to be a **Lincoln's sparrow**. Lincoln's usually hide in thick foliage and tangles close to the ground. They are so timid that they are not usually seen, even though they are common over most of North America. I remember being told once that if a sparrow sings like a house wren, it is a Lincoln's. I waited, hoping for a song, but no sound came from the brush pile.

When I reached the parking lot, harsh calls of *keeek, keeek* came from above. Two **black terns** flew over the open expanse of the parking lot in agile, floppy flight, like large swallows. They were black, rather than the typical light color of terns. There is national concern for their survival, due mostly to the loss of their preferred habitat. They have been nesting here in the adjacent ponds for as long as anyone knows. Sharon Skelly of the Braddock Bay Bird Observatory has been monitoring their nesting efforts for a number of years, accumulating many miles in her canoe. The results have not been encouraging. Nests are built on hummocks or debris close to the water, but fluctuations in water level have drowned many of the nestlings. More stable water levels may help the colony to survive. With special appreciation, I watched them fly toward nearby Buck Pond.

As I walked across the parking lot, a **killdeer** called out in disgust for having been disturbed. She flew a short distance, deliberately holding her wings as though she were injured, calling loudly again, then repeated the procedure several more times. With this characteristic behavior, she was trying to lure me away from her nest, which was probably somewhere in the parking lot among the small pieces of crushed limestone. The nest would be hard to find, because it would consist of nothing but a small, slightly cleared area, with the eggs hard to differentiate from the surrounding stones. With all the birders coming and going, it must have been a trying time for the mother killdeer. I hoped no one would unknowingly step on the nest or drive over it with a car.

Millions of birds had been in the air the previous night, winging their way northward, and many chose to stop here as dawn arrived. Everywhere I turned this morning there was another species to see. A variety of melodies filled the air, with many discordant choruses. The climax of the annual pageant—spring migration—was near its peak.

I was thrilled to have experienced this morning's marvelous display. It was the kind of day I wait for all year. I had not yet seen everything available this morning. To sample the Pageant as broadly as possible, I must now sample other nearby habitats. Hawk Lookout is just a few miles away.

70. The Lakeshore Acts as Magnet to Many Species

At Hawk Lookout, Jerry Liguori was on duty at the observation platform, along with his usual complement of dedicated hawk watchers. Very strong winds prevented thermals from forming, so hawks and turkey vultures were taking advantage of the tailwinds by flying low, fast, and on a direct route that took them near the observation platform.

Every few seconds another **sharp-shinned hawk** shot by the platform, several quick wing flaps followed by a short glide. One of the sharp-shinneds, on a direct path toward us, suddenly dove into the scrubby growth of osier bushes at the edge of the cattails. It had apparently seen something that would make a good lunch. Jerry remarked on the unexpected change of course: "Sharpies, being accipiters, have short wings designed for pursuing prey on the wing into dense vegetation." Someone imaginatively added, "The sharp-shinned's version of a fast-food stop along the highway!"

A continuous flow of **broad-winged hawks** had been going by using the same direct, low-level route. I wasn't sure what species of hawk they were at first, because their shape looked very different from the way it does when they soar on thermals. One of the experts next to me remarked about the difference and explained, "In a soar, the tips of the wings are pointed forward, making the leading edge of the wings a straight line, and the trailing edge curved. In the active method of flight we're seeing now, the leading edge of the wings is curved back at the wing tips, making the trailing edge a straight line. The result is two different, essentially opposite, profiles."

It was an ongoing parade of sharpies and broad-wingeds. Jerry interrupted the routine, calling out, "Two **ospreys** far to the west." They were much larger than the hawks we had been seeing, their profile very different, and easily recognized: long, narrow wings with a pronounced backward bend midway along the length of the wing. The bend is what some birders call the "wrist," but to me their "wrist" looks like an elbow. A bird's "fingers" are proportionally much longer than ours, its lower arm far less developed, and consequently its "wrist" is midway along the length of its wing.

For an hour we watched the parade, including the resident **harrier** making intermittent appearances over the marsh. It would fly over the woods across the bay, and then turn to patrol over the cattails. At a very low altitude, usually at less than ten feet, it would search for rodents or frogs. It would then disappear, perhaps going to another marsh nearby. Later it would reappear to repeat its search, hoping another mouse had ventured out since its previous patrol run. Several times it hovered, then dove into the cattails, but it emerged quickly without a catch. Once, however, when it remained on the ground longer than usual, I guessed it had been successful and was eating its catch.

The number of hawks going by gradually reduced to a trickle. Hawk watchers fill such times with their favorite pastime of telling more recently arrived visitors what they had just missed. Today, I heard about the bald eagle that had gone by just before I arrived.

With more time between sightings, and the storytelling and jokes becoming less numerous, I became lost in thought. Why does this site have so much attraction for me? There is the serenity and vastness of scenery, and of course there is the presumption, given favorable conditions, that many migrating hawks will be flying by. The migration is more than hawks, however; a variety of water-loving birds are attracted to the lake, as are many other migrants. Above all, it's the likelihood of the unexpected that draws the usual conclave to the lookout. There is often an unexpected sighting—a surprise to the Pageant!

A shorebird, larger than the small least or semipalmated sandpipers we often see, shot up from shore. It gave a two-noted flight call, flew parallel to the water's edge for a short distance, then dropped down to be hidden again by a row of cattails. It had a white spot near its rump, long legs extended well back from its body. One of the hawk watchers called out, "Yellowlegs!" Jerry, after hearing the call note, said "Lesser yellowlegs." He explained his identification. "The two-noted call told us it was a lesser yellowlegs; the similar but larger greater yellowlegs has a three-noted call." Later a **Wilson's snipe** flew up from where the yellowlegs had come, following a similar flight path across the cattails. The snipe was undoubtedly following a migration route similar to that of the yellowlegs: across the country, then on to Canada. The two shorebirds' appearance, however, were very different: the snipe's body was compact, legs short.

There were many birds among the cattails. Approximately twenty **red-winged blackbirds** and several **grackles** busily flew about, chattering their incessant call notes. Perhaps the yellowlegs and snipe had found the noise so disturbing that they moved to a quieter area of the marsh.

Someone announced, "Ten **double-crested cormorants** flying across the mouth of the bay." They looked like geese, stretched out in a long line, one behind the other. One at a time they found a spot to land on the dead tree branches that protruded from the water at the tip of the west spit. It was their favorite perching spot, and the colony's home base. About fifty more cormorants were already perched on the branches; at least that many more were swimming nearby. With the help of a twenty-power spotting scope, we saw that some of those swimming were fishing: diving, coming up briefly, diving again. Cormorants are excellent fishermen. Because the legs are attached far to the rear of the bird's body, they provide efficient propulsion, like propellers on a boat. Cormorants use their specially adapted wings too, to "fly" underwater. Unlike ducks, the cormorants' wing feathers are structured to not be buoyant, which also reduces their waterproofness. That is why we see cormorants perched on branches, sun-drying their feathers after a swim. They are so well known for their fishing capability that in China and Japan, fishermen use pet cormorants to catch fish. The fisherman places a ring around the bird's neck to prevent its swallowing the catch. Later, the ring is removed so the bird can eat a measured portion of the catch.

Two of the hawk watchers had observed small groups of cormorants patrolling the shoreline at considerable distances both east and west of here. Presumably, they were from this colony, for they are known to cruise far along the shore looking for a school of fish. In recent years, the colony has nested here at Braddock Bay. Before then, we would see only a few, just during migration. They winter somewhere along the Gulf Coast. My curiosity stirred me to wonder just where on the coast this colony had spent the winter. Had they all been together during the winter, or is this just a summer colony? How many of those here now are permanent members of the summer colony, or are some migrants, stopping here for brief socialization?

All spring there had been ducks on the bay, the species varying as migration progressed. Today, however, there were no ducks. Even the recently numerous **red-breasted mergansers** had moved on. I felt an emptiness for not seeing the ducks, whose migration, which I had so conscientiously followed all spring, was now over. However, I had a feeling of accomplishment for having tracked their migration so attentively to completion.

But Mother Nature never ceases working, and she was about to introduce me to yet another aspect of her Pageant. Flocks of small birds flew along the shoreline, and some were passing directly overhead. Among them was a group of **American goldfinches** with their characteristic undulating flight. Following them was another group of birds, flying in a looser formation, and their bodies were larger than the goldfinches. I didn't see any identifying flight mannerism, and the backlighting kept me from spotting any distinguishing marks or colors. I was wondering what they were when one flew very low and close to the platform. The change in angle caused light to reflect from his black body and white wings, and I was even close enough to see the yellow patch on the nape of his neck. A very handsome male bobolink!

Jerry pointed out a flock of **pine siskins** trailing the bobolinks. "Notice their small size and short tails compared with the larger bobolinks." The siskins were closer in size to the goldfinches but did not have the goldfinches' unique undulating flight pattern.

Jerry announced the next group: "A flock of about ten **American pipits** following the same route. Listen to their flight notes, calling their name." I heard *pipit* from several of the birds as they flew directly over us. "Pipits almost always give their flight notes," he added.

I told Jerry how surprised I was by this aspect of spring migration at the observation platform; "It's supposed to be for hawk watching." He explained, "Flights of **siskins, pipits, bobolinks, goldfinches,** and **evening grosbeaks**—I have seen several flocks of grosbeaks this morning—are often seen at the platform this time of year. The flocks are usually between five and thirty birds. We see them here at the observation platform, and other points along the lakeshore, flying an easterly course. Like hawks, they skirt the lake rather than flying across it."

Back home, I sat down at the kitchen table to count the number of species I'd seen for the day. A **ruby-throated hummingbird** came by to sample the flowers just outside the window. Adding it to the day's count brought the total to seventy-four. Such an impressive total was a measure of how much of the Pageant I had experienced.

As I sampled the Pageant over the past several weeks, I had been continuously reminded of its scope. This is a huge event I am observing, and it is not just a local phenomenon.

I leafed through my field guide for the geographical distribution maps of the day's species. Most of the birds I saw today can be seen across much of the eastern half of the United States. Thousands of birders all over the East are utilizing the same knowledge of these species that I use to find and identify them. I could picture the birders, old and young, some spending the day in the field, others squeezing in an hour before work, tramping through whatever habitats existed in their locale. We were all experiencing parts of the Pageant, but because of our different skills, and times and locations of sightings, each of us was seeing different parts of the Pageant. What if we could, somehow, combine our experiences over time and geography, into a gigantic, multifaceted composite? What an enormous amount of information would be revealed to study the ebb and flow of the various species as they progress across the country. How much more we could learn about the Pageant!

71. A Super Day for Warblers and Other Migrants (May 18)

According to the late-night TV weather map, warm, brisk, southerly winds were covering a large area of the eastern part of the country. That suggested ideal conditions for a large migratory flight. I went to bed hoping a large movement of migrants was under way.

Just before dawn, I was awakened by rain against the window. I wondered if the northward-flying birds had first encountered rain as they arrived here. If that were the case, the rain would have caused them to abort their flight, and to land in the sanctuary of the woods along the lakeshore, rather than continuing on across the lake. I was eager to see if we had a fallout. I had to sample several habitats and sites to explore what had come in on the flight.

My first stop was at a place where, in late August, I had witnessed swallows gathering to migrate. It was there, along the shoreline of Lake Ontario at the west side of Braddock Bay, that there is a huge old willow tree, just feet from the shore. Behind it is a small woodlot and hedgerow. The site is an irresistible stopping point for migrants not yet wanting to proceed across the unforgiving expanse of the lake.

I had just shut the car door when I saw on the right side of the willow a dull, dingy warbler. It was a drab olive color on both the upper and lower body. I couldn't find a clearly identifying characteristic. I studied it carefully as it worked its way along a horizontal branch looking for something to eat. By a process of elimination, and by checking my field guide, I decided that it was an **orange-crowned warbler**. They are uncommon here in the East.

Higher and to the right, another small bird was exploring the willow's branches in typical warbler fashion: flitting every few seconds to another nearby location. Twigs and swelling buds were blocking my view, and its incessant movements added to the difficulty in finding an unobstructed look. Finally, after moving to one side just the right amount and crouching down, I had a clear view. Then, as though he knew he was being watched, he turned to show the reddish-brown patch in the center of his yellow face, and sang his high-pitched, very thin, *seet-seet-seet* song. An adult male **Cape May warbler**! I was delighted; Cape Mays are hard to find here along the lakeshore. Unlike the challenging identification of the orange-crowned, the Cape May was easy to recognize. Females, however, lack the face patch and can be tricky to identify. My hunch that this would be a great day for birding had been immediately reinforced by two notable sightings. I couldn't wait to see what else had arrived!

The branches of the enormous willow contained many other birds moving among its twigs and buds. In the lower branches were several **yellow warblers**, a **ruby-crowned kinglet**, and a **magnolia warbler**. Higher were two **Baltimore orioles** canvassing the upper branches—they like to be high in tall trees. Six species were taking advantage of the willow's inviting location.

Away from the tree, the air was filled with swallows going in all directions. Some were flying low, inches above the lake's surface. Others were hawking for insects twenty or thirty feet above the adjacent field. Two of the low flyers came close, and banked a turn by spreading their long, pointed tails—**barn swallows**. There were so many swallows in the air that it was hard to sort them out. Eventually, I had them all identified. Those flying low were barn swallows; those higher, with less pronounced tails, were **tree swallows**.

An endless tide of **blue jays** was flowing east along the lakeshore. At least a dozen were in view almost all the time—not flocked together, but flying individually, as is their nature. They do not fly in tight flocks like starlings, scaup, or some species of shorebirds. A wedge of **double-crested cormorants** appeared just offshore. They were probably going to their colony's gathering site at the mouth of the bay, a few hundred yards away—they were already dropping in altitude in preparation for landing. Several **ring-billed gulls** sat on the large rocks protruding out of the water in front of the willow tree. The location's mixed habitat of lake, marsh, hedgerow, large trees, and fields had quickly proven its value as a site for me to sample the migration.

A path, parallel to the hedgerow, leads away from the lake and willow. On the left of the path is the bay's cattail marsh, which was noisy with red-wings' chatter. On the right is the field patrolled by swallows. I stopped a few steps down the path to listen to a song that was clear and robin-like, but more musical. I scanned the green and gray hedgerow until I was halted by a large, bright red, triangular patch. Above the red was a black head; below, a white breast—distinct and striking colors. The heavy, stocky bird was sitting very still in the top of a maple sapling, a welcome behavioral change from the small, flitting, hard-to-follow warblers I had been seeing. It was a male **rose-breasted grosbeak**! It had recently arrived, perhaps just the night before, taking many days to come from Central America. Unlike many of the migrants I had been seeing on their way farther north, the grosbeak may decide to nest here. I hope so. It would be pleasant to enjoy its sight and sound throughout the summer.

Below the grosbeak, in the lower branches of the hedgerow, close to the path, several tiny birds were busily feeding. There was a good look at the common migrant **Nashville warbler's** gray head contrasting with its yellow throat. There were several more **yellow warblers**, and a male **chestnut-sided**, one of my favorite warblers because of his artistic color pattern. A **black-throated blue warbler** sang and showed himself. A **yellowthroat** popped its head up from the undergrowth. From the nearby bushes a **redstart** sang a selection from its varied repertoire.

It was not yet eight o'clock. I was excited about the prospects for the remainder of this already spectacular day. My desire to experience as much as I could of what the Pageant had brought today caused me a dilemma: should I walk very slowly, stopping to thoroughly check out every movement and sound, or would I be better off not being so slow, thus permitting me to canvass a larger area? I decided to compromise. I'd keep moving until I found an area that obviously had many birds that I needed to identify. I would sort them out as quickly as possible, then move on.

At the end of the path was a large grove of ash saplings about twenty feet high, growing close together, allowing for only a few low branches. A band of **bay-breasted warblers** was working its way out to the end of the high branches in search of insects. Sometimes they would hang upside down to find food on the underside of leaves. Their movements were deliberate, providing me sufficient time to savor their rich chestnut and gray beauty.

Close to the ground a twig moved, directing my eye to a bright yellow head with a black patch on its crown—a male **Wilson's warbler**. It was thoughtful of him to face me, tilting his head downward to show off his prime identifying characteristic.

From well back in the underbrush came jumbled, varied vocalizations; most phrases were repeated, thereby designating a **brown thrasher**. It sounded much like its more commonly heard relative, the **gray catbird**, but a catbird does not repeat phrases. A similar-sounding relative, the **northern mockingbird**, repeats its changeable phrases at least three times before going on to the next phrase. After serenading me for a while, the grackle-sized thrasher flew out of its hiding place. He was rich reddish-brown with a long tail, flying low to the ground, then dropping into another spot of heavy undergrowth.

The thrasher had just ducked out of sight when from a considerable distance, echoing through the scrub growth, came a soft, cluck-like call, *cu-cu-cu cu-cu-cu*. A **black-billed cuckoo**! It was the first, and very possibly the only one, I would hear this year. Most years I hear only one or two in the spring or early summer, when they are establishing their nesting territories. Their low-pitched calls carry well—much farther than the calls of most other birds. Seeing a cuckoo is much less likely than hearing one. That is because they move slowly, and are usually well hidden by dense foliage, while searching for their favorite food—tent caterpillars. I decided there was no chance of seeing this one—it was too far away, and hidden in a large tract of scrub growth.

As I walked back to my car, six **purple martins** circled high above, looking for their breakfast of flying insects. Even at such a great height it was easy to see they were martins, because they were so much larger than other swallows. Two were males, all one color, bluish-purple. The other four, females, had white breasts. The martins were probably building nests in one of the nearby apartment houses that had been erected for them by people living along the lakeshore.

The martins were cutting back and forth across the same air space that the **blue jays** were using. Since arriving this morning, I had frequently looked skyward. Each time, I would see at least twenty jays flying east toward the bay. Thousands must have passed while I was here.

The blue jay migration across the bay is such a well-known occurrence that it has been suggested that a formal jay count be conducted, similar to the hawk count. It would be interesting, perhaps valuable, to know how many jays pass this site during spring migration, year after year, and to gather information related to their flights, such as weather conditions and time of day.

It started to rain. Sometimes a rain causes birds to come down lower in the woods, where it is drier. Thinking of the dense upper canopy of Island Cottage Woods' very tall oaks, maples, basswoods, and beeches, I decided that was to be my next stop.

Many cars were parked at the Island Cottage Woods parking lot. Several longtime birders, whom I have seen every spring for years, were taking a coffee break. One reported, "There are many, many warblers, and a wonderful variety of other migrants! You'd better get started; it will probably be the best day of the year."

I started down the entrance path, immediately overwhelmed by so many birds that I couldn't decide which ones to identify first. Everywhere I looked there were more to see. Sprinkled among low branches were **Blackburnian, palm, black-and-white, magnolia, Tennessee,** and **yellow-rumped** warblers. **Black-throated greens** were singing from several directions.

Farther into the woods I was able to identify, by either sight or sound, **red-eyed vireos, white-throated sparrows, gnatcatchers, ruby-crowned kinglets, goldfinches, warbling vireos, catbirds, orioles, house wrens,** and **chickadees**. There were birds of all shapes, sizes, and colors, in all directions! Also, there was singing from many species reverberating from many directions and distances. It was difficult to listen to one song at a time in order to identify it.

I came upon an old friend. We agreed that there had been a huge flight last night, and that the rain had brought the birds low to the ground for uncommonly close views. She had heard a **northern parula**, but regretfully admitted that she had not seen the especially beautiful and uncommon warbler. It had been singing near the large oak tree on the path toward the back part of the woods, but had stopped singing before anyone could find it. I walked in that direction.

Standing near the oak tree were several other birders listening for its song. After several minutes, hearing nothing of the parula, we dispersed, each to his own idea of where the best birds might be. I walked farther along the main path, deeper into the woods, seeing and hearing many birds, but none were species I had not already found. It would be tough to add to my already long list of findings. I turned around, walking back toward the central part of the woods, when I heard it. The parula!

Its song was an upward trill ending with a final note that abruptly dropped in pitch. Several of us were within hearing distance; we immediately headed toward the song. The bird sang again as we came closer. He was in the same large oak tree where he had been heard earlier, and where we had been looking for him just a few minutes before. As is usual for a parula, he was very high. We strained our backs and necks to look almost straight up at him. Fortunately, there were no leaves to block our view, because oaks are the last to leaf out in spring. Being almost directly underneath him, we couldn't see much of his plumage—only the rust and black band across his yellow breast. He stayed for a few minutes and sang periodically, permitting everyone to find him. Then he disappeared.

A cool onshore breeze from across the lake suddenly overpowered the warm, but weaker, southerly winds, dropping the temperature by what felt to be at least ten degrees. Insects, and hence the birds, too, stopped what they were doing, became silent, and disappeared from view.

When I returned to my car, I went through the checklist, counting the number of warblers I had found during the morning at both Braddock Bay and Island Cottage Woods. The total was seventeen! We finally had a good warbler day—the kind we typically have only three or four times during the spring.

72. A Checkpoint on the Progress of Warbler Migration

After lunch, I sat at the kitchen table analyzing how the warbler migration had progressed. First, I listed the more common warblers in the order in which they typically arrive [See plate 15]:

Very early arrivals	pine, yellow-rumped, palm, black-and-white, northern waterthrush
Early arrivals	yellow, black-throated green, Nashville, black-throated blue, yellowthroat, ovenbird, Blackburnian, redstart
Mid arrivals	parula, Cape May, chestnut-sided, magnolia, golden-winged
Late arrivals	Tennessee, orange-crowned, bay-breasted, hooded, cerulean, Canada, blue-winged, Wilson's
Very late arrivals	mourning, blackpoll

Then I compared the list to the warblers I had seen to date. The mid-migration arrivals were well represented, with a smattering of late arrivals. Neither of the very late group had been seen.

While in the mood for categorizing, I thought of another useful classification of warblers. When experienced birders look for a specific species, or try to make an identification under poor conditions, they draw on their knowledge of how far off the ground a species is often found. Some species are almost always seen on or near the ground, others in low bushes, others higher, and some prefer the upper canopy of the tallest trees. Some species, however, can be seen at almost any height, depending upon the situation. Strong winds, rain, or extended cool weather may cause all birds to come lower. Keeping in mind that there are exceptions, the following groupings can help find the bird one is seeking.

On or near the ground	northern waterthrush, ovenbird
Low bushes, undergrowth	yellowthroat, palm, hooded, Canada, Wilson's, mourning
Less than 20 feet	yellow, yellow-rumped (can be at any height), black-throated blue, redstart, magnolia, chestnut-sided
Up to 40 feet	black-and-white, black-throated green, Nashville, Cape May, blue-winged, golden-winged, bay-breasted, pine, blackpoll, orange-crowned
Tops of high trees	Blackburnian, cerulean, parula, Tennessee

73. Late Arrivals Fill the Woods (May 25)

Last night's winds came from the north, lowering my expectations for the arrival of new migrants. When I entered Island Cottage Woods, however, I was pleasantly surprised. Mother Nature had tricked me once again. Along the entrance path I heard **yellow warblers, yellowthroats, redstarts, house wrens, robins, red-eyed vireos,** and **great crested flycatchers.** They were only part of the contingent of new arrivals. Other calls were intermixed in the chorus that I couldn't separate sufficiently for identification. In the treetops, I saw **bay-breasted warblers**, richly colored in chestnut, gray, and black. They had been traveling for over a month, starting in Colombia or Venezuela, gradually working their way across Texas and the Midwest, and were now approaching their nesting grounds in Ontario or Quebec.

From the corner of my eye was a flash of blue; a male **indigo bunting** had flown to the top of a large oak. I had an unobstructed view of the bunting's alighting in the leafless oak, as well as his deeply rich blue plumage, intense in the sunlight. Two more male buntings joined him. I had never seen three buntings together before, especially three males. They are usually seen alone or with a mate. One of them was a first-year bird, with brown blotting his blue plumage; next spring he will be all blue.

Moving from the scrub growth near the entrance to somewhat larger trees, I stopped and listened. **Tennessee** and **blackpoll warblers** were singing. As I moved closer, many more of both species came within hearing range, becoming increasingly louder in all directions. The Tennessees were the loudest. I remembered this to be an annual occurrence. There are several days each spring when the Tennessees arrive in such large numbers, and sing so loudly, that it seems as though they have completely overtaken the woods. There were many blackpolls singing too, but their soft, very high-pitched, thin notes were nearly drowned out by the Tennessees. Perhaps the highest-pitched of all the warblers', the blackpoll's is the first call one misses as one ages and the ability to hear at high frequencies is reduced. I was pleased that I was still able to hear them.

The arrival of Tennessees, and especially blackpolls, marks the warbler migration's climax. The fullness of the emerged foliage—basswood, ash, and cherry; most of the trees and shrubs in the woods, except for the oaks—is another indication that migration is well along. The time of year that I have looked forward to for so long has finally come. I will enjoy it to the fullest now, and in a few days it will ebb.

I walked farther down the path, seeing and hearing even more warblers, not a lot of birds at any one time, but just gradually coming upon them. I heard a **Tennessee**, then a **yellow**. I followed the direction of a **magnolia's** song to where I could see its head tilted back, mouth open, as its familiar notes emerged. A **Wilson's** sang; another showed itself. A **Canada warbler** gave its abrupt and easily heard call from low bushes along the path. I spotted more **bay-breasteds** in the top of an oak. More **Tennessees** and **blackpolls**, hidden by the canopy, sang from high in maple and ash trees.

There was the resonant song of a **veery**: *veery-veery-veery*. The veery has a haunting song that descends in both pitch and volume. Its unusual-sounding tremolo is made possible by its unique voice box, the syrinx, that produces two harmonious notes simultaneously. A summer resident here, we may hear him anytime we walk through the deep woods.

At the base of a huge old willow, I heard one of the few remaining warblers I could expect to find for the season, a **mourning warbler**. It was singing *cheery-cheery-chorry*, out of sight, under the cover of mayapples.

Last night's cool north winds must have been just a local occurrence, perhaps influenced by the lake. South of here the wind must have been warm and southerly. Whatever the explanation, there had been an excellent incoming flight last night. My expectations for the day were now high, because a good day this late in the migration provides the potential for finding many more species compared to the earlier days, when many species were not yet scheduled to arrive.

Most of the warblers I have seen recently have similar ranges: they winter in Central America, or northern South America, and nest mostly in Canada. They travel the distance between the two ranges twice a year, giving birders across the Eastern United States several weeks to enjoy their incredible numbers, great varieties of plumage colors, and their intricate vocal compositions. Being able to watch the warblers each year, in perhaps the greatest act of the Great Pageant, is a great gift to us Easterners from Mother Nature! She provides a similar display in the Western states too, but it is in diminished variety.

Moving on, I was now among very tall mature trees. Their well-enclosed canopy permitted little vegetation at ground level. The habitat shift caused a corresponding change in bird species. I found a male and female **scarlet tanager**, a **rose-breasted grosbeak**, **red-eyed** and **warbling vireos**, and **phoebes**. Eastern wood-pewees had just arrived to join their much earlier-arriving cousins, the phoebes.

A thrush was hopping along a well-decayed log lying among a patch of mayapples. I was hoping it would be a gray-cheeked thrush, an uncommon thrush here, and a late migrant—it was now time for it to be here. The bird on the log was facing away from me, so I couldn't see its identifying face pattern. When I moved for a better angle, it turned slightly in response, showing its buff-colored cheek—meaning that it was a **Swainson's thrush**. I spotted another thrush. Its face was turned away, but this time, that was the angle I needed. It showed a reddish-brown back, making it a **veery**, another species of thrush. The Swainson's and gray-cheeked thrushes have dark, olive-brown backs. Perhaps it was the veery I had just heard singing so beautifully. Unlike the Swainson's, that are on their way to nest in southern Canada, veeries nest here and throughout the Northeast; we can hear them sing here in the mature woods well into summer.

Something small moved in the branches at about eye level. My immediate reaction was that it was a warbler. However, it was heavier and acted much more sluggishly than a warbler. It must be a vireo. I moved side to side, hoping to see a distinguishing characteristic to tell me which vireo it was. Finally, the necessary look came into view: plain olive overall, verifying it was a vireo, and, importantly, a slight yellow wash on its belly. A **Philadelphia vireo**! Another excellent find for the day. Philadelphias are much less common than our nesting red-eyed and warbling vireos. They are here only briefly during migration.

When I returned to my car, I counted through the list of warblers in the field guide to see how many species I had found this morning: eighteen! It was an outstanding measure of last night's flight. Of course, there was a large selection of other birds too: thrushes, vireos, flycatchers, and many others. After having figured that the cool north winds during the night would not be good for birding today, I was astounded by my findings. That's part of birding; when second-guessing Mother Nature, you are often wrong.

74. A Pileated, Always a Thrill (May 26)

Something large shot across the backyard. When it landed, just outside my kitchen window, I could see that it was black, the size of a crow. It was not a crow, though, because its large head was adorned with streaks of red. It had a long, heavy, sharp bill, in the shape of a powerful chisel. It was tearing open a huge gash in the base of a rotting stump, searching for insects, or anything tasty that might have burrowed into the old trunk. Minutes before, there had been no hole at all.

It was a **pileated woodpecker**, the largest woodpecker one might see in North America (the nearly extinct ivory-billed is three inches larger). For me, it is its size; the handsome, colorful features; and most of all, the awesome power it displays when at work, that provides such a thrilling sight.

To take its picture, I moved to the garage, poking my spotting scope and digital camera through a narrowly opened rear garage door. The big bird seemed not to be aware, or perhaps didn't care, about my presence, as he focused intently upon his mission. He had a male's red mustache, and red on the forehead. After about ten minutes, he flew to another tree for a moment, posing for a full view of his magnificent body, and then flew across the adjacent field.

His wings spread nearly thirty inches from tip to tip. With every wing beat's upward sweep, conspicuous large areas on the underwings flashed, mostly white, edged in black. The manner of flight was deliberate, suggesting strength; straight, direct, with a slight swoop, different from most other woodpeckers, which have an undulating manner of flight. He was soon out of sight. Watching his flashy flight was nearly as exciting as seeing him brandish his powerful bill.

Once or twice a year, pileateds visit the trees in my backyard, usually in spring or early summer. Sometimes, loud call notes announce their approach. One sighting was a female; she lacked the red mustache and the red on the forehead, but still had considerable red on the top of her head. Their seldom, but repeated, appearances make me believe that the pileateds are nearby permanent residents, for they do not migrate. They require huge areas for scavenging, so their nest could be more than a mile away. There are several modest-sized woodlots with huge, mature trees nearby that could provide nesting sites, and in aggregate, sufficient scavenging opportunities. Their nest is built in a large cavity in a tree trunk, excavated from a knot hole or other opening that they enlarged. The trunk would have to be huge to provide, at the height above ground of at least forty feet, a cavity large enough to accommodate four fledgling-sized offspring. [See plate 13]

75. The Later Migrants Arrive, and
Summer Residents Settle In (May 28)

Southerly winds caused last night to be warmer than it had been for several days. Migrants that had been resting and feeding in Island Cottage Woods had probably taken advantage of the preferred conditions and left for Canada. It is late in the migration, so only a few migrants are yet to arrive from the southern states. What birds would I find in Island Cottage Woods? Perhaps stragglers, summer residents, or a few late migrants?

I was still walking across the parking lot, approaching the woods, when I started hearing **yellow warblers** and **redstarts**. As I followed the path into the woods, the increasing closeness and volume of the singing became almost deafening. Some of the yellows and redstarts may still go on to Canada, but I guessed most were staying. Both species are common summer residents of the wood's edges here.

Progressing farther into the woods, I left the yellows and most of the redstarts, and started seeing **red-eyed vireos**. Some were singing their slowly repeated, singsong vocalization, *hear-I-am-where-are-you*. Many more **red-eyed vireos** were slowly searching for insects among the buds and recently emerged leaves. Red-eyeds were in all directions. My first thought was that there had been a large vireo flight last night, but then I realized that this was a very late date for so many to have just arrived. Perhaps they had been accumulating here recently, some stopping to consider spending the summer, others delaying their departure to Canada.

Several **wood thrushes** sang. They were close to the ground, and deep in the woods. The closed cover of the overhead canopy amplified their melodious, flute-like voices, causing their songs to echo throughout the woods. As I had entered the woods a few minutes ago, I had heard yellow warblers and redstarts from the undergrowth. Now, I was being serenaded by vireos and wood thrushes from the canopy of tall, mature trees.

Farther was a congregation of **blackpoll warblers** singing their high-pitched, thin-noted songs. Most were hidden by the foliage, now completely out. I did manage a good look at a very dingy female that lacked the identifying black cap of the male. There were **bay-breasted warblers** too. They would leave as soon as conditions permit. A late-departing female **Cape May warbler** was a difficult identification. I had to go back and forth several times between looking at the bird and checking the plumage in the field guide. It lacked the chestnut-colored face patch of the male, and it showed very little yellow over the rest of its body. The subdued colors indicated that she was a first-year female Cape May. No other similar species shown or described in the field guide—orange-crowned, myrtle, magnolia, blackpoll, palm—matched her appearance.

As I continued down the path, moving to a mixture of tall trees and shorter scrub growth, the chorus all but ceased. An occasional yellow warbler, vireo, or redstart, all summer residents, sang briefly to break the silence. It reminded me that we were approaching the time when the migrants would be gone, and we would be hearing only summer residents. It occurred to me that the palm warbler, which I had been seeing all spring, was now gone—it is one of the first early migrants to complete its flights. At this late point in migration, the experienced local birders were looking for late migrants that they had not yet seen, such as the yellow-bellied flycatcher and the gray-cheeked thrush.

A sparrow hopped out from the underbrush at the path's edge, remaining in view just long enough for me to see its finely streaked breast with buff-colored background—a **Lincoln's sparrow**. I was lucky to have seen it, for, by this late date, most Lincoln's had arrived at their nesting sites in Quebec. They are secretive birds, almost always hard to see well enough to identify them. Other sparrows—such as the white-throated, white-crowned, and song—are not nearly as wary. They are much easier to see.

Just past the Lincoln's, I heard, then spotted, a pocket of activity; there were several **chickadees** and **house wrens** singing along with **blackpolls** and **redstarts**. I noticed that the **redstarts'** song was different from the one I had heard them sing a week ago. At that time, the song had increased in volume, and abruptly dropped off. Today, it was more even in pitch and volume. Perhaps the change indicated a change in their life cycle, from finding a mate to nesting.

A **ruby-throated hummingbird** methodically explored the blossoms of a honeysuckle bush. While hovering in place at a blossom, its wings moved so fast—fifty-five times per second, the books say—that they became invisible. The ultra-fast wing beat enabled him to hover with such precision and stability that he could place his long thin bill down the throat of a honeysuckle blossom, and hold the position long enough to extract the nectar. Even more amazing was that this tough little guy had flown all the way from Central America, and will return in the fall. At first, I saw no identifiable color at all, as though he were in deep shade, which he was not. But when he moved to explore another flower, changing the angle to the light, his body turned into a brilliant green, and his throat showed the ruby red of a male. The colors had a shimmering character, indicating that they were caused by iridescence. Iridescent color does not come from pigment in the feathers, like most birds' colors, but from the angle at which light strikes the microscopic structure of the feathers.

I decided to check out the large cattail marsh that surrounds Round Pond, just a few hundred yards away. I heard the *fitzbew* calls of **willow flycatchers** as I followed the path among osier bushes. After having recently heard many least flycatchers' calls, *chebeck*, today's willow flycatchers calls marked a shift in flycatcher arrivals. Both species will spend the summer and nest here.

With the osiers' upland habitat and willow flycatchers to my back, I looked down the embankment to the water's edge ten feet below. A short distance out into the pond, a pair of **Canada geese** swam by; they had three tiny goslings, no larger than robins. I laughed as one flapped its stumpy wings, still without flight feathers. Its a treat to see the large graceful adult birds, gliding along the pond, herding their young with them. Only a decade ago it was rare to see them nest in the vicinity; now it is common. Not far away was a mother **mallard** with her brood of twelve ducklings. The scene was a bustling nursery.

Three **black terns** patrolled up and down the finger of the pond. Their black plumage had never made much of an impression on me before, because I had always viewed them from a distance, causing the black body and gray wings to appear somewhat drab. But now, with them only twenty feet away, in direct sunlight, I was impressed by how very suave they looked, as though they were dressed for a formal ball.

Barn swallows skimmed low over the water, making repeated trips back and forth before me, long pointed tails and blue backs in full view from my higher vantage point. Among the barns was a brown-colored swallow. I followed it with my binoculars, trying to see its throat to determine which of the two species of brown swallows it was, the **bank swallow** or **rough-winged** swallow. Several times it flew near, but never at an angle for me to see its throat in good light. Finally, the dusky throat of the rough-winged was revealed, unlike the distinct brown band across a bank's white chest.

Experienced birders identify the two brown species by their manner of flight—it's easier than the struggle I just went through to get a good look at its throat. I studied the rough-winged's flight characteristics carefully, hoping to make an easier identification in the future. The rough-winged flies like a barn swallow, wings swept back at the end of a deeper wing beat. The bank swallow flies in a more floppy manner, and is little smaller. I wished there was a bank swallow flying along with the rough-winged for comparison.

Near the water, but from drier scrub growth, came the *fee-bee-o* call of an **alder flycatcher**. Then I heard the alder's close relative, the **willow flycatcher**, sing *fitzbew* again. Perhaps it was the same bird I had heard a few minutes before. Both birds continued to call, almost as though they were taking turns. I took advantage of the lucky coincidence and analyzed the two calls. The difference between the two is slight: the willow's first note has a rising inflection; the alder raises its pitch between the first and second notes. The alder's second note ends abruptly downward, the "o" in *fee-bee-o*. The nature of both calls was somewhat raspy.

The two small flycatchers, along with the more common **least flycatcher**, look so much alike that they can be told apart only by their calls. In fact, some years ago, the alder and willow were considered to be one species, known as the Trail's flycatcher. Today the name Trail's is still used when a bird is seen and is not singing.

The overlook where I had been standing, although near water, is of upland habitat, favored by the willow flycatcher. Nearby, at the edge of the marsh, there are cattails and alder growing, which is attractive to the alder flycatcher. The least flycatcher avoids wet habitat and is found in orchards, parks, hedgerows, and dry wood edges. The three species are nearly identical in appearance, and their preferred habitats vary slightly, but their songs are distinctly different.

76. In Search of the Final Four (May 29)

Except for the few late migrating shorebirds, the end of May means migration is essentially over; birders' activities will be shifting to more mundane activities such as gardening. At Island Cottage Woods' concrete slab was a handful of diehard birders searching for the last few species. They were especially looking for the notable four late migrants: **yellow-bellied flycatcher**, **olive-sided flycatcher**, **common nighthawk**, and **gray-cheeked thrush**.

Bob Marcotte arrived about the same time as I did, even though we had not coordinated our plans. We were told there was a **cuckoo** singing an unusual song. The birders we were talking to were not sure whether it was a yellow-billed or black-billed. We listened to the call, a slow soft *cow-cow-cow-cow*—not the usual call of either cuckoo. It was well back in heavy growth, impossible to see. Cuckoos are secretive birds. Their habit of sitting very still in thick foliage makes them very hard to find; birders are more apt to hear a cuckoo than see one.

We slowly walked down the path into the woods listening to other calls and checking out what few birds could be seen. Nearly all the birds we saw or heard were nesting birds. There were many **redstarts**; a few **yellowthroats**; **gnatcatchers**; **marsh wrens** singing from the distant marsh; and **yellow warblers**. There was an especially large number of **red-eyed vireos** singing, but since the leaves were out fully, we saw many fewer than we heard.

Continuing farther, we heard the unusual cuckoo song again from almost directly overhead. We saw the bird clearly among thinly leafed branches just twenty yards away. It was obviously a **cuckoo**: a good-sized, slender bird with a long tail, brown-olive above and white below. Its long, slightly down-curved bill had a yellow lower mandible; the large white spots on the underside of the tail and the rufous patches on its folded wings made it definitely a **yellow-billed cuckoo**. After we watched the bird for a few minutes and listened to him sing several more times, he flew away, trailing his very long, slender tail behind him.

We wondered whether this was the same bird we had heard earlier or whether there was more than one cuckoo in the woods. It was an excellent find. Cuckoos are usually difficult to see; rarely does one have such a clear view as we just had. Also, the yellow-billed is much less common than the black-billed cuckoo. Bob mentioned how cuckoo populations fluctuate considerably with infestations of caterpillars, especially the tent caterpillar. Cuckoos help to limit such infestations.

We walked in the direction of a persistently singing **Canada warbler** until we spotted him. Bob intently watched him sing to imprint the Canada's song upon his memory. Bob can identify most warblers by their song, but enjoys improving his skills in diverse situations. There are variations to the songs of the same species. Also, distance can sometimes make the song sound different by masking some of the notes that don't carry as well.

We discussed how the human mind learns bird songs. One can take an intellectual approach, listening to audio recordings and making note of the distinguishing characteristics of each call so they can recognized in the field. Another approach is to use the subconscious capabilities of the mind, or imprinting. This works best for me by listening to the bird's call, and watching the bird sing, both at the same time. When I hear a song that I have heard many times before, the identity of the bird pops into mind. I do not have to analyze the key characteristic of the song.

We are very aware of our frequent reliance upon logical mental processes, but I think we use our subconscious or innate abilities more than we realize. For example, a friend calls on the telephone and I recognize his voice immediately. It just happens. Likewise, I can identify the more common birds by the character of their voices, perhaps from just the first note or two.

While walking back to the parking lot, Bob suggested we go to Badgerow Park, a large tract of land with excellent, varied birding habit, about two miles to the southeast. Bob lives near the park. He has conducted extensive bird census studies there that he hopes will influence town officials as they consider development and plans for the park. He suggested we look there for the Final Four.

We soon arrived at the park, where, in past years, Bob had found the uncommon **olive-sided flycatcher**, one of the Final Four. He pointed down the path that leads from the playground to a tall tree standing in the open. "Most of the olive-sideds I have seen here have been in that tree, perched on the dead branch that extends well above the rest of the tree." The branch was empty.

Two **broad-winged hawks** came our way, flying low due to a strong wind. They were clearly molting, for both birds had big gaps of missing flight feathers on their wings, as well as missing tail feathers. One had so many missing tail feathers that I wondered how much its flight had been affected. More broad-wings flew by; several more groups followed. Bob said that flights of several hundred can occur as late as the second week of June.

We walked about five hundred yards to an open field next to a hedgerow. A **kingbird** was flying back and forth along the edge of the field, catching flying insects. It would fly just a few feet off the ground and then stop to rest on a branch. It almost always gave its twittering flight call when it took off again. Bob pointed out two characteristics of the kingbird, a member of the flycatcher family, that help in identification. "The first is its flight mannerism: when flying it looks like the wings never come above the body, but are held in a bowed downward position. The other characteristic is the white band at the end of its tail. The two visible characteristics, along with the kingbird's unique flight call, make the bird unmistakable, even from a distance."

Bob pointed to a tall tree, also with dead branches in the top, and was about to say that that was another potential site for the olive-sided, when he noticed there was something sitting there. The large flycatcher was facing us, showing a white breast with olive markings on both sides, like a vest. Its tail was relatively shorter than other flycatchers. It was an **olive-sided flycatcher**! The coincidence was astonishing—olive-sideds are rare here even at their favorite habitats and dates, late May and late August. It flew off for about two seconds, then landed again on the same perch. It repeated quick flights for catching insects several more times. A white patch on each side near the tail would be a positive identification, but it was not visible. A blue jay flew in, causing the olive-sided, to fly off in the direction from which we had just come. We quickly returned to the original tree with the dead branch that Bob had pointed out before. There was the olive-sided, sitting on the dead branch where Bob had earlier said it should have been! We watched the olive-sided for several more minutes as he periodically flew off to catch insects. He caught a good-sized bee and we watched him have considerable trouble swallowing it. At one point, he dropped the bee and had to retrieve it in midair and return to his perch—what quickness. We moved a few feet to one side, to where we had a different viewing angle. The bird's white breast with olive-shaded sides were very distinctive in the bright sunlight, but it was not until it shook its feathers that we could finally see the other identifying characteristic we were looking for: a white spot on its side near the base of the tail.

It was later than Bob had planned to stay, and I was getting hungry; it was time to call it a day. Before we left, Bob suggested we walk over to the row of cottonwoods next to where our cars were parked and listen for the **yellow-bellied flycatcher**. We did not have to wait long until we heard its *churee* call. Bob picked it up first. It seemed very faint to me, almost inaudible, but he was standing closer to the hedgerow. The bird cooperated, for my benefit, I'm sure, repeating its call several times. I could then hear it clearly, and identified it for certain. This gave me two of the Final Four this morning. It was time for lunch.

77. Evening Birding and Nighthawk Migration (May 30)

It was 7:30 p.m. when I arrived at Beatty Point for a relaxing stroll. It was a beautiful, clear evening, sunny, the temperature mild, with a light breeze coming from the west.

The walk from the parking lot down to the water's edge was like listening to a choir rehearse; each species was singing a different part: **song sparrows, yellow warblers, common yellowthroats, American goldfinches**, and **gray catbirds**. Flying overhead were **red-winged blackbirds** and **common grackles**, adding their flight notes to the jumble, while ring-billed gulls flew silently. Farther down the road, in a row of trees near the water, a **warbling vireo** added its warbling song. These were all birds that would be spending the summer here; most had undoubtedly started to nest.

I was especially relaxed. The birds seemed more easygoing, too. They were not as active, and were moving more deliberately. Perhaps we were more tranquil because the day's activities were over and evening is the time to take it easy. Possibly the birds felt relieved after having completed a long and demanding migratory journey. I too, had just completed a journey of sorts, monitoring the past month's busy migration, its changing phases, getting up early every morning, spending much time in the field. Now the busyness, the daily pressure to pay attention to the progress of the unfolding migration, is essentially over. Whatever the reason for the special feeling, I enjoyed it immensely.

A **common nighthawk** called *peent* as it flew overhead. Its long, slender, floppy wings, peculiarly marked with elongated white spots across their middle, zigzagged through the evening sky catching insects. It would dive almost to the ground, then shoot back up to a high altitude again, acrobatically. The nighthawk is one of the few species that feeds mostly in the evening, often hundreds of feet above the darkening landscape. Its name is a misnomer. It has no strong beak to grasp a prey, but it is equipped with a large, wide mouth, like a swallow, to catch flying insects. A number of years ago I would see and hear nighthawks on summer nights as they flew among the tall buildings of the downtown business district; they liked to nest on the flat gravel roofs. I also remember seeing them chase insects in the stadium lights at night baseball games. But in recent years, I seldom see them, and only around the first of June; they are late spring migrants. On several occasions I have been fortunate enough to be in the field when there was a prominent flight along the lakeshore. The bird I just saw had probably been migrating today, and was now hunting for food before stopping to rest.

I stood on the bridge where Larkin Creek empties into the marsh that surrounds Buck Pond. Every year, a colony of **barn swallows** attaches its nests of mud to the bridge's interior walls. I listened as their twittering echoed against the walls, ceiling, and stream inside the bridge. Several swallows flew over the edge of the marsh, and then back to the bridge. As they passed under the bridge just a few feet below me, I could see what normally was not visible: small white spots that bordered their long and pointed V-shaped tails.

Two more **nighthawks** flew by, appearing more interested in their intended destination than in catching insects. They were followed by another flying so low that I could see the barring on its chest. I had stumbled upon a little-known part of the Pageant: one of the last species to migrate are the nighthawks, and they do so during the day. They winter in South America and nest throughout much of North America. The birds I had seen today might be going to Canada.

I left the bridge and walked along the large field where six weeks ago I had heard nighthawks performing their spring mating ritual. Several sparrows flew into the short grass at the edge of the lane. Clear breasts and pink bills marked them as **field sparrows**. On the other side of the trail a **Savannah sparrow** sang *sit–sit–sit–seeeee–saaaaay* while perched at the top of a berry bush, showing his yellowish eye line. When he flew, his color, manner of flight, and profile looked similar to a song sparrow, but with a shorter tail.

I was experiencing how productive birding open fields can be, a habitat I often overlook in my field trips. This large field was adding to my discoveries. Fluttering over the open field was a male **bobolink**. He held his wings down in a bowed fashion, not bringing them above the horizontal. which is a flight characteristic of two other birds I had seen this spring—the kingbird and spotted sandpiper. The bobolink hovered in place for a moment while twittering his song; then he landed atop a tall weed. He watched me carefully while I studied him. He had a large, conspicuous, buff-colored patch on the back of his head, which contrasted to his black body. Then he flew, showing even more distinctive aspects of his plumage. A large white rump and white shoulder patches gave the impression that he had a white body—the opposite impression of color one gets when he is perched. His appearance in flight was one of black wings with a white body, a striking image. Bobolinks live in colonies, so I scanned the field looking for others, alert for sparrow-appearing females. I saw none. I wanted to ask my lone sighting if he were migrating or going to nest here, and where were his friends? Had he somehow lost them during the long flight from South America? I will look for him and others here again, to see if they stayed to nest.

I was back to the barn swallow colony. It had been almost an hour since I first stopped to watch them; with the sun dipping to the horizon, the swallows had stepped up their attacks on swarms of mosquitoes out in force over the water. The swallows' sorties appeared to be successful if their very frequent, quick flutters were any indication. Swallows, like nighthawks, feed as heavily, if not more so, in the evening as in the morning.

The lane closely skirted the marsh. From the cattails, two **marsh wrens** "sang" their click-like rattle. It was not at all surprising to hear them sing this late in the day; in fact, it is not unusual to hear marsh wrens sing well into the night. Farther out into the marsh, several more sang from the inter sanctum of heavy cattail growth. There were obviously a number of marsh wrens in the vicinity, but I saw none. I found myself thinking of how important birding by ear has been in determining what birds are around, enhancing my awareness of how Mother Nature's Great Pageant was progressing. When I walk this route in the morning, I hear both marsh wrens and the similar-sounding swamp sparrows. Now, because swamp sparrows don't sing as often at night, I was hearing only the wrens.

Many **red-wings** were being very vocal. I stopped and listened to their calls. There was the song that sounded like *konk-a-ree*, their typical or most characteristic call. They were also using their call note, *check*. This, I presumed, was used to keep track of where others were in the dense foliage of the cattails, and perhaps for communicating some simple status information. They used another call note occasionally, the higher-pitched *tear*. If only there were a dictionary of red-wing vocabulary.

June

78. Migration Is Over (June 2)

By the end of May, most birds have completed their migration, although there will be late stragglers. (Neil and Laura Moon counted 3,200 broad-winged hawks going over Hawk Lookout June 1–10, 1979). Other raptors, shorebirds, waxwings, gulls, and terns are still seen moving along the lakeshore in early June. They may be non-breeding immature birds in no hurry to get to their ancestral nesting grounds, where they will be raising young in future years. Over the last six weeks, the migration's momentum had been building. I had been spending more and more time in the field as the pace of the migration increased to a frenzy. I sensed the frenzy personally, feeling the rush, focus, urgency, stresses, and crush of events that millions of birds were experiencing. It peaked just a few days ago. Now, it was over! I took a quick walk through Island Cottage Woods, and along the west side of Braddock Bay. The only birds I saw or heard were summer residents. I had a strange, let-down feeling. I hadn't planned on migration withdrawal symptoms.

79. A Moment for Reflection: A Full Year of the Great Pageant

I fondly remember the silent, reclusive beauty of the scarlet tanager. The little house wren singing almost incessantly all day long, keeping me entertained, making the neighborhood more pleasant. There was the raucous, take-charge personality of the blue jay. The inquisitive joyousness of the chickadee. The shamelessness, adaptability, and cunning of the crow. I enjoyed the beauty of a magnolia warbler framed with apple blossoms, the pleasant sound of the hermit thrush's flute-like song.

The fact that we can have these experiences each year, that the magnolia warbler looks as excitingly beautiful as it did when I first saw one as a young boy, or that the hermit thrush sings the same song as it did those many years ago, is to experience the timelessness of the Great Pageant.

Over the past year, I was privileged to witness a small part of a divinely inspired and directed play. It has been presented each year for millions of years. It is so extensive and complex that no mortal can see it all or know it all. It can be viewed from an infinite number of locations, each revealing different aspects of the play. What more would I have seen if I had watched the Pageant from a site a hundred miles to the south, or to the north, or from an island in the Bering Sea, or the northern tip of the Red Sea, or from the chain of islands in Indonesia?

Following the Pageant unfold throughout the year was like monitoring the pulse of Mother Nature, her powers unfathomable, a spiritual experience.

I fervently hope you will experience the Great Pageant too, as I have—firsthand, extensively, revealingly, joyously!

Map of Birding Sites

(birding sites described in the journal's text are shown in bold type)

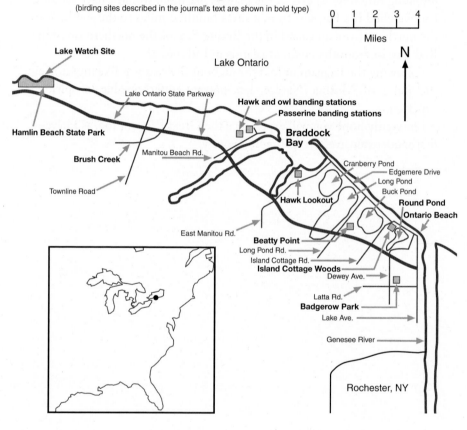

Index of Topics

(Bold type page numbers are principal discussions)

Index by Species

(bold type page numbers are principal discussions)